sport diver
manual

International Standard Book Number 0-88487-009-X
©1975 Jeppesen Sanderson, Inc.
8025 E. 40th Ave.
Denver, Colo. USA 80207

First Printing May 1975
Second Printing July 1975
Third Printing January 1976
Fourth Printing April 1976

R4761C

foreword

Welcome to the exciting and spectacular world of underwater diving. You are going to see and do things that go far beyond your dreams and expectations. Diving is never adequately described; it must be experienced.

Divers are penetrating what could prove to be man's last frontier on earth. Three-fourths of our planet's surface is covered with water, and most of it is not only unexplored, but has not even been seen by man. This thrilling realm is open to every certified diver in the world. Becoming a certified diver permits you to join an international diving community that explores, collects, photographs, works, and does research in both salt water and fresh water.

Diving is not limited to a few "uniquely trained specialists." Anyone with ordinary swimming ability and normal physical fitness can gain certification with adequate instruction. Today's certified diver is educated and highly trained in the classroom, pool, and open water.

A certified *skin diver* is competent in the use of the mask, fins, snorkel, and buoyancy compensator during breath-hold dives. The certified *scuba diver*, in addition, has the knowledge and skill of using underwater breathing equipment. (Scuba is a word coined from the first letters of **S**elf-**C**ontained **U**nderwater **B**reathing **A**pparatus.) Dive shops and air stations will not sell air or rent equipment to divers who cannot show proof of certification.

There are several recognized agencies and instructor organizations that issue certification. They issue a "C" card when a student has passed an examination and has completed the required hours of combined classroom and water training, plus supervised open water instruction.

This Manual and its supporting Workbook are designed to supplement, under the guidance of a qualified instructor, classroom instruction and water training, helping you toward the goal of becoming a certified sport diver. First, the subject is studied in the Manual; then, the corresponding section in the Workbook is completed. The Workbook contains self-study exercises designed to focus attention on practical problem-solving techniques necessary to the education of sport divers, and helps the student evaluate his retention of the knowledge studied in the Manual.

A look at the Manual's table of contents will quickly define the sections. They are carefully sequenced into a logical order; however, they can be studied independently or in conjunction with other sections. For example, in one study session, the section on *equipment* used for underwater breathing might be combined with the section on the *science* of breathing underwater.

The Manual includes the basic information for the sport diver without being overly technical and presents these essentials in a manner designed to interest the novice and "old timer" alike. Its emphasis is on teaching how to perform in real-life diving situations. You will find that it will be an excellent reference text throughout your diving career.

Although basic skills are discussed in the Manual, specific instruction techniques and the "how to do" are left up to the instructor. The Manual is divided into four parts:

PART I THE EQUIPMENT

Skin and scuba diving equipment is presented in the order in which the student learns its use. The skills and techniques needed by the student to select, maintain, and use the equipment are also included in this part.

PART II THE DIVER

The diver's mind and body are discussed in Part II. Physics, physiology, and safety procedures are introduced to give a thorough understanding of what the diver can expect under water and what he must do to safely enjoy this sport.

PART III THE ENVIRONMENT

The diver is introduced to his surroundings in this part. It builds appreciation for how the fresh waters and salt waters were formed, how and why water moves, and water's effect on the diver. A discussion of underwater animals and how man affects their environment also is presented in this part.

PART IV THE DIVE

The full spectrum of skin and scuba diving activities is covered. Everything from amateur collecting and photography, to advanced wreck and commercial diving is previewed, along with information on other professional diving careers.

Becoming a qualified diver is easy and enjoyable and is the key to a lifetime of exciting adventure. So let's get started. Good diving!

table of contents

PART I the equipment

PART II the diver

PART III the environment

PART IV the dive

PART I the equipment

introduction

Man can enter and enjoy a different environment, safely and comfortably, if properly equipped. With the necessary equipment, man can easily see, move and breathe in water—transforming an alien, sometimes hostile world into a delightful new home.

The waters of the world have always fascinated man, but until recently, only the most highly trained and equipped experts regularly ventured into the sea. Before the 1950's, skin and scuba diving were known to only a few people, for one reason—no equipment. Diving below the surface meant entering a blurry, confusing, and cold place for only a short time. The evolution of sport diving, then, has been primarily dependent on the development of diving equipment. Advances in underwater technology, once begun, continue to increase rapidly every year.

The diving pioneers, who experimented and invented diving equipment, were curious and brave people who encountered obstacles that demanded solutions. Overcoming each problem required a unique piece of equipment or a special procedure. Through progressive effort and change, sport diving has become established as an exciting, comfortable, and safe sport.

Now that you are preparing to launch your career as a sport diver, it is important that you begin by studying each piece of equipment and its function. Knowing how each piece of diving equipment solves a problem will help you understand it.

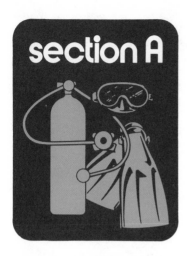

section A

seeing and swimming

- MASKS
- FINS
- SNORKELS

MASK, FINS, AND SNORKEL

The major challenges that faced early divers were basic ones of seeing and moving under water. To accomplish this, the basic equipment of the skin diver—the mask, fins, and snorkel—was developed to restore crystal clear vision and to increase the mobility of the swimmer.

MASKS

Try to remember the first time you opened your eyes under water. Everything was blurry, out of focus, and confining. The human eye, especially designed for seeing through the light density of air, does not work well in the heavy medium of water. Surrounding the eyes with air was found to be the simplest solution for attaining underwater visibility. Early divers wore goggles with polished, tortoise-shell lenses, similar to those pictured in figure 1-1. The lenses provided air spaces in front of the eyes which restored vision.

Fig. 1-1 Early Tortoise-Shell Swimming Goggles

Swimming goggles are still available with tempered glass lenses and rubber straps, but these are of no use to today's skin or scuba divers. Goggles can be used safely by surface swimmers to protect their eyes from chlorine and irritants. But when a diver descends even a few feet, the increasing water pressure tends to squeeze the air spaces in the goggles. This is painful and can cause injury at greater depths.

The first goggles solved the vision problem, but they also created a pressure problem that was not solved until about 1865 when the first modern mask was invented. Instead of two small lenses with two airtight spaces, one big lens that covered the eyes and nose in one common air space was used. (See figure 1-2.)

Fig. 1-2 Early Single-Lens Mask

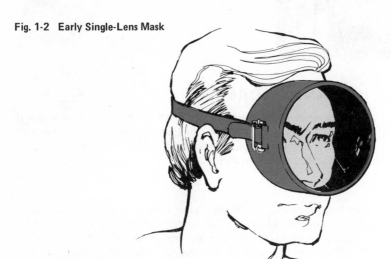

The single-lens mask allows the diver to exhale through the nose to increase the air pressure inside the mask so it equals the water pressure outside the mask. The basic design of this early mask has changed very little.

SELECTING A MASK

There are many types of masks in use today. To help clarify the main differences and to better discuss them, we will create three general classifications: low volume, wide-angle and a general-use mask. See figure 1-3 for a typical example of each mask.

The skin diver, with his limited air supply, needs a low-volume mask. He cannot afford to blow a great amount of air into a large-sized mask to equalize the pressure. The lens in a skin diving mask fits closely to the diver's face and has a pocket provided for the diver's nose. This keeps the air space inside the mask as small as possible.

Scuba divers, on the other hand, can use large-volume masks because they can exhale as much air as needed into the mask to equalize pressure. For this

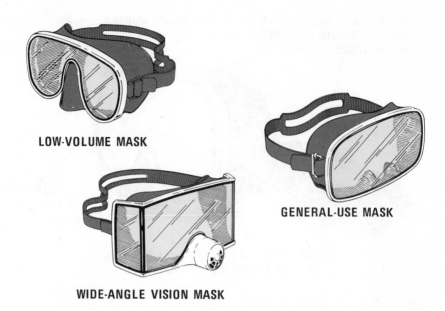

LOW-VOLUME MASK

GENERAL-USE MASK

WIDE-ANGLE VISION MASK

Fig. 1-3 Diving Masks

reason scuba masks can be designed primarily for wide-angle vision. The wide-angle mask, as shown in figure 1-3, has three plates of tempered glass. The two small plates on the sides of the mask expand the scuba diver's peripheral vision.

If you need a mask for both skin and scuba diving, you may want to select a general-use mask. This type offers medium-volume with medium visibility.

WHAT TO LOOK FOR IN A MASK

Once you have decided on a type of mask, look for the following features: (See fig. 1-4.)

1. Notice the quality of material and manner of construction. Black rubber is stronger and lasts longer than colored materials.
2. Make sure the lens is tempered or safety glass. The word "tempered" or "safety" should be printed directly on the lens. Plastic lenses can crack, craze, or break, and scratch easily. They also fog badly.
3. The band that holds the lens in place should be made of some type of noncorrosive material, such as hard plastic or stainless steel, and it should be removable in case you need to replace the lens.
4. The mask strap should be easily adjustable with strong buckles and a positive locking device. The strap should also be split to fit over both the upper and lower parts of the back of your head. A one-piece strap slips up or down too easily.

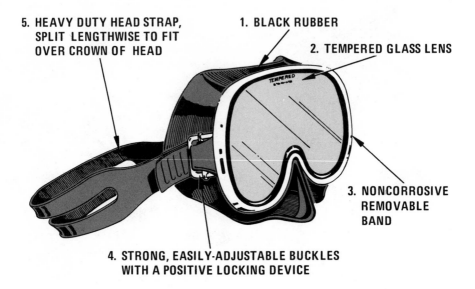

5. HEAVY DUTY HEAD STRAP, SPLIT LENGTHWISE TO FIT OVER CROWN OF HEAD

1. BLACK RUBBER

2. TEMPERED GLASS LENS

3. NONCORROSIVE REMOVABLE BAND

4. STRONG, EASILY-ADJUSTABLE BUCKLES WITH A POSITIVE LOCKING DEVICE

Fig. 1-4   What to Look for in a Mask

MASK FEATURES

As you descend, water pressure increases. The pressure in the air spaces inside your head must be equalized with the surrounding pressure; otherwise, you will feel pain in your ears or sinuses. Some people can equalize by yawning or swallowing, but many have to hold the nose, close the mouth, and blow lightly. Because of this, many masks are available with built-in finger or nose pockets so the diver can seal off his nostrils to equalize; note figure 1-5. Equalization is discussed in detail in Part II, Section C.

Fig. 1-5   Equalizing Features for Masks

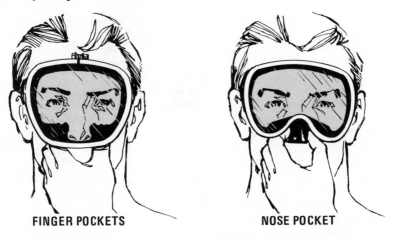

FINGER POCKETS   NOSE POCKET

Masks do not stay perfectly dry inside. Small amounts of water leak in and must be cleared regularly. The purge valve, as shown in figure 1-6, is a feature that helps remove water. It is a one-way valve that lets air and water out of the mask when you exhale, but does not let water enter the mask. The larger the purge valve, the quicker it will clear the mask completely, even if the mask is full of water.

 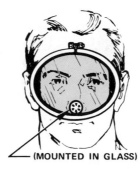 

(MOUNTED IN GLASS)   (MOUNTED IN SKIRT)

LARGE PURGE VALVE   **SMALL PURGE VALVES**

Fig. 1-6 Purge Valves

The diver who wears prescription glasses or contact lenses has several options. There is no reason why contacts cannot be worn while diving. As in any active sport, however, losing a lens is always possible, especially if a mask is suddenly flooded. Many prefer masks with built-in corrective lenses. These are available through dive stores and optical companies that specialize in prescription diving masks. Figure 1-7 shows four different ways of wearing corrective lenses under water.

OPTICAL EYE PORTS   **BONDED OPTICAL BLANKS**

CORRECTION GROUND INTO GLASS   **LENS FRAME**

Fig. 1-7 Masks with Corrective Lenses

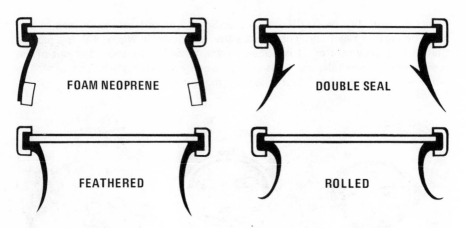

Fig. 1-8 Mask Sealing Edges

To keep water from leaking into the mask, the rubber skirt must form a good seal with your face. Four kinds of sealing edges, shown in figure 1-8, are designed to form a tight, but comfortable airtight seal.

MASK FIT

One of the most important things in selecting the right mask is finding one that fits the size and general shape of your face. The soft rubber skirt of the mask should conform to your face without pinching or pressing harder in one place than another. To make sure a mask fits properly, hold it lightly in place without using the strap. The sealing edge should touch your face everywhere, with no air leaks, gaps, or pressure points. Inhale gently. This should pull the mask close to your face without letting air leak into it. If the fit is good, you will be able to hold it in place with light air pressure alone, as illustrated in figure 1-9. It will feel secure and comfortable. Try this test with several different models until you find the best possible fit.

Fig. 1-9 Testing Mask Fit

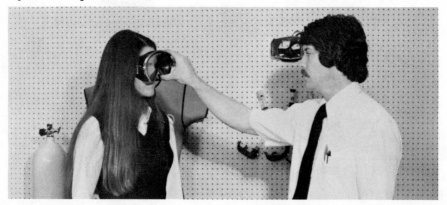

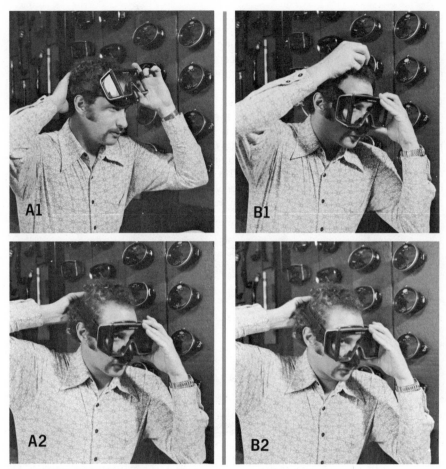

Fig. 1-10 Putting a Mask in Place

MASK USE

A diving mask should have sturdy, easily adjustable strap fasteners attached to both sides. The strap should be worn tightly enough to keep the mask firmly and comfortably in place.

There are two basic ways of putting on the mask. Put the strap on the crown of your head with one hand, then pull the body of the mask down over your forehead, as shown in figure 1-10A. The best and most desirable way is to put the mask in place first, and then pull the strap back. (See 1-10B.) When putting the mask on under water, exhale slightly through your nose to avoid the feeling of water being forced into your nostrils.

Before getting the mask wet, be sure to coat the inside of the lens with an anti-fogging solution. Otherwise, the warm humid air inside the mask will condense and fog the lens which is cooled by the surrounding water. Some chemical solutions prevent water droplets and fog from forming in the mask lens. Such things as liquid dishwashing detergent and saliva also work, but usually are not as effective as chemical wetting agents. If the lens fogs over during a dive, let a little water inside the mask to rinse it away.

One skill you must master in order to use a mask effectively is mask clearing—removing all the water from the mask and replacing it with air while under water. This skill is easier than it sounds, even when the mask is completely flooded. By pushing the top part of the mask against your forehead and exhaling quickly and forcefully through your nose, you create a greater pressure inside the mask than out. This forces the air and water out of the bottom of the mask or through a purge valve, as shown in figure 1-11. Exhaled air replaces the water that escapes from inside the mask.

1 PRESS TOP OF MASK AGAINST FOREHEAD AND EXHALE

2 WATER IS FORCED OUT BOTTOM OF MASK AS AIR COLLECTS AT TOP

Fig. 1-11 Mask Clearing

When clearing a mask with a purge valve, the valve should be as low as possible so all the water drains out. Masks without purge valves can be cleared in almost any position as long as the highest part of the mask is firmly sealed against the face during exhalation. Figure 1-12, for example, shows a diver clearing his mask from the side.

As you descend, you should equalize the pressure inside the mask and inside your ears. To equalize the mask, gently breathe air into it through your nose; otherwise, the increasing water pressure will tend to squeeze the mask against

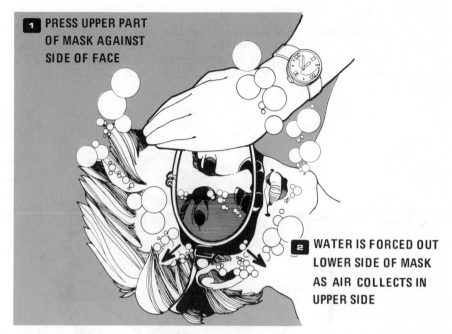

1 PRESS UPPER PART OF MASK AGAINST SIDE OF FACE

2 WATER IS FORCED OUT LOWER SIDE OF MASK AS AIR COLLECTS IN UPPER SIDE

Fig. 1-12 Mask Clearing from the Side

your face. A severe mask squeeze can be painful but is extremely uncommon with trained divers.

To avoid an ear squeeze, use the equalizer pockets in the mask to seal your nose, then blow gently. You can also wiggle your jaw from side to side, swallow, or yawn. Whatever method or combination of methods you use, be careful not to blow too hard—this can damage your ears. Just blow until you feel a fullness in your ears or until any discomfort disappears.

If you tend to have problems equalizing your ears, stop periodically or ascend a few feet until the pain disappears or subsides. Always equalize at a shallow depth before going deeper. Do not, in any case, ignore any discomfort that might develop in your ears. For a closer look at equalizing, see Part II, Section C.

FINS AND FOOTWEAR

Under water, a good swimmer can move fairly well for short periods of time without equipment. But prolonged swimming, even for a highly trained athlete, demands an extraordinary amount of strength and endurance. The advent of rubber foot fins in the 1930's was an important breakthrough because of the increased mobility it gave to skin and scuba divers. Fins substantially increase the power of the naked foot. They enable the diver to swim greater distances for longer periods of time without tiring.

SELECTING FINS

Fins fall into two general categories: the full-foot and the open-heel types, as shown in figure 1-13. Full-foot fins are built like rubber shoes with blades attached. They come in as many as 10 different shoe sizes, from ½ to size 14. Open-heel fins usually come in four different sizes: small, medium, large, and extra-large.

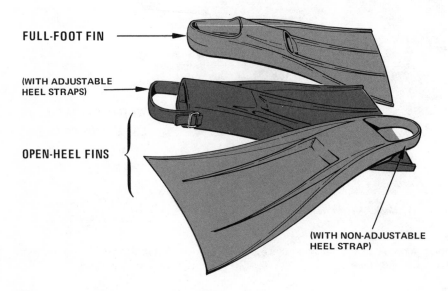

FULL-FOOT FIN ——→

(WITH ADJUSTABLE HEEL STRAPS) ——→

OPEN-HEEL FINS

(WITH NON-ADJUSTABLE HEEL STRAP)

Fig. 1-13   Fin Types

WHAT TO LOOK FOR IN FINS

Fins with large stiff blades are more powerful than those having small, more flexible blades, but you need strong legs to use them for long periods of time. As in selecting the proper mask, it is necessary to know what features to look for when choosing the right fins for your feet. The essential features to consider are as follows:

Materials. Notice the quality of the rubber and manner of construction. Black rubber is stronger and lasts longer than colored materials.

Buoyancy. Some fins sink, some float, and some are neutrally buoyant (neither sink nor float). If you plan to dive in relatively deep water with limited visibility, fins that float might be better since you won't lose them as easily. On the other hand, when diving in clear shallow water, it might be easier to keep track of fins that sink, especially if there is a current or heavy surf in the area.

Fit. Adjustable heel strap fins have obvious advantages in achieving a perfect fit over fins that are not adjustable. A fin that is too tight can restrict circulation and cause cramps, while a loose-fitting fin can rub, chafe, fall off, or cause cramps from trying to keep it on your foot.

The vented fin blade, pictured in figure 1-14, is another fin design feature worth considering. Vented fins have several slots, or vents, located near the diver's foot to effectively redirect the flow of water through and along the fin blade toward the fin tip. This provides for less tiring leg strokes and gives maximum power on the back stroke. Vented fins are purported to produce more thrust with less effort than fins without vents. The vented part of the fin also forms a second blade area close to the foot, that otherwise would do little to increase the speed or power of the fin.

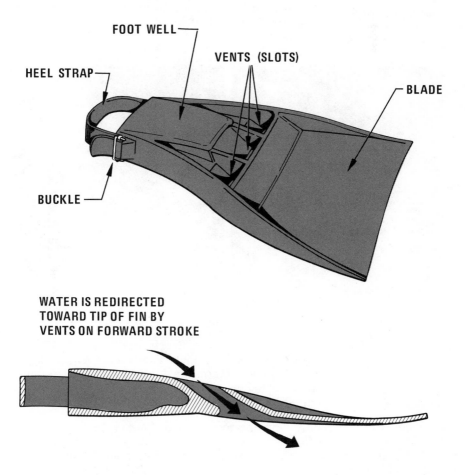

Fig. 1-14 Water Flow through Vented Fins

FIN FIT

When selecting fins, try them on over a pair of wet suit boots. Adjust the straps so the fins are firmly in place, and then try to kick them off, as shown in figure 1-15. They should feel secure without binding, cramping, or pinching. Remember, fins loosen in the water. If possible, experiment with the fins in water before making a final decision.

Selecting fins that fit properly over boots depends on the size of the foot pocket and the strap. Boots are made out of wet suit material and are necessary for warmth during cold water diving. (See figure 1-16.) Warm water divers also use boots for protection from rocks and coral. The foam neoprene serves as a good cushion between the foot and the fin pocket, and minimizes the possibility of blisters. Tennis shoes and socks are poor substitutes for boots even though both are sometimes used by divers. They do not protect against cramps and cold, and they do not stop sand and other abrasives from causing blisters.

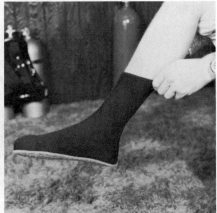

Fig. 1-15 Testing Fin Fit   Fig. 1-16 Wet Suit Boots

FIN USE

There are a few tricks to putting on fins. See figures 1-17 and 1-18 for illustrated examples. Make sure your feet, boots, and fins are wet so the fins will slip on easily. If you are using full-foot fins, fold the heel back to form a "handle" to pull on the fins. With open-heel fins, work the fin over the foot as far as possible and then slip the strap up over your heel.

Few things feel as clumsy as trying to walk with fins on your feet. In fact, walking while wearing fins is nearly impossible. Walking backward on a pool deck, beach, or in shallow water is much easier and safer and climbing boat or pool ladders should be avoided when wearing fins. The safest approach is to remove them first in the water and throw them into the boat or up on the pool deck. If you prefer, you can hold the fins in your hand, or slip the straps over your wrist when climbing up the ladder.

Fig. 1-17 Putting on Full-Foot Fins   **Fig. 1-18 Putting on Open-Heel Fins**

When you enter the water, fins become graceful and powerful extensions of your own body. In fact, fins are so effective that your arms and hands are not used when swimming with fins. Instead, you can let your arms hang naturally at your sides, or use your hands for other functions such as exploring or carrying extra equipment.

Kicking

The flutter kick, pictured in figure 1-19, is the most widely used kick in diving. It is a slow, steady kick that moves a lot of water with each stroke. Legs are kept as straight as practical and ankles swing back and forth like hinges. There is no reason to swim fast—doubling your speed in water takes four times the effort. When doing the flutter kick at the surface, be sure to keep your legs and fins well under water.

Fig. 1-19 Flutter Kick

The scissors kick is sometimes used for variation. The first stroke is almost identical to the flutter kick. Notice the similarity in figure 1-20. The power stroke, however, stops when your feet come together. After gliding for two to three seconds, repeat the first stroke with the same leg coming forward and the same one going back. Because of the glide feature in the scissors kick, it is a relaxing, restful stroke for any distance.

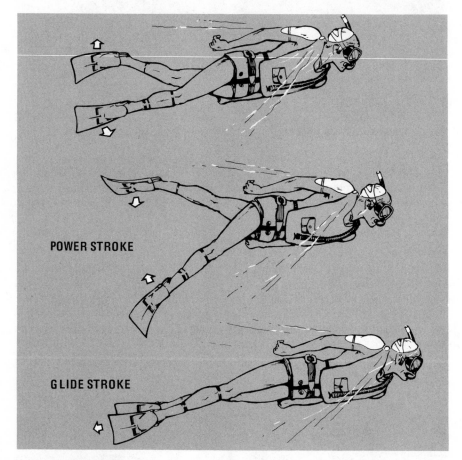

POWER STROKE

GLIDE STROKE

Fig. 1-20 Scissors Kick

The frog kick is not commonly used in diving, but it is a good powerful stroke with a relatively long and restful glide. Variation in kicks is important, especially for long surface swims. Occasionally changing to the frog kick, for example, requires using different muscles than in either the flutter or scissors kicks. As a result, your legs won't tire as easily and will be less likely to cramp. The frog kick begins with a slow separation of your legs, as shown in figure 1-21. The power stroke brings your legs together forcefully and ends in a long easy glide which lasts until you lose most of your forward momentum.

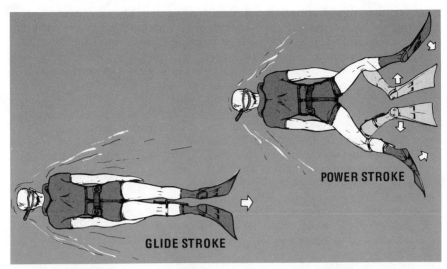

Fig. 1-21 Frog Kick

The dolphin kick is a useful variation underwater. As seen in figure 1-22, both legs stay together and work with the upper part of the body. Begin the dolphin kick in a horizontal position. Bring your fins up by bending your legs at the knees; then, bring your legs down in a power stroke by straightening your legs and bending slightly at the waist. The next step is to bring your fins up again by bending at the knees slightly and, at the same time, straightening your body at the waist and arching your back. As you gain speed, your body moves forward in a wave-like motion in the same way that a dolphin or whale swims.

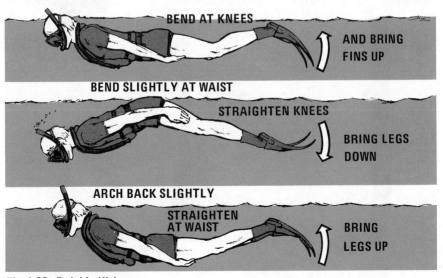

Fig. 1-22 Dolphin Kick

What happens if you accidently lose a fin while diving? The flutter, scissors, and frog kicks all depend on two fins moving in opposite directions. The fins balance each other and convert side motion into forward motion. With only one fin, this balance is missing. The dolphin kick does not depend on two legs and two fins balancing each other. It is the only kick that works well with one fin.

SNORKEL

Breathing tubes of one kind or another have probably been used for over 2,000 years, but it wasn't until the snorkel joined with the modern mask and fins that man was able to swim and relax effortlessly on the surface. The snorkel, with its curved tube and mouthpiece, enables you to swim on the surface without constantly lifting your face above the water to breathe. Your face can remain submerged as long as desired with the aid of a snorkel. With your head down and body relaxed, you have maximum buoyancy and can remain comfortable for hours. You can hang motionless at the surface and breathe through the snorkel without expending any effort to stay afloat.

The snorkel is both a skin and scuba diving tool. The scuba diver uses it to conserve air while swimming on the surface, to and from the dive sites, and while surveying a dive area.

SELECTING A SNORKEL

For discussion, we are going to establish two general classes of snorkels: skin diving snorkels and scuba diving snorkels. Figure 1-23 shows both types of snorkels. The skin diving snorkel generally has a large internal bore for easy breathing, so the air supply is not reduced even when the diver is working hard. The scuba diving snorkel is usually more flexible than the skin diving snorkel. This snorkel often has an accordion shaped curve that permits the mouthpiece to drop easily out of the way when the scuba regulator is in place.

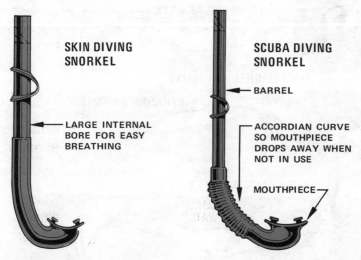

SKIN DIVING
SNORKEL

SCUBA DIVING
SNORKEL

←— BARREL

←— LARGE INTERNAL
BORE FOR EASY
BREATHING

┌— ACCORDIAN CURVE
  SO MOUTHPIECE
  DROPS AWAY WHEN
  NOT IN USE

MOUTHPIECE —┐

Fig. 1-23 Skin and Scuba Snorkels

WHAT TO LOOK FOR IN A SNORKEL

Two major things to consider when selecting a snorkel are breathing resistance and comfort. An easy breathing snorkel has a large bore and clean, simple lines with gentle curves. Do not use snorkels with nonreturn valves at the top of the tube. These increase air resistance and can stick in an open or closed position creating an unsafe condition. A snorkel does not have to be long to work well. Excessive length, in fact, increases breathing resistance and dead-air space. Figure 1-24 shows a number of different snorkel features that increase breathing resistance.

Fig. 1-24 Snorkels with Breathing Resistance

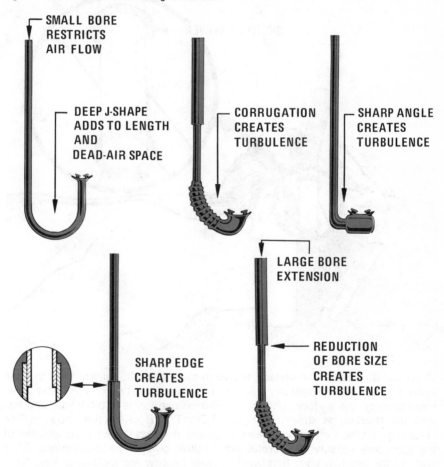

A mouthpiece that does not fit can be extremely uncomfortable. Be sure to test the mouthpiece before selecting a snorkel. Mouthpieces come in many different sizes, shapes, textures, and degrees of flexibility. Some can even be molded for a personalized fit. Try a number of different snorkels until you find one that feels comfortable and meets your needs.

SNORKEL USE

As shown in figure 1-25, the snorkel is always worn on the left side to avoid confusion with the scuba regulator hose and mouthpiece which are routed over the right shoulder. The snorkel is attached to the mask strap with the help of a small rubber snorkel keeper. Adjust the position of the snorkel keeper on the snorkel and along the mask strap until the mouthpiece feels comfortable and the snorkel itself is nearly vertical when you are swimming on the surface with your face in the water.

Fig. 1-25   Position and Location of the Snorkel

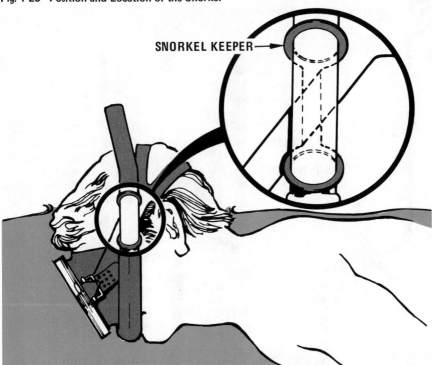

SNORKEL KEEPER

When you dive below the surface, the air in the snorkel bubbles out the top and water fills the tube. There are two different ways to get rid of this water when you return to the surface. The most common method is to blow hard and fast into the snorkel, as shown in figure 1-26. This is called the "popping" or "blasting" method of snorkel clearing because it forces the water up and out of the tube very quickly. Be careful not to blow around the mouthpiece. After clearing the snorkel, your first breath should be slow and shallow to keep from inhaling any water that may remain in the tube.

When swimming at the surface, it is not uncommon for water to spill into the snorkel. When it does, simply clear it. This soon becomes second nature and you will automatically clear your snorkel regularly.

Fig. 1-26   Popping Method of Snorkel Clearing

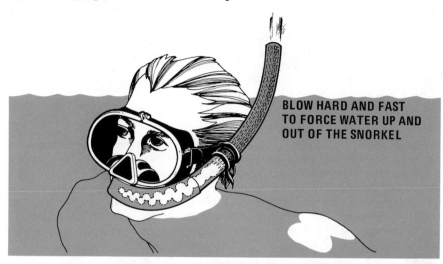

BLOW HARD AND FAST
TO FORCE WATER UP AND
OUT OF THE SNORKEL

The expansion or displacement method of snorkel clearing can be used when returning to the surface. As you ascend, look up toward the surface. This points your snorkel down. (See figure 1-27.) As you approach the surface, exhale lightly into your snorkel. The air expands naturally and clears the snorkel automatically. This method is easier than popping the snorkel clear, but it only works on ascent.

Fig. 1-27   Snorkel Expansion Method

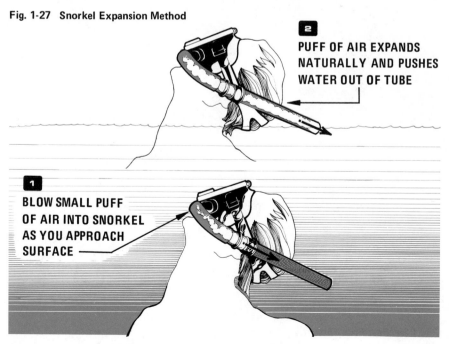

2
PUFF OF AIR EXPANDS
NATURALLY AND PUSHES
WATER OUT OF TUBE

1
BLOW SMALL PUFF
OF AIR INTO SNORKEL
AS YOU APPROACH
SURFACE

USING THE MASK, FINS, AND SNORKEL TOGETHER

ENTRIES

The object is to enter the water the easiest and safest way possible without causing disorientation. It should be a transition, not a collision. Once in the water, your mask, fins, and snorkel should be in place and ready to use. You should be more or less oriented soon after making the entry with a good idea which way is up and which way is down.

Make sure the water is deep enough at the point of entry and be aware of any currents in the area. Before grasping your mask and entering, look at the water: Is your buddy well clear of the entry point? What about other divers or swimmers? If you are entering before your buddy, make sure he is ready to enter and knows that you are going first. No matter which entry you use, grip your face mask firmly with one hand to keep it from being torn off your face from the impact with the water. Once in the water, come to the surface and clear the entry area for your buddy. Watch while your buddy makes his entry.

BOAT, DOCK, AND POOL DECK ENTRIES

If the boat or dock is high off the water, a feet-first entry is best. This allows your feet to break the water first and to absorb the shock of hitting any unseen objects. It also keeps you in an upright position so you will maintain underwater orientation. Figure 1-28 shows three different techniques for making feet-first entries. These include walking or stepping off the edge,

WALKING   **JUMPING**   **GIANT-STRIDE**

Fig. 1-28 Feet-First Entries

jumping with feet together, and jumping feet-first into the water in giant-stride position. The idea of the giant-stride is to keep your legs spread and arms extended until you touch the water. At that point, bring your legs together and your arms down forcefully against the water to slow your speed and to keep your head above the surface. The giant-stride entry can cause injury from great heights, but from lower entry points it is a good technique to use if the water is shallow or if you want to stay near the surface.

The front roll and back roll entries, shown in figure 1-29, are used often by divers in movies and television. They are impressive and splashy entries, but they leave you disoriented and offer no protection against objects under the surface. When diving from a small boat or rubber raft, a back roll from a seated position might be useful to keep the boat from rocking.

BACK ROLL ENTRY

FRONT ROLL ENTRY

Fig. 1-29 Front and Back Roll Entries

The controlled seated entry should be used whenever possible. From a low pool deck or low boat, sit on the side with your feet in the water. Hold on to the side of the boat or pool and just slip gracefully into the water, as shown in figure 1-30. This is a completely controlled entry because you stay in contact with the boat or pool deck at all times, and there is hardly any impact with the water. You remain oriented and in full control of the situation.

Fig. 1-30   Controlled Seat Entry

SHORE ENTRIES

When making an entry from a shore, you will have to decide whether or not to wear your fins. If you have to climb over rocks or through mud, it is safer and easier to carry your fins into the water until it is deep enough to support your weight. Then, put on your fins and dive.

When making an ocean-beach entry through surf breaking near the shore, put on your fins, walk backward into the water until it is deep enough to swim, and then turn around and swim out through the surf. If the surf is breaking far out from the shore, carry your fins out to knee-deep water and put them on there. This will help keep sand out of your fins. Remember, do not try to walk forward with fins on your feet. Walk backward and shuffle your feet to help keep your balance. Part 3, Section B gives further information on shore entries.

SURFACE DIVES

There are two basic kinds of surface dives: the head-first and feet-first. The purpose of both types is to lift as much of your body out of the water as you can so your body's weight can push you down into the water. If done properly, the head-first dive will drop you 15 to 20 feet below the surface without kicking.

The head-first surface dive, pictured in figure 1-31, starts from a face-down floating position with your legs near the surface. The first step is to bend your body at the waist to force the top half of your body straight down. Then, lift your legs up completely out of the water. This is the key to the head-first surface dive. The higher you can get your legs out of the water and over you, the more downward force the weight of your legs will create.

1 BEND AT THE WAIST, FIRST

2 THEN LIFT YOUR LEGS UP
COMPLETELY OUT OF THE
WATER

3 LET THE WEIGHT OF YOUR
LEGS FORCE YOU DOWN

Fig. 1-31   Head-First Surface Dive

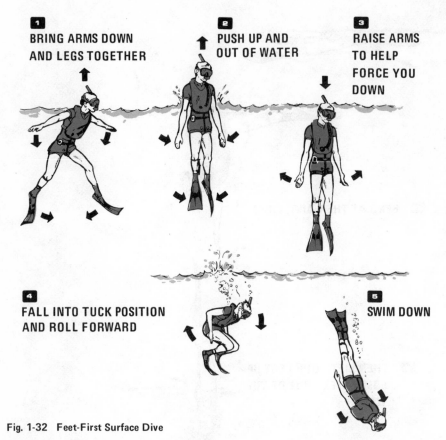

1 BRING ARMS DOWN AND LEGS TOGETHER

2 PUSH UP AND OUT OF WATER

3 RAISE ARMS TO HELP FORCE YOU DOWN

4 FALL INTO TUCK POSITION AND ROLL FORWARD

5 SWIM DOWN

Fig. 1-32 Feet-First Surface Dive

The feet-first surface dive, while skin diving, is used primarily in kelp where there is not enough room to swim or float horizontally at the surface. It lets you begin in a floating, vertical position. (See figure 1-32.) The object is to lift yourself as far out of the water as possible. Start by separating your legs and bringing your arms up; then, kick hard and bring your arms down quickly. As you shoot up and out of the water, keep your arms against your sides and drop straight down beneath the surface. When below the surface, raise your arms to help force you down. When you stop descending, tuck into a ball, turn your head down, and swim toward the bottom.

SEEING AND SWIMMING UNDER WATER

The mask, fins, and snorkel are basic, not only to skin diving, but also to scuba diving. They may feel awkward and clumsy at first, but they add so much to your ability to see, move, and breathe under water, that you will soon feel practically immobile without them. You will also learn the importance of good, comfortable, and reliable equipment and know how to intelligently purchase your gear according to function and cost. The most expensive mask, for example, may not be the best for you. The best mask is the one that meets your needs, fits your face, and feels comfortable, regardless of the price.

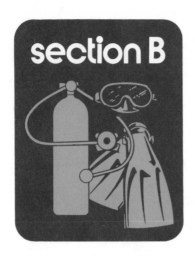

section B

warmth and buoyancy

● WET SUITS
● WEIGHT BELTS
● BUOYANCY COMPENSATORS

WET SUIT, WEIGHT BELT, AND BUOYANCY COMPENSATOR

The mask, fins, and snorkel solved the problems of seeing and swimming under water, but they also led to a new problem: cold. It is tempting to prolong diving time when wearing basic skin diving equipment. But skin divers lack the whale's protective blubber or the otter's thick, oily fur to insulate them. Divers must wear protective suits to retain body heat.

The wet suit satisfactorily solves one problem, but creates a conflict in another area—the wet suit's material increases buoyancy. For a diver, excessive floating is just as bad as excessive sinking. The simplest way to counteract the buoyancy of the wet suit is by adding a weight belt. The puzzle of maintaining warmth and controlling buoyancy was solved by a three-part system, consisting of the wet suit, weight belt, and buoyancy compensator (sometimes called a vest).

WET SUIT

Water absorbs body heat 25 times faster than air. Because of this, a temperature that might be uncomfortably warm in air could be uncomfortably cold in water. A resting diver, for example, chills in one to two hours when the water temperature is between 75° and 80°F (approximately 25°C). Cold water, however, is not only uncomfortable, but also is dangerous. People have died in an hour in 40°F (4° - 5°C) water.

During the first attempts to solve the problem, divers wore long underwear covered with a waterproof rubber dry suit, as shown in figure 1-33. The smallest

Fig. 1-33
Early Dry Suit

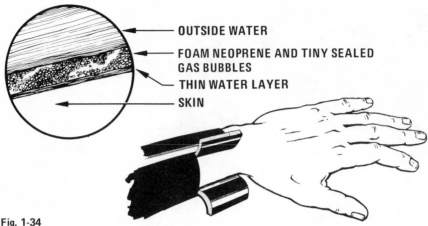

OUTSIDE WATER

FOAM NEOPRENE AND TINY SEALED GAS BUBBLES

THIN WATER LAYER

SKIN

Fig. 1-34
Cross Section of Foam Neoprene

leak or tear in the dry suit, however, ruined everything: divers quickly found soggy underwear and thin rubber suits were undependable insulators.

Divers finally discovered that they did not have to be bone dry to stay warm. Preventing body heat from escaping required an insulating material to stop it from passing into the water. A wet suit made of foam neoprene, three-sixteenths to one-fourth inch thick, proved to be an effective insulator.

Foam neoprene consists of flexible rubber filled with tiny bubbles of gas, as shown in figure 1-34. The insulation concept of the wet suit is based on a thin layer of water seeping in between the suit and skin where it is quickly warmed. Heat escapes slowly through the neoprene thus the body retains most of its natural heat. The body and the water layer next to the body stay warm.

Nothing is more important to diving comfort than a good wet suit. This is especially true in water temperatures below 75°F (24°C), where most sport diving takes place. In many areas, the wet suit extends the diving season from a few summer months to all year. The wet suit also protects against the sun and almost anything else that could irritate, bruise, chafe, or harm delicate human skin. The wet suit also provides reserve buoyancy.

SELECTING A WET SUIT

Sport divers commonly dive in water between 40° to 75°F (4° - 24°C). In this temperature range, you must cover your entire body with a full wet suit, including hood, gloves, and boots.

In warmer water, you may only need a one-eighth inch thick jacket. In cooler water, a hooded vest and high-top pants, sometimes referred to as "Farmer Johns," will help keep your torso warm. Figure 1-35 portrays three types of wet suit protection.

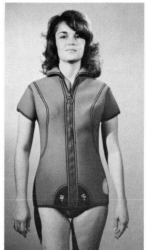

Fig. 1-35 Scuba Diving Suits

The extent of body coverage and thickness of necessary wet suit protection depends on many things. Thin divers, for example, need more protection than heavy divers. Extremely active divers need less protection because they produce more body heat. All divers require extra protection when diving in deep water, since temperature drops as depth increases.

When selecting a wet suit, you can choose between a standard-size or a custom-made suit. The correct fit is extremely important for maintaining warmth. If the suit is too large, water sloshes in and out of the suit at the ankles, wrists, waist, and neck. The warm water seeps out and lets in cold, uncomfortable water. A tight-fitting suit can keep you warm, but it also restricts breathing, circulation, and freedom of movement. This is unsafe. Custom-made suits insure a perfect fit, but stock sizes are acceptable if they fit snugly and feel comfortable.

WHAT TO LOOK FOR IN A WET SUIT

After deciding on the type of wet suit protection you need, study the neoprene material and see how it is made. Wet suits lined inside and out with four-way stretch nylon fabric are the most durable. The inside lining makes it easier to climb into; it works like a dry lubricant. The external lining slightly reduces the flexibility of the suit, but the increase in strength and suit life is worth this small disadvantage. Suits without nylon, or only on one side, are equally warm.

WET SUIT FEATURES

Zippers at the ankles and wrists are not necessary, but they make dressing and undressing easier. Usually an extra strip of neoprene under zippers restricts water leakage. (See figure 1-36.) If you plan to dive in extremely cold water, avoid wet suits with zippers since some water seeps through them.

Fig. 1-36 Wet Suit Zippers   Fig. 1-37 Wet Suit Features and Options

Wet suit jackets are available with a spine pad, which is an extra strip of foam neoprene that fits into the depression along your spine. The spine pad prevents cold water from entering into this area. Pockets, reinforcing patches, knee and elbow pads, and special knife or tool holders also can be built into wet suits, as shown in figure 1-37. Neoprene socks or boots are available with hard rubber or felt soles to protect both boots and feet when walking over sharp rocks or coral.

The one wet suit feature that is *not* optional is a good fit. A suit should feel snug all over your body without binding or pinching. There should be no gaps or spaces under the arms, at the neck, or in the crotch. The ankles, waist, wrist, and neck openings should be tight enough to keep water from sloshing in and out, but loose enough to allow free body circulation. In short, your wet suit should fit like a second skin.

WET SUIT USE

Using a wet suit is easy. Once you have it on, you can forget about it and enjoy its warmth. Getting it on and taking it off is the challenging part. Dressing can be frustrating, time consuming, and exhausting for the new diver. To avoid any confusion, follow these steps when preparing for entry on your first dive, especially when you don't own the equipment. Normally all equipment would be adjusted prior to leaving for the dive site.

1. **Pants.** Pants go on first. Fold the pants down over the knees as though you were turning them inside out. This insures a good fit from the ankle to the knee. Once the pants are on up to the knees, simply roll them up your legs checking that the crotch fits snugly. (Fig. 1-38)

2. **Boots.** Roll the tops of the boots down, and inside out, just past the heel. Then work the foot into the boot as far as you can before pulling it over your heel and ankle. Zippers in pant legs are helpful because the boots *must* tuck under the wet suit pants. (Fig. 1-39)

3. **Fins.** Get your fins and boots wet and put the fins on over your boots to make proper adjustments. Then, lay them near the water so they will be handy when you make your entry. Have all the equipment you need near the entry point before putting on your wet suit. You can become overheated if you delay entry while wearing a wet suit. (Fig. 1-40)

4. **Jacket.** Pull the wet suit jacket on like any ordinary shirt or jacket, one arm at a time. Make sure the sleeves are up all the way to your arm pits so there are no gaps under your arms. Jacket arms that are not up all the way will pull and bind at your shoulder. This is uncomfortable and limits arm movement. Before zipping the jacket, fasten the crotch strap to help hold the flaps together. (Fig. 1-41)

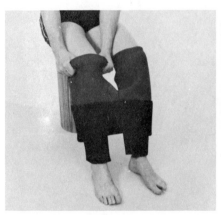

Fig. 1-38 Wet Suit Dressing: Pants

Fig. 1-39 Wet Suit Dressing: Boots

Fig. 1-40 Wet Suit Dressing: Fins

Fig. 1-41 Wet Suit Dressing: Jacket

Fig. 1-42 Wet Suit Dressing: Vest

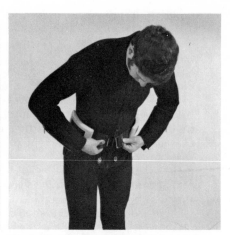

Fig. 1-43 Wet Suit Dressing: Weight Belt

Fig. 1-44 Wet Suit Dressing: Hood

Fig. 1-45 Wet Suit Dressing: Mask

5. **Buoyancy Compensator or Vest.** Inflate the buoyancy vest completely (if you fasten a deflated vest, it will be too tight after inflation). Adjust and tighten the waist strap first and then the crotch strap. Deflate the vest, and position the buckle on the right side so it will not be confused with the weight belt and backpack buckles. Then, take vest off. (Fig 1-42)

6. **Weight Belt.** The belt is the last thing to go on and the first thing to come off, but it should be adjusted now so it will be ready to go when you are. Make sure the weights are evenly balanced somewhere near the front of the belt. Also, the belt should not be too long. If it sticks out of the buckle more than eight inches, cut it off and burn the end (if made out of nylon) to keep it from unraveling. Take the belt off and put it next to your other equipment. (Fig. 1-43)

7. **Hood.** Put the hood on next. Pull it from the front of your forehead down and toward the back of your head so it will pull your hair out of the way. The lower skirt of the hood should be tucked under the collar of the wet suit jacket. (Fig 1-44)

8. **Mask.** Put the mask on to make sure it is adjusted properly. The mask skirt should be sealed firmly against your face underneath the hood. After adjusting both mask and snorkel, lay them next to your other equipment. (Fig 1-45)

9. **Gloves.** Gloves are the last thing to put on. Wet suit gloves go on like ordinary gloves, but diving gloves must be pulled on completely. A glove only half on is clumsy and tiring. Your buddy can help in tucking the gloves under your sleeves at the wrist. (Fig. 1-46)

Fig. 1-46 Wet Suit Dressing: Gloves

Fig. 1-47 Wet Suit Drying and Storage

WET SUIT CARE AND MAINTENANCE

After the dive, remove your equipment and wet suit in the reverse order that you put it on. Rinse the wet suit inside and out in clean, fresh water. Turn it inside out and hang it on wide wooden or plastic hangers in an open, shaded area to dry, as shown in figure 1-47.

For permanent storage, do not fold the suit. Folds and creases in neoprene compress and weaken the material. Excessive heat and direct sunlight also are harmful.

Use neoprene cement to mend small tears. Lubricate metal fittings and zippers with silicone spray, candle wax, or a bar of soap to keep them working smoothly. Occasionally, wash the wet suit with a mild detergent in lukewarm water. Many divers use the bathtub for washing and the shower-head for rinsing. Open all snaps and zippers and push the suit up and down in the tub water for about five minutes.

Heat and sunlight damage foam neoprene and so does ozone, a chemical contained in smog. If you live in a smog-filled city, store your suit in an airtight plastic bag. Otherwise, hang it on two-inch wide hangers or lay it flat to help distribute the weight evenly. A good wet suit will last indefinitely with proper care and maintenance.

WEIGHT BELT

A diver in the water wearing only a full wet suit floats very well. So well, in fact, it is impossible for him to dive below the surface for any length of time. A medium-size, one-fourth inch thick wet suit at the surface of fresh water has about 18 pounds of buoyancy. It is like wearing a thin life jacket all over your body. The diver wearing a wet suit will be warm and comfortable, but without a weight belt to counteract the buoyancy of foam neoprene, he is trapped at the surface. The lead weight belt is the solution to the buoyancy problem caused by the wet suit.

Fig. 1-48   Neutral Buoyancy

SELECTING A WEIGHT BELT

How heavy should a weight belt be? Each diver must experiment to find out for himself. Your goal is to be neutrally buoyant at the surface with or without a wet suit. Normally, you need 10 to 20 pounds of weight to be neutrally buoyant. Put on all the equipment you will wear when you dive. Get in the water and start adding and subtracting weight until you sink slightly after you exhale, and rise slightly when you inhale. Ideally, your eyes will be at the surface of the water when you have completely inhaled and your body is in a vertical position. (See figure 1-48.) Make sure your buoyancy compensator is completely empty.

Since you are somewhat more buoyant in salt water than fresh, remember to add between two and five pounds of lead when going from fresh to salt water. These are only general guidelines. Weight needs are individual, and often change depending on the age and condition of a wet suit, body type, experience, and equipment. Even the food you eat before the dive has an effect. Usually, you are more buoyant after a meal because digestive gases are present in your stomach and intestines.

Fig. 1-49   Weight Belts

NYLON WEB

RUBBER

WHAT TO LOOK FOR IN A WEIGHT BELT

Figure 1-49 shows the two basic types of materials used for weight belts—nylon web and rubber. Nylon is the most common and durable. Rubber will not last as long, but it stretches, which is an advantage to the descending diver. When pressure increases, the gas cells in the foam neoprene are compressed, which makes the wet suit thinner. If the diver is wearing a nylon belt, it will become loose as he descends. A rubber belt, on the other hand, pulls into the space vacated by the suit, compressing with the increasing depth, and stays tight around the diver's waist. A nylon belt equipped with a depth-compensating device is shown in figure 1-50.

Fig. 1-50   Depth-Compensating Nylon Weight Belt

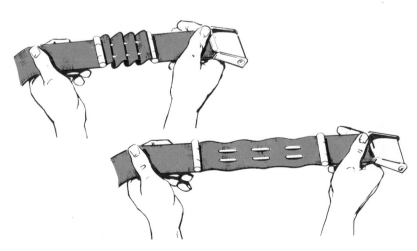

The weight belt must be a quick-release type, as shown in figure 1-51. You should be able to release it immediately with either gloved hand. The clasp-type quick-release buckle is one of the most common. The wire buckle is especially useful because it is unlike any other scuba equipment buckle and, therefore, prevents confusion with the buoyancy compensator or backpack buckles.

Fig. 1-51   Quick-Release Weight Belt Buckle

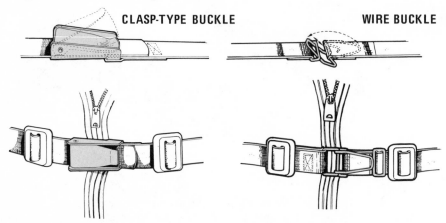

CLASP-TYPE BUCKLE   **WIRE BUCKLE**

There are different kinds and sizes of lead weights as shown in figure 1-52. Some have slits so they can be donned or taken off without unbuckling the belt. Hip weights are available in 6 to 10 pound sizes and should be used as pairs and worn to balance each other.

The shot-filled weight belt, pictured in figure 1-53, does not use ordinary lead weights. It uses a mass of tiny lead balls, or shot, contained in a vinyl compartment. Shot is added or removed to adjust for difference in buoyancy. This is more complicated than changing lead weights and the vinyl compartment is more bulky—but it is a comfortable belt because the shot conforms to the body.

Fig. 1-52   Weights

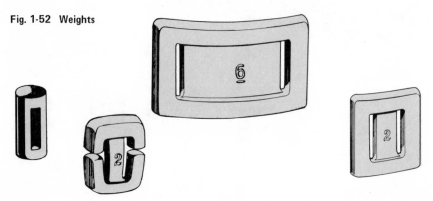

USING THE WEIGHT BELT

The weight belt lets you approach neutral buoyancy at the surface. It is also extremely important as a safety device because it gives you buoyancy the instant you take it off. This is why you must put it on last and take it off first. *The weight belt must not be held in place by other straps or equipment.*

A quick-release buckle enables you to ditch the weight belt immediately in an emergency. Simply unfastening the buckle is not enough. You must pull the belt completely away from your waist as far as you can to let it drop freely and clearly, as shown in figure 1-54. Otherwise, it could get hung up on other straps, a knife handle, or even a fin.

Fig. 1-53 Shot-Filled Weight Belt

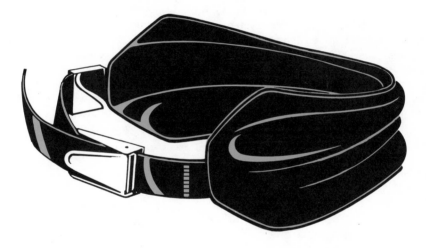

The wet suit-weight belt combination is a dynamic safety pair. They keep you warm and let you achieve instant buoyancy whenever you want or need it. If you should run into a problem while diving, do not hesitate to drop the belt. You can always go back down and get it and, even if you cannot find it again, the cost of a weight belt is a small price to pay for the security of almost instant buoyancy.

**Fig. 1-54
Ditching the Weight Belt**

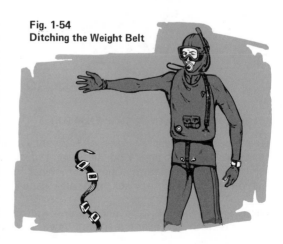

BUOYANCY COMPENSATOR

At this point, complete buoyancy control is not yet solved. The weight belt adequately counteracts the buoyancy of the wet suit at the surface, but buoyancy changes when you descend because of wet suit compression. If a medium size wet suit has 18 pounds of buoyancy at the surface, for example, the same suit will have an extreme loss of buoyancy at a depth of 100 feet. The diver who wears 18 pounds of lead to achieve neutral buoyancy at the surface may find himself as much as 10 pounds too heavy at 100 feet.

The solution to the problem of changing wet suit buoyancy had been around for a long time, but divers only discovered it in the late 1960's. Previously, the "solution" was used to solve another problem—keeping downed pilots, airplane passengers, and sailors afloat in an emergency. The life jacket sometimes called a safety vest, or "Mae West," usually came equipped with a small tube or inflator so the person using it could blow it up orally. It also had an emergency carbon dioxide (CO_2) inflation system, as shown in figure 1-55. Divers began using war surplus life vests in the 1950's and early 1960's as safety vests. The vests were never considered tools since they had been designed only as emergency devices and the oral inflator tubes were small and usually located in the wrong place. The CO_2 mechanisms were not designed for repeated use. They often became clogged or blocked. These emergency vests were relatively small in volume and not particularly comfortable when inflated. It was not until the late 1960's that a true buoyancy compensator was designed especially for the skin and scuba diver.

Fig. 1-55 Early Navy Type Life Vests

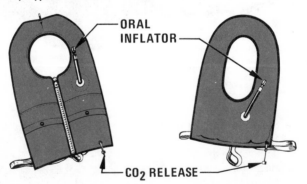

ORAL INFLATOR

CO_2 RELEASE

SELECTING A BUOYANCY COMPENSATOR

There are three general types of buoyancy compensators or vests. The first model, shown in figure 1-56, has been redesigned to fit the diver's particular needs. The oral inflation tube is somewhat longer and larger, and is attached high on the collar of the neck to let air escape easily when deflated.

These vests, like all buoyancy compensators used with scuba, should be equipped with an over-expansion valve to prevent the possibility of over

Fig. 1-56 Buoyancy Compensator

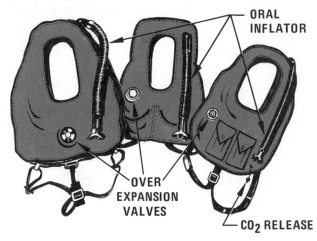

ORAL
INFLATOR

OVER
EXPANSION
VALVES

CO₂ RELEASE

inflating during ascent. Like the original life vest, this model is often equipped with a CO_2 cartridge inflation mechanism.

The buoyancy control vest, illustrated in figure 1-57, is the second kind of buoyancy compensator. It was designed specifically as a diving tool. It has a larger, three dimensional shape than the old style CO_2 vest, and the oral inflator is larger and easier to use. The buoyancy control vest can include an automatic inflator hose from the scuba tank to the vest or oral inflator. By pushing a button or lever, you can inflate the vest with air directly from the scuba tank.

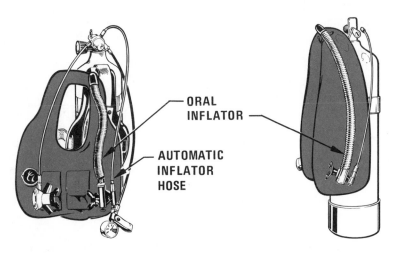

ORAL
INFLATOR

AUTOMATIC
INFLATOR
HOSE

Fig. 1-57
Buoyancy Control Vest

Fig. 1-58
Buoyancy Control Pack

The buoyancy control pack, as shown in figure 1-58, is the third alternative. It works like the vest, but it is attached to the backpack instead of the diver's chest. It is usually a horseshoe shaped unit with an oral and an automatic inflator. For long swims at the surface, it is best to take this type of tank and buoyancy control pack off and lie on top of it.

WHAT TO LOOK FOR IN A BUOYANCY COMPENSATOR

Compensators made out of sealed, rubberized nylon are strong and reliable, as are those with double bag construction. Seams should be heat sealed or taped inside and out to insure a good airtight seal. The vest should expand away from your body without pulling or tightening the straps. It should have a small amount of flotation around and behind your neck, with most of the air space low on the chest and abdomen. When fully inflated, the vest should stay in place without riding up around your neck.

Large diameter inflator hoses which are attached high on the vest at the collar are easy to inflate and deflate. The larger the volume of the vest, the greater the buoyancy. The overpressure valve also should be large and located relatively low on the vest so that all buoyancy will not be lost if the valve breaks or leaks.

BUOYANCY COMPENSATOR USE

Never dive without some form of buoyancy compensation device. It is one of the most useful diving tools. It is a valuable emergency device. Keep your vest at least partially inflated while on the surface. Using energy to stay at the surface is unnecessary; let the buoyancy compensator do the work.

Filling a vest with an automatic inflator is easy, but you also should learn to fill it orally in case of an equipment failure. The bobbing technique is one of the easiest and safest methods. Simply kick to the surface, take a deep breath, and relax while you exhale into the vest. You might sink slightly during the exhalation, but when you have finished, just kick back to the surface for another big breath of air and repeat the procedure. (See figure 1-59.) You will establish good positive buoyancy in two or three breaths.

When resting or swimming at the surface, stay in a facedown position. It might seem easier to swim on your back, especially with a fully inflated vest, but it is much more exhausting. The reason is that in a facedown position, the upper part of your body is resting on the vest which partially lifts your lungs above the surface of the water. This reduces the pressure surrounding your lungs and makes breathing much easier. If you have difficulty staying on top of your vest, release some of the air until the position feels secure and comfortable, as shown in figure 1-60.

When deflating your vest, hold the inflation tube above the vest so air can escape easily, as shown in figure 1-61. Either press the deflate button, or depress the mouthpiece, depending on the type of vest you are using.

Fig. 1-59 Inflating the Buoyancy Vest at the Surface (Bobbing Technique)

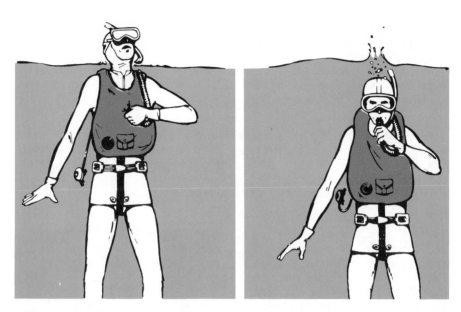

When underwater, inflate your vest either mechanically or orally until you begin to rise above the bottom. Then, deflate the vest until you hang suspended. Using this technique, together with controlling air in your lungs, enables you to maintain a state of neutral buoyancy throughout any dive at any depth. When ascending, be careful to allow expanding air to escape from the vest so you maintain a slow ascent rate.

Fig. 1-60 Resting at the Surface

Fig. 1-61 Deflating the Vest

CARE AND MAINTENANCE OF THE BUOYANCY COMPENSATOR

After every dive, fill the buoyancy vest about one-third full with fresh water and slosh it around, as shown in figure 1-62. Hold the inflator hose down and open the mouthpiece valve to let the water run out. Just before it is completely empty, taste the water and make sure it is clear and clean. If it tastes salty, repeat the rinsing procedure. If it is clean, remove the CO_2 cartridge and let the water flow through the opening to the CO_2 mechanism. Again, taste the water to make certain all salt has been flushed.

After the inside is clean, rinse the outside of the buoyancy compensator, taking special care to clean push-button valves, inflation mechanisms, and other parts. Dry out and lubricate these parts with silicone spray. Lubricate the CO_2 cartridge threads and puncture disc with vaseline, white all-purpose grease, or some other kind of waterproof material to prevent corrosion.

Test for leaks by inflating the vest and submerging it in the bathtub or sink. Look for tiny air bubbles. Repair any leaks before the next dive. When you store the vest, leave it half full of air to keep the insides from sticking together.

With proper care, your buoyancy compensator, weight belt, and wet suit will work together as a warmth-and-buoyancy control team for many years. Take care of it and it will take care of you.

Fig. 1-62 Rinsing the Buoyancy Compensator

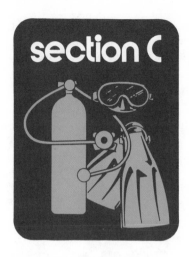

section C

breathing underwater

- TANK ASSEMBLIES
- REGULATORS
- BUDDY BREATHING

TANKS, REGULATORS, AND BUDDY BREATHING

No matter how comfortable the skin diver is under water, time reminds him that he is not a fish. After what seems like only seconds, the skin diver must return to the surface to breathe. The problem of staying under water for a matter of hours instead of minutes was solved long before skin diving became a sport.

Diving bells, hoods, underwater boats and deep sea hard hats, illustrated in figure 1-63, were used, or at least thought of, for centuries. But these contraptions limit the one thing always dear to the sport diver's heart: freedom of movement. You cannot swim in a hard hat rig. With the air hose and lifeline attached, it is like being a fish, all right—but a fish caught on a hook.

Fig. 1-63 Early Underwater Breathing Apparatuses

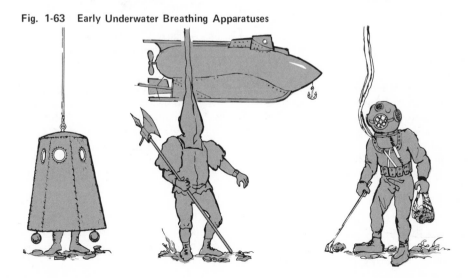

The sport diver needed a *self-contained* air supply to give him both time and freedom of underwater movement. He needed two things—a large amount of air in a small container and a way to control the release of air so he could breathe. Amazingly, these two things existed almost 80 years before a true self-contained underwater breathing apparatus (SCUBA) unit was invented.

In 1825, W. H. James, an Englishman, invented a self-contained diving suit with a supply of compressed air. (Note figure 1-64.) But no one was particularly impressed or interested in the outfit.

Fig. 1-64
James' Self-Contained Diving Suit

Fig. 1-65 Rouquayrol's Apparatus in
20,000 Leagues Under The Sea

Some 41 years later, Benoist Rouquayrol of France patented the first *demand regulator*. When connected to a supply of high pressure air, Rouquayrol's regulator delivered air to the diver whenever he inhaled. When he stopped inhaling, the regulator stopped letting air flow. For some reason, Rouquayrol did not bother to attach his regulator to a container of compressed air like the one James had used. Jules Verne, the only person who did make this connection, used it in his book, *20,000 Leagues Under the Sea*, as shown in figure 1-65.

In 1925, Frenchman le Prieur took a tank of high pressure air and attached it to a diving mask, as shown in figure 1-66. By this time, however, Rouquayrol's demand regulator had been forgotten, so the diver had to manually turn the air on and off, wasting a lot of the limited air supply.

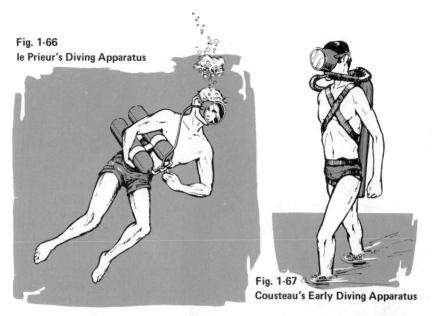

Fig. 1-66
le Prieur's Diving Apparatus

Fig. 1-67
Cousteau's Early Diving Apparatus

Finally, in 1943, Jacques Cousteau of France and Emile Gagnan, an engineer from Canada, put everything together. They had been skin diving for several years with masks and fins. They wanted the freedom of skin diving along with the extended time that a compressed air supply would offer. One June afternoon in the south of France, Cousteau attached a demand regulator to a high pressure tank and tested the world's first fully automatic compressed air diving apparatus, shown in figure 1-67. It worked. Diving was revolutionized.

Never before had man carried this much air on his back—air that was supplied to him automatically, whenever he inhaled. It also delivered air at the correct depth pressure. Cousteau called it the passport to the underwater world, and that is exactly what it was.

TANK

The scuba tank used by sport divers has changed little since Cousteau made the first scuba dive. It is a simple device—a seamless metal container with threads at the neck for a valve. But the manufacture of this and all other high pressure containers is a carefully controlled process. From the time it comes from the factory, until it is retired, the tank is regularly tested and inspected. It would be difficult to find, let alone buy, a new scuba tank that is not good. You should, however, understand tanks well enough to select, use, and take care of one intelligently.

SELECTING A TANK

The first two decisions to make when selecting a tank concern size and materials. Tank sizes are measured by how much air they contain at a certain maximum pressure. They run from 18 cubic feet to 100 cubic feet, as shown in figure 1-68. The 71.2 cubic foot tank is the most common size tank used by sport divers. Smaller tanks are lighter and easier to handle for young or lightweight divers, but larger tanks have a greater air capacity.

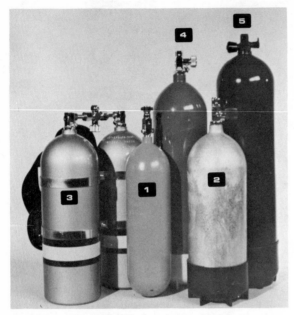

1   18 CU. FT.
STEEL

2   40 CU. FT.
STEEL

3   50 CU. FT.
ALUMINUM

4   71.2 CU. FT.
STEEL

5   80 CU. FT.
ALUMINUM

Fig. 1-68 Different Size Tanks

The *seventy-one*, however, is a good compromise between weight and air capacity. It weighs about 28 to 35 pounds depending on whether it is empty or full. It is a little over two feet long, six to eight inches wide, and is designed to hold air at a maximum of 1800 to 3000 pounds per square inch (psi) of pressure depending on design.

A full *seventy-one* contains about the same amount of air as a telephone booth. How long does the air last? This is a common question that has no correct answer. It depends on depth, lung capacity, activity level, water temperatures, and other factors that will be discussed in Part II, Section C.

Until 1970, all sport diving tanks were made out of steel. Since that time, they also have been made out of an aluminum alloy. The main difference between steel and aluminum is the way the two metals corrode—rust forms on steel, and aluminum oxide forms on aluminum.

When a metal corrodes, oxygen combines with it to form a new substance, usually the original ore. Rust resembles the ore used initially in making steel. It is much softer than steel, so it crumbles and flakes off. (See figure 1-69.)

This oxidation process happens faster when water or water vapor is present; salt water increases it even more. With enough oxygen, water, and salt rust can gradually eat through a steel tank wall.

Fig. 1-69   Rust: Oxidation Process of Steel   Fig. 1-70   Aluminum Oxide

Rust does not form on all metals. A gray coating called aluminum oxide forms on aluminum when it is combined with oxygen. As illustrated in figure 1-70, aluminum oxide is hard and clings tightly to the metal underneath. It clings so well, that it actually prevents more oxygen from coming in contact with the aluminum. Without oxygen, corrosion cannot take place, so the aluminum oxide protects the metal it covers.

For all practical purposes, aluminum scuba tanks will not corrode as long as the protective aluminum oxide coating stays in place.

Steel tanks corrode if water and salt leak into the tank, but steel is just as durable as aluminum if the tank is kept clean and dry, inside and out.

WHAT TO LOOK FOR IN A TANK

Coatings

There are a number of inside and outside coatings for scuba tanks which protect them and make them more attractive. All steel tanks should be galvanized to protect outside surfaces from water and air—two things necessary for rust. Vinyl and epoxy coatings are sometimes painted over the zinc coating for color and additional protection, but if any of these coatings are punctured or scratched, rust forms underneath. Ordinary paint is not durable enough to either protect or beautify a steel tank for any length of time. Aluminum tanks do not need any coatings or undercoatings, but they are available with vinyl or epoxy coatings to add color.

Steel tanks are not coated with zinc inside since zinc can be toxic in heavy doses. Only the outside of the tank is galvanized. Epoxy paint is used to coat the inside of steel tanks. It protects the bare metal from corrosive effects of air and water, but the coating works only if the epoxy maintains a perfect seal over the steel. Moisture can penetrate underneath the epoxy even through a tiny hole. When this happens, rust forms *under* the coating where you cannot see it.

Another way to protect the inside of
a steel tank, which is currently under
development, is with a polyvinyl
tank liner, shown in figure 1-71.
Placing a tank liner into a tank is
like blowing up a balloon inside the
tank to protect it from outside air
and water. The liner can be removed
for inspection and replaced with a
new one, if necessary.

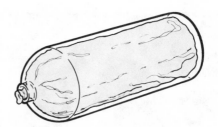

Fig. 1-71   Polyvinyl Tank Liner

Tank Markings

Like all high pressure containers, scuba tanks must conform to regulations set
by the Bureau of Explosives and the U.S. Department of Transportation. The
manufacturing, transporting, and testing of scuba tanks is a carefully controlled
process. All tanks sold in the United States must have either DOT (U.S.
Department of Transportation) or ICC (Interstate Commerce Commission)
stamped on the neck, along with a series of other markings. The numbers,
letters, and symbols stamped on the tank describe and identify the tank and
also provide a record of testing validations. The meanings of these markings are
shown in figure 1-72.

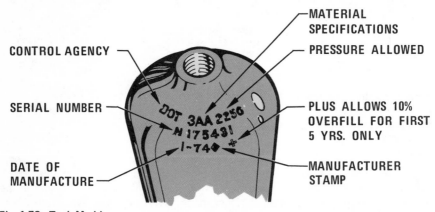

Fig. 1-72   Tank Markings

Without correct markings, a tank is illegal. Reputable dive stores will not fill
illegal tanks. You should understand the meaning of tank markings so you can
recognize an illegal tank. This is especially important when buying old or used
equipment.

Tank Valves

Tanks have one of two kinds of valves at the top to turn the air on or off. The
body of the valve is threaded and screws into the tank neck. The tank valve
stays in place continuously, except for tank inspections. The nonreserve, or
"K" valve, as it is usually called, is a simple on-and-off valve. The "J" or
constant reserve valve, has an extra level connected to the special spring-loaded

reserve mechanism. It serves as a warning device to prevent the diver from accidentally running out of air. The reserve valve stays open until the pressure inside the tank gets down to about 300 psi. Then the spring pressure shuts off the air flow. Pulling down the reserve lever opens the valve manually so the diver can use the remaining 300 psi of air for his ascent. "K" and "J" valves have a number of safety, or convenience features, as shown in figure 1-73. The small black "O" ring that surrounds the air outlet forms the seal between the tank valve and the regulator yoke. Without the "O" ring, a tank valve is useless, so make a point of carrying an extra. (Divers often carry extra "O" rings between the wing screw and the yoke on the regulator.)

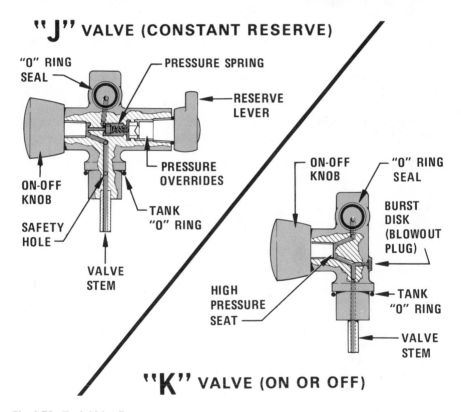

Fig. 1-73   Tank Valve Features

The *burst disk assembly* or *blowout plug* is an important safety feature, especially against overfilling. Air expands when heated. If a full scuba tank is heated as a result of being left in the sun, in the trunk of a car, or in some other similar area, the air can expand greatly. If it were not for the blowout plug, an over-heated tank could explode. Instead, the thin metal disk ruptures and lets the expanded air escape harmlessly. The burst disk, illustrated in figure 1-73, is designed to give way somewhere between 125 and 166 percent of the tank's stamped working pressure. Valves without a blowout plug are *illegal*.

Fig. 1-74   Tank Boots

Fig. 1-75   Self-Draining Tank Boot

Before removing a tank valve, be sure to release all of the air. Unscrewing the valve with high pressure air behind it could be dangerous. Because of this, some valves have a small safety hole, as shown in figure 1-73, drilled into the threads. This lets any pressurized air escape before you have unscrewed the valve more than a few turns. This should never be done except by professional repairmen.

The valve stem extends into the tank and helps keep water, rust, or other impurities (that should not be in your tank), out of your regulator. Even if you turn a tank upside down and turn on the valve, water will stay in the tank because it cannot get past the two inch valve stem. (See figure 1-73.)

Tank Boots

An upright tank is unstable and might fall over unless someone is holding onto it. Tank boots, like those in figure 1-74, were designed to protect the tank, floor, deck, foot—anything an unbalanced tank might fall on. Most boots let the tank stand upright by itself, but this is obviously not their primary purpose.

Some tank boots are designed like a large rounded cup that encloses the bottom of the tank. This design also traps water and can lead to serious corrosion. Other boots, like the one shown in figure 1-75, are designed to let water flow out the bottom. If possible, boots should be removed and washed occasionally. This is especially true of non-galvanized steel tanks coated with vinyl or epoxy.

Backpack

Early scuba divers simply strapped the tank or tanks to their backs with a tank harness. (See figure 1-76.) This basically secured the tank to the body, but it allowed too much movement of the tank which affected both balance and comfort. The tank harness was even less comfortable and secure out of the water. The backpack, also shown in figure 1-76, is a more comfortable and stable way to attach the scuba unit to your back. It has two shoulder straps and one waist strap. This is an extremely comfortable and secure design for use both in and out of water.

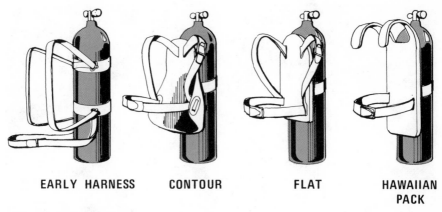

EARLY HARNESS CONTOUR FLAT HAWAIIAN PACK

Fig. 1-76 Early Tank Harness and Modern Backpacks

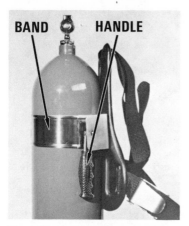

BAND HANDLE

Fig. 1-77 Tank Retaining Band

When selecting a backpack, look for quick release buckles at the waist and on at least one shoulder strap. Everything on the pack should be made out of non-corrosive materials. The tank retaining band holds the tank onto the backpack. The band holds the tank with either cam operated handles, for quick change to another tank, or simple nut-and-bolt and screw-type methods for more permanent attachment. (See figure 1-77.)

Make sure the tank band is tight before each dive. Adjust the backpack so that your head does not hit the tank valve when you lean back.

There are a number of different ways to put on a scuba tank. Your buddy can hold it for you while you slip your arms through the shoulder straps, fasten the shoulder and waist buckles, and adjust the straps. Because of the scuba tank's weight out of water, don't try to put it on like a jacket or a knapsack. Rather, let the tank rest on the floor, slip your arms through both shoulder straps past your elbows, and lift it up and over your head in one smooth operation, as depicted in figure 1-78.

CARE AND MAINTENANCE OF THE TANK

Scuba tank care, for the most part, means keeping out moisture. Like all diving equipment, the exterior should be rinsed thoroughly with fresh water after each dive and washed with mild soap and water when it gets dirty. To keep water out of valve and tank, keep at least 50 pounds of air pressure in the tank.

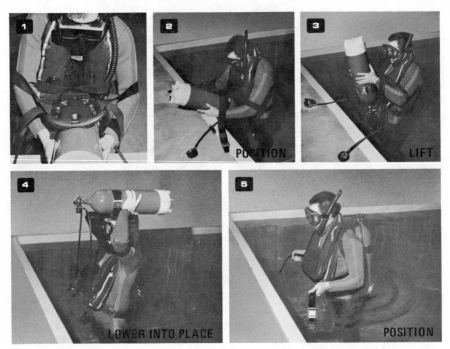

Fig. 1-78 Putting on the Scuba Tank

When carrying the tank in a car, either lay it sideways on the floor or lengthwise in the trunk, with the valve towards the rear. (See figure 1-79.) Wrap the valve in thick cloth, such as a beach towel, and lash it down or block it so it cannot move.

If you are traveling by air, leave 40 pounds of pressure in the tank—this is considered empty by the Department of Transportation. Most airlines, however, require open valves and a completely empty tank.

Rust will form inside a warm tank full of high pressure air, where the oxygen from the air is concentrated. Steel tanks, therefore, should be stored in cool areas with no more than 100 psi of air inside. The metal in the tank is thicker at the bottom than around the side, so it is better to store it standing up than lying down. Aluminum tanks and perfectly dry steel tanks can be stored in any position. Wherever you store your tank, tie it down and keep it away from children.

Fig. 1-79 Traveling with a Scuba Tank

Visual Inspections (Internal and External)

There is only one way to make sure that a tank is clean, safe, and rust-free. Thorough visual inspection once a year by a professional inspector is not required by law, but is highly recommended by most equipment dealers. Aluminum tanks do not rust, but they should be inspected to be sure no conminants are inside.

It is easier to prevent the problem of a contaminated tank than to solve it. Never release *all* the tank air. If you release it accidentally, shut the valve immediately to keep water from entering the tank. When you push the regulator purge valve with the tank valve open and the tank empty, there is a direct and open route into the tank. This increases the possibility of contamination.

Water can also get inside your tank if air is released too quickly. For example, suppose you want to store a full tank for several months. If you open the valve far enough, most of the air will escape in a matter of minutes. But, since gases cool when they expand (refrigerators and air conditioners are based on this principle), the air, and the tank itself, will become very cool. As a result, water vapor will condense on the inside of the tank. To prevent this, take a few hours to let all the air out of a tank. You can also put it in water to keep the tank's temperature from dropping too much.

When filling a tank or when attaching the regulator, make sure all fittings, openings, and "O" rings on or attached to the tank valve are clean and dry. Filling a tank with a wet valve is a sure way to introduce water into the tank.

Between annual visual inspections, look, smell, and listen to your tank for hints of water inside.

1. **Look.** Turn the valve on and check the air coming out. Damp air is white. Dry air is clear and you cannot see it.

2. **Smell.** Pure, clean air does not smell. If the air coming out of your tank smells damp and metallic, there could be water, oil, or rust inside.

3. **Listen.** Put your ear next to the tank. Turn the tank upside down so that anything inside will fall to the other end. You should not be able to hear a sound.

If you have cause for suspicion, take it in for a visual inspection. Otherwise, take it in once a year. A full-service dive store is usually equipped to inspect and test tanks. Hydrotesting firms specialize in servicing all kinds of high pressure cylinders.

The visual inspection begins when the inspector examines the tank's exterior after removing the tank band and boot. He looks for any dents, scratches, or corrosion. Then, he slowly lets all the air escape and removes the tank valve. He uses a special light or series of lights to see inside.

Rust, water, salt, flaked epoxy linings, and especially pits or rough and scaley surfaces must be cleaned. The inspector fills the tank half full with some kind of abrasive materials, such as carbide or aluminum oxide chips. After capping the tank, he lays it down on two rotating rollers to tumble, as shown in figure 1-80. The abrasive chips scrape the inside of the tank clean so the inspector can see clearly how much damage has been done. Some hydro-testing firms use a rotating chain or sandblasting machine to clean the inside, but these methods are neither thorough nor complete. *Never* let a hydrotester use chemicals inside the tank—fumes can be toxic.

Fig. 1-80 Tank Tumbling

After tumbling, the inspector looks inside again to see if corrosion was only on the surface, or if it was more serious. Then, he retests the tank. If it fails hydrotesting, the inspector will not stamp a new test date on the tank. He may also stamp out the DOT or ICC markings on the neck of the tank.

Hydrostatic Testing

Every five years, you must have your tank hydrostatically tested. The Department of Transportation and the Bureau of Explosives set testing standards, govern the interstate transportation, and investigate testing viola-tions. Illegal hydrostatic testing operations do exist, so ask your diving instructor or dive store to suggest a reputable hydrotester. He must be authorized by the Bureau of Explosives and he should have a current letter of authorization.

After a complete visual inspection, the hydrotest begins. It is designed to measure the elasticity of the metal within the tank. A good strong tank will stretch and then return to within 10 percent of its original size with very little, if any, permanent expansion.

The tank is filled with water, connected to a high pressure water pump, and submerged in a sealed container that is also filled with water. (See figure 1-81.) Water is forced into the tank at five-thirds of its working pressure which makes the tank expand. The expanding tank forces the surrounding water in the sealed testing chamber through a tube and up into a thin glass measuring tube called a burette.

The testing pressure is held for 30 seconds and then released to let the expanded tank return to normal. To pass the test, the tank's permanent expansion cannot be more than 10 percent of the total expansion. If the tank passes, a new test date is stamped under the old one on the neck of the tank.

If the examiner feels the tank is in good enough condition to be filled 10 percent over its working pressure, he will stamp a plus sign after the new hydro date. However, this is not always done. The tank must have this 10 percent overfill to actually hold 71.2 cubic feet; otherwise, it only holds about 65 cubic feet. A tank is eligible for a plus if it has a high "K" factor. This is a number determined by measuring the thickness of the tank wall, its expansion, elasticity, and several other things. If the "K" factor is too low, your tank will not get a plus. The examiner can simply refuse to give a plus sign; it is his choice whether to use it or not. Aluminum tanks never have plus signs because the pressure stamped on them is their full rated pressure.

What happens if the tank ruptures during the hydrostatic test? Nothing much. Unlike a tank filled with air, a water-filled tank is not explosive. If the tank should break, it relieves the water pressure almost immediately without much expansion.

After the hydrotest, the tank must be thoroughly dried with hot air from the inside. Usually, hot air is blown into the tank through a tube. Heating the tank from the outside does not work—it causes steam to form which later condenses in the tank when it cools.

Hydrotesting is safe, reliable, and cheap, especially when you consider the insurance it provides. It is comforting to know your tank will hold almost twice the amount of internal pressure you will ever put into it. Feel free to hydrotest your tank more often but it must be hydrotested at least every five years.

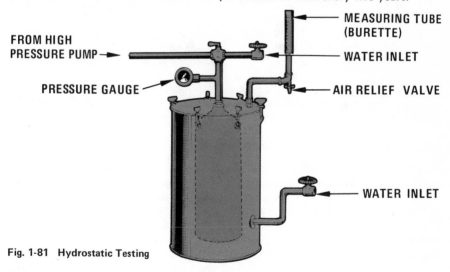

FROM HIGH PRESSURE PUMP →

PRESSURE GAUGE

MEASURING TUBE (BURETTE)

WATER INLET

AIR RELIEF VALVE

WATER INLET

Fig. 1-81 Hydrostatic Testing

THE REGULATOR

Squeezing air into a cylinder at over 150 times its normal pressure is easy, compared to making that air usable for the diver. An ordinary on-and-off valve on top of the tank lets the air escape, but the diver using that air does not need it all the time. When he does, he needs only a small amount of air at just the right pressure. Regulating the air flow becomes pretty complicated for a simple valve; even if the diver could manually control the air flow, he would have to devote all his time and concentration on it.

This is why the demand regulator was so important to the growth of diving. Without it, a diver would have to turn the air on and leave it on—wasting most of his limited supply in a hurry. With the regulator, the diver gets just the right amount of air, at the right pressure, and at the right time.

SELECTING A REGULATOR

Illustrated in figure 1-82 are the two basic regulator designs used in sport diving. The double hose regulator was used by divers until the late 1950's, when a more compact single hose regulator came into use.

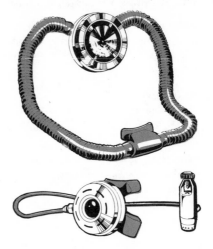

Some divers still choose the double hose design for a number of reasons. They favor the balance of a mouth-piece with a hose on each side. Since the hoses are filled with air, they are buoyant, which makes the mouth-piece lighter and more comfortable on long dives. Some photographers prefer the double hose design because they like having exhaust bubbles re-leased at the tank valve, well out of the way of cameras.

Fig. 1-82
Double and Single Hose Regulators

The single hose regulator, however, is far more popular. It is usually less expensive, more rugged, and easier to maintain. It does not free flow like the double hose model, and the purge valve makes it easier to clear.

WHAT TO LOOK FOR IN A REGULATOR

Regulators are finely adjusted and precise pieces of equipment designed for reliability and durability. Some regulators, however, breathe easier and more smoothly than others. A regulator that is difficult to inhale from or exhale into has *breathing resistance*. This is annoying at best and extremely tiring at worst.

Breathing resistance is caused by a number of things. Hard work and cold water make you breathe much harder. Most regulators have very little breathing resistance at the water surface. The real test occurs near the end of a long hard dive, in deep water, when the tank is almost on reserve. Here, heavy breathing, increased water pressure, and decreasing air pressure inside the tank all tend to increase breathing resistance.

What makes one regulator easier to breathe through than another? To understand the answer, and to know what to look for in a regulator, you must have a basic understanding of regulator operation. Regulators use a system of valves, springs, diaphragms, and levers to reduce tank pressure in stages to usable breathing pressure.

A one-stage regulator reduces pressure all at once. Unfortunately, you may have to inhale very hard to open the air valve, and when it does open, it could give you air faster than you can inhale it. To solve this problem the two-stage regulator was developed. In the two-stage regulator, the first stage reduces the high tank pressure to about 140 psi over ambient pressure. The second stage further reduces that pressure to a workable breathing pressure. It is smoother and more reliable than the old single-stage regulator system.

The double hose, two-stage regulator was a great innovation for the diver. It provided him with nearly effortless breathing in almost all conditions, but it had disadvantages. When the diver is under water in a vertical or upright position, both the two-stage regulator on the tank and the diver's lungs are on about the same level. (See figure 1-83.) This makes breathing easier.

When the diver is swimming in a horizontal, facedown position, the mouthpiece is below the regulator, as shown in figure 1-83. This forces him to pull tank air downward against increased pressure to the mouthpiece. In this position, the double-hose regulator requires more breathing effort.

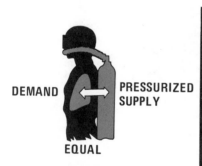

DEMAND — PRESSURIZED SUPPLY

EQUAL

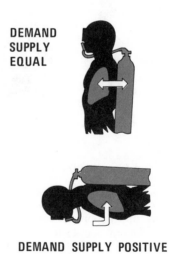

DEMAND SUPPLY EQUAL

PRESSURIZED SUPPLY

DEMAND SUPPLY NEGATIVE

DEMAND SUPPLY POSITIVE

DEMAND SUPPLY POSITIVE

PRESSURIZED SUPPLY

DEMAND SUPPLY NEGATIVE

Fig. 1-83
Breathing with Double Hose Regulator

Fig. 1-84
Breathing with Single Hose Regulator

When the diver is on his back, the mouthpiece is above the two-stage regulator. (See figure 1-83.) In this position, the air in the hoses has a natural tendency to flow up to the surface. This lowers the pressure in the inhalation hose in the same way that a diver lowers the pressure when he inhales. The result is a constant, free flow of air—not an altogether comfortable feeling.

With the advent of the single hose, two-stage regulator, some of the double hose problems were overcome. The single hose regulator puts the second stage next to the mouthpiece, so breathing is nearly equal, no matter what position the diver assumes.

If the diver is upright or vertical in the water, once again the two stages are level and breathing is similar in both types of regulators. In a normal swimming position, the second stage is below the lungs. (See figure 1-84.) Because of this, air has a natural tendency to flow up from the mouthpiece and into the lungs. This is why the single hose regulator makes breathing easier in a normal swimming position.

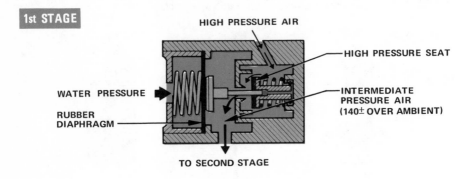

Fig. 1-85   The First-Stage Diaphragm

There are two designs used in the first stage of the single hose, two-stage regulator: the diaphragm and the piston. The diaphragm design is essentially the same as the double hose, two-stage regulator. The first stage diaphragm, shown in figure 1-85, is flexible rubber. On one side of the diaphragm is a spring that pushes about 140 pounds of pressure against it. On the other side is a spring with about 140 pounds to counteract the first spring.

When you inhale, you create a vacuum which overrides the springs. This opens the high pressure seat and allows air to flow into the collecting chamber. When you descend, water pressure pushes against the diaphragm and helps the outer spring maintain the 140 pound balance over ambient pressure.

The advantage of a diaphragm regulator is that you can adjust it precisely. The disadvantage is that there are several adjustments and parts which require care and maintenance.

The piston first-stage is similar to the diaphragm, but a piston, instead of a diaphragm, controls the air flow. In flow-through pistons, air flows directly through the center of the piston. In a partial flow-through piston, air flows from a collecting chamber, through the side of the piston, and then into the hose of the single hose regulator. (See figure 1-86.)

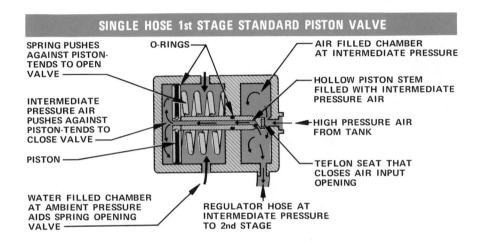

SINGLE HOSE 1st STAGE STANDARD PISTON VALVE

SPRING PUSHES AGAINST PISTON-TENDS TO OPEN VALVE

O-RINGS

AIR FILLED CHAMBER AT INTERMEDIATE PRESSURE

HOLLOW PISTON STEM FILLED WITH INTERMEDIATE PRESSURE AIR

INTERMEDIATE PRESSURE AIR PUSHES AGAINST PISTON-TENDS TO CLOSE VALVE

HIGH PRESSURE AIR FROM TANK

PISTON

TEFLON SEAT THAT CLOSES AIR INPUT OPENING

WATER FILLED CHAMBER AT AMBIENT PRESSURE AIDS SPRING OPENING VALVE

REGULATOR HOSE AT INTERMEDIATE PRESSURE TO 2nd STAGE

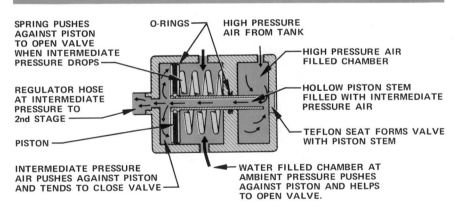

SINGLE HOSE 1st STAGE BALANCED FLOW-THROUGH PISTON VALVE

SPRING PUSHES AGAINST PISTON TO OPEN VALVE WHEN INTERMEDIATE PRESSURE DROPS

O-RINGS

HIGH PRESSURE AIR FROM TANK

HIGH PRESSURE AIR FILLED CHAMBER

REGULATOR HOSE AT INTERMEDIATE PRESSURE TO 2nd STAGE

HOLLOW PISTON STEM FILLED WITH INTERMEDIATE PRESSURE AIR

TEFLON SEAT FORMS VALVE WITH PISTON STEM

PISTON

INTERMEDIATE PRESSURE AIR PUSHES AGAINST PISTON AND TENDS TO CLOSE VALVE

WATER FILLED CHAMBER AT AMBIENT PRESSURE PUSHES AGAINST PISTON AND HELPS TO OPEN VALVE.

Fig. 1-86 The Flow-Through and Partial Flow-Through Piston Regulators

The hose pressure stays at about 140 psi over the ambient pressure. This intermediate pressure is further broken down to ambient levels by the second stage at the mouthpiece.

Early one hose regulators used a *tilt valve* in the second stage. As the term implies, the tilt valve opens by tipping to one side when you inhale, as shown in figure 1-87. But this constant tipping tends to deform the valve seat and causes leakage.

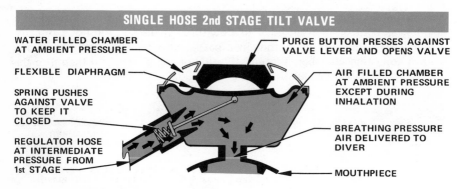

Fig. 1-87 Single Hose Upstream Regulator

The downstream lever action valve solved the problem of the tilt valve deforming the valve seat. *Downstream* refers to a valve that opens *away* from the pressure and with the airflow. The *upstream* valve opens *toward* the pressure and against the flow of air. High pressure air tends to push the downstream valve open, so this type opens very easily and smoothly. The downstream valve is flat and sits directly against a flanged seat. When it opens, the lever simply pulls the valve away and allows the air to flow into the second stage without deforming the valve seat. (See figure 1-88.)

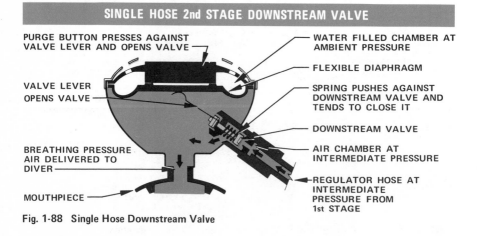

Fig. 1-88 Single Hose Downstream Valve

All one hose demand regulators have a large rubber diaphragm in the second stage. As water pressure increases, it presses against the rubber diaphragm which puts pressure against the lever inside the second stage. The water pressure acting directly on the diaphragm and lever aids the diver in compensating for the ambient water pressure surrounding his chest and lungs. Because of this, the second stage valve opens with an absolute minimum of effort. In fact, most high quality regulators manufactured today almost breathe for you; they require very little breathing effort.

A high quality regulator is important. The regulator is the lifeline to your complete system; without it, nothing else works. While most regulators manufactured today are good, there are important differences between the low cost and the more expensive models.

The differences are in durability and dependability. Most low cost piston regulators have chrome-plated brass inside, while most expensive regulators are machined stainless steel. You find higher quality parts in the more expensive diaphragm regulators and the method for reducing air pressure is more sophisticated and dependable than in the lower cost models.

Reserve Options

The diver who runs out of air under water has no excuse. With the right reserve device and good planning, he can easily finish every dive with the minimum 100 psi left in his tank.

The "J" valve is a common reserve. It is designed to warn you when your air supply reaches approximately 250 to 500 psi. To work, however, the "J" valve lever must be in the up position until you pull it down to use the reserve air. If it accidentally gets knocked down, or if you forget to set it before the dive, it will not work.

One solution to the problem of a nonworking lever is to omit it altogether so it cannot be accidentally knocked down. The sonic, or sound, reserve is built into the first stage of some regulators. It is automatic. When your air supply gets down to the warning level, the sonic alarm buzzes or clicks every time you inhale. When this happens, both you and your buddy know you are breathing reserve air and that it is time to ascend.

Both the "J" valve and the sonic alarm warn you, but they do not give information about your air supply until you go on reserve. The underwater pressure gauge, shown in figure 1-89, tells you exactly how much air you have left in your tank at any time. It has become a standard piece of equipment for scuba divers and should be considered mandatory. The pressure gauge is like a fuel gauge in a car—it does no good unless you look at it. Get in the habit of checking your pressure gauge regularly during the dive. It's a very important piece of equipment—don't ever dive without one.

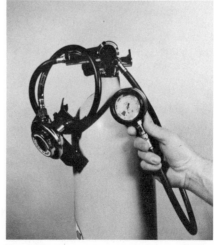

Fig. 1-89 The Underwater Pressure Gauge

Pressure gauges are connected to the first stage of the regulator at the high pressure port. Together with a "J" valve or sonic alarm, the pressure gauge lets you monitor your air supply throughout the dive, while the warning device works as a backup system to warn you when you go on reserve.

USING THE REGULATOR

The outside of the regulator is a rugged metal container. The inside is more delicate and should be kept as clean as possible. Protect the mouthpiece from sand and dirt, and always keep a plastic dust cap firmly in the first stage regulator yoke, as shown in figure 1-90. Never move or store a regulator that is attached to the tank valve. Remove it as soon as you finish diving.

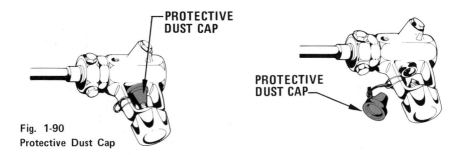

Fig. 1-90
Protective Dust Cap

Assembly

Attaching the first stage to the tank valve is a critical operation. The opening in the tank valve should be clean and dry to keep dirt out of the regulator. Begin with the tank in front of you and the backpack on the opposite side, as demonstrated in figure 1-91, picture no. 1. When you attach the regulator to your tank, follow these five steps:

1. Check the "O" ring in the valve. If it is nicked or broken—replace it. (picture no. 2)

2. Hold the second stage of the regulator in your right hand, the first stage in your left, and put the yoke over the tank valve. (The air hose always comes over your right shoulder when the tank is in place.) (picture no. 3)

3. Turn the regulator yoke screw until it is snug. If you tighten it too much, you will damage the "O" ring. (picture no. 4)

4. Turn the valve knob counterclockwise to turn on the air. Always hold the pressure gauge down and away from your face in case it ruptures. Carefully open the valve all the way turning it very gently. Listen for leaks. If you hear one, turn the valve off and check it.

5. Press the purge valve. You should hear air flowing freely. Then, place the mouthpiece in your mouth, inhale and exhale to make sure it is working. If the exhaust is stuck shut, place the second stage in water for a few moments, then blow hard into the mouthpiece.

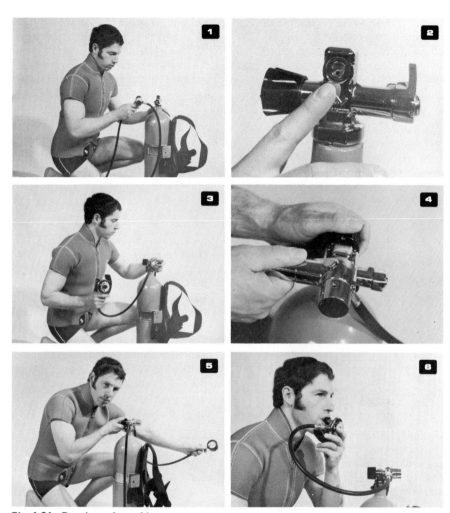

Fig. 1-91   Regulator Assembly

REGULATOR CARE AND MAINTENANCE

If clean fresh water is nearby, rinse the regulator and tank before taking them apart. Flush water into the mouthpiece and through the exhaust ports, as shown in figure 1-92. Be careful not to ever press the purge button while rinsing the second stage inside, however it is alright while rinsing the outside. This will keep water from entering the air hose which should always stay clean and dry.

Fig. 1-92   Flushing the Mouthpiece

Before removing the regulator, turn off the air and press the purge button to let intermediate pressure air escape. Dry the dust cap before putting it in place. When storing the regulator, do not hang it by the regulator yoke. This can bend the hose and weaken it at the point where it attaches to the first stage. Instead, store it in a protective bag to prevent dust and abuse from shortening the regulator's life.

REGULATOR CLEARING

When you take the regulator out of your mouth under water, water fills the mouthpiece and air chamber. There are three different ways to clear it: blowing, purging, or swishing. Blowing the regulator clear is a matter of putting the mouthpiece in your mouth and exhaling into it.

Fig. 1-93 Purging the Double Hose Regulator

If you are short on air in your lungs, however, you may have to purge the regulator with tank air. With a double hose regulator, lift the mouthpiece up above the regulator housing, as pictured in figure 1-93. This causes it to free flow, which purges the mouthpiece automatically. With a single hose regulator, just push the purge button lightly and then put the mouthpiece in your mouth.

If you cannot reach the purge valve when you are out of air, you can still swish the regulator clear. Simply take a mouthful of water and squirt it out through the regulator. This creates a vacuum and causes air to flow in and replace the water in the second stage.

After clearing the regulator, inhale cautiously. There may still be water in the regulator air chamber. If there is, clear again. When using a regulator under water, breathe deeply and regularly. Do not breathe at a faster than normal rate and do not breathe slower in order to save air. *Remember, never hold your breath under water while using scuba. Always keep breathing, especially during ascent.* (See Part II, Sections B and C for a detailed discussion of breathing.)

How do you find a lost mouthpiece? One sure way to find it is to reach back over your shoulder and find the place where the regulator hose or hoses are attached to the regulator housing, as shown in figure 1-94. Then move your hand down the hose until it runs into the mouthpiece. If the single hose mouthpiece is not in place, it will usually be draped over your shoulder or hanging back along the right side of your tank.

Fig. 1-94 Finding a Lost Mouthpiece

Double hose regulators float because they are filled with air, so to find a double hose mouthpiece, roll over on your back until the mouthpiece is in front of your face. Then reach up for it. Figure 1-95 illustrates how a diver can replace a double hose mouthpiece.

Fig. 1-95 Replacing the Double Hose Mouthpiece

BUDDY BREATHING

With good equipment care and dive planning, there is little chance you will ever lose your air supply. But you cannot eliminate the possibility of equipment breakdowns and diver mistakes. Therefore, you should know how to *buddy breathe*, or share air with your buddy.

Buddy breathing begins when the diver who needs air, the *needer*, notifies the diver who has air, the *donor*, that he needs help. As pictured in figure 1-96, when the needer draws his finger or hand across his throat, this means he is out of air.

At this point, it is the donor's job to take control. The needer is physically and mentally handicapped because of his immediate need for air. It is up to the donor to keep a firm grip on the regulator mouthpiece at all times. The donor must also control the breathing and ascent rate.

Buddy breathing techniques depend on the situation and the equipment being used, but the basic methods are the same. The donor takes a big breath and gives his mouthpiece to the needer. The donor maintains a firm grip on the regulator and continues to exhale slowly while the needer purges the mouthpiece and takes two big breaths. The donor then gets the mouthpiece back again and takes his two breaths. This rhythm continues as the two divers make a steady ascent to the surface.

Fig. 1-97
Buddy Breathing with Single Hose Regulator

Fig. 1-96   The Out of Air Signal

The donor wants to do everything possible to help the needer, but it is foolish for both people to pay for one person's mistakes. So, in case of emergency, the donor must maintain a position which gives him complete control of the situation, as shown in figure 1-97. Buddy breathing with a single hose regulator follows this sequence:

I.   The donor should always position himself on the right and the needer on the left.

2.   The needer places his right hand on the donor's tank valve for stability.

3.   The donor places his right hand on the second stage (he should never let go at any time).

4.   The needer places his left hand on top of the donor's on the second stage. The regulator is then passed back and forth as described above. This position allows the donor to keep one hand free to maintain stability and control.

Buddy breathing with a double hose regulator is a little more difficult. The divers must face each other, as shown in figure 1-98. Each diver should hold onto the other's tank harness. The donor holds the mouthpiece with his right hand and turns it down and around to the needer to keep out water.

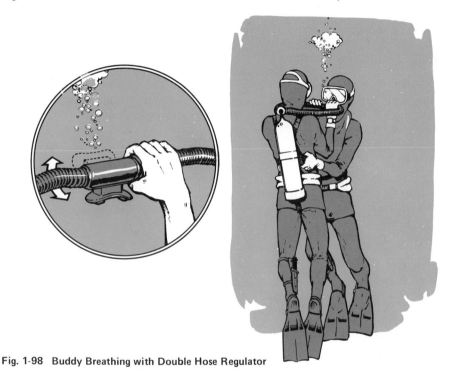

Fig. 1-98   Buddy Breathing with Double Hose Regulator

The best way to buddy breathe while swimming sideways is shown in figure 1-99. It is the same method used with the double hose face-to-face method. Notice that the donor is swimming with his left side down. This makes it easier to clear the regulator as they pass it back and forth, because the exhalation hose on the left is lower than the inhalation hose on the right.

Fig. 1-99   Face-to-Face Buddy Breathing Swim

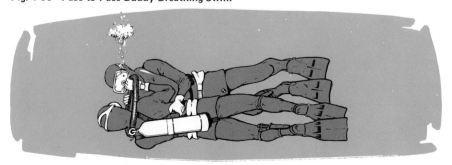

Buddy breathing in a pool or on a training dive is a complex skill that needs repeated practice and drill for it to work smoothly in an emergency. Don't forget to exhale continuously. When the mouthpiece is not in your mouth, your first instinct is to hold your breath. Don't. Make a point to blow a stream of bubbles out of your mouth at all times and make sure your buddy does the same. If he does not, stop your ascent until he starts exhaling.

The self-contained underwater breathing apparatus was little more than a recurring dream for over 2,000 years. Almost suddenly, science fiction became scientific fact in the middle of this century. With a complete understanding of how this "breathing machine" works, the underwater realm is yours. When wearing a scuba tank and regulator, you can easily imagine what it is like to live under water with the freedom and agility of a fish.

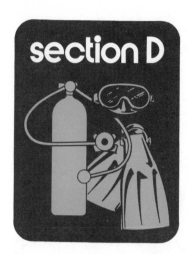

section D
underwater information

- PRESSURE GAUGES
- WATCHES
- DEPTH GAUGES
- COMPASSES
- DECOMPRESSION COMPUTERS
- THERMOMETERS

PRESSURE, TIME, AND DIRECTION DEVICES

Living on land is a relatively flat, two-dimensional experience. The position of the sun, countless clocks, convenient roads, and other landmarks help determine time and direction. Terrestrial air supply is normally unlimited.

The underwater realm, however, is an uncharted, three-dimensional place. The regular time indicators disappear. Ordinary direction markers are obscured, making all directions indistinguishable. A diver's air supply is definitely limited.

This, of course, is part of what gives the diving environment its magic. But without correct information, it can lead to disorientation. The diver needs equipment to inform him of exactly how much air remains in his tank, where he is, and how long he has been there. Like all diving gear, this equipment has one primary purpose—safety.

SUBMERSIBLE PRESSURE GAUGE

At one time, the submersible pressure gauge was a fancy option. Now it is a standard piece of a diver's equipment. It is the *only* way to assess accurately how much time you can continue to dive. Diving without a submersible pressure gauge is like driving a car without a fuel gauge.

SELECTING A PRESSURE GAUGE

The pressure gauge attaches to a high pressure port at the tank valve or first stage of the regulator, as shown in figure 1-100. Since the gauge is directly connected to the high pressure tank air, it must be calibrated above normal tank pressure so overheated or overfilled tanks will not damage it.

To withstand high interior tank pressure, the pressure gauge should have a shatterproof mechanism. Durable materials, such as rubber exterior coatings, protect gauge and diver. A swivel head and large luminous dial also make the gauge more readable under water.

USING THE PRESSURE GAUGE

Figure 1-101 illustrates pressure gauge use. When you turn on the tank valve, hold onto the high pressure hose near the gauge, not the gauge itself. Never look at the gauge while turning on the air, in case of accidental shattering. Of course, this is extremely rare, but it is a good idea to keep the pressure gauge at arm's length.

Fig. 1-100   Submersible Pressure Gauge

Fig. 1-101   Using the Pressure Gauge

While you are submerged, attach the pressure gauge to a tank strap or tuck it under your buoyancy compensator. If it hangs loose, there is a chance it will snag or break. Wherever you put it, don't forget to use it. Develop the habit of regularly monitoring your gauge, air consumption, and remaining air supply. Checking your pressure gauge every few minutes should become automatic, especially at greater depths, where air consumption rates increase greatly.

CARE AND MAINTENANCE OF THE PRESSURE GAUGE

Rinse the pressure gauge thoroughly after every dive, being careful not to let water enter the high pressure hose. This could introduce contaminants into the gauge and tank regulator. When storing the gauge, do not crimp the hose. Keep it straight or in a gentle curve.

DIVING WATCH

It is almost impossible to correctly estimate the passage of time under water, because the sun cannot be seen and your attention is usually focused intensely on other things. Diving is an extremely active sport, requiring concentration on your buddy, the equipment, the environment, and yourself. With so much happening, time passes quickly. Below 30 feet, the time factor becomes critical. Your time on the bottom must stay within certain limits to avoid decompression problems. (See Part II, Section D.) A diving watch is a necessary piece of equipment when descending below 30 feet at any point during a dive.

SELECTING A DIVING WATCH

Not all water-resistant or waterproof watches can withstand increased underwater pressure. A diving watch should be labeled and pressure tested to at least 220 feet (660 feet preferred). It should have a solid stainless steel machined case with a 17-jewel movement.

The movable bezel, surrounding the watch face, marks elapsed time. Notice this part in figure 1-102. It should have a positive hold to eliminate any accidental movements. A large, serrated edge makes the bezel easier to set, especially when you are wearing gloves. Some watches have internal bezels set by small knobs. Divers who prefer the look of a dress watch may wear these.

A diving watch must fit correctly. Try on the watchband while wearing a wet suit to be certain the band fits. A large, readable watch face is important when visibility is limited.

DEPTH GAUGE

Underwater timing is not necessary if you never dive deeper than 30 feet, but you should still know how to measure your depth limit. When you dive below 30 feet, you must know exactly how deep you are diving to estimate the rate of air consumption and to avoid problems with decompression. (See Part II, Sections D and E.) Because of this, a depth gauge is considered standard equipment for the scuba diver.

MOVABLE
BEZEL

Fig. 1-102 Diving Watch

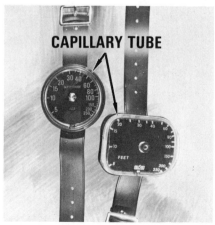

CAPILLARY TUBE

Fig. 1-103 Capillary Depth Gauge

SELECTING A DEPTH GAUGE

There are three kinds of depth gauges: the capillary, bourdon tube, and liquid or gas-filled gauge.

The capillary gauge is the simplest and least expensive. It has no moving parts and is extremely accurate down to 35 feet. "Capillary" refers to the thin plastic tube shown in figure 1-103. It has one open end, so when the diver descends, increased water pressure compresses the air and allows water to enter the tube. At 33 feet, for example, the air in the tube is compressed to half its original volume; at 66 feet, it is compressed to one-third; at 99 feet, one-fourth, and so on.

The tube is placed on a circular or rectangular dial that records depth in feet. The depth reading is the point on the dial where air and water in the tube meet. The wide spacing of the numbers in the first 33 feet makes it easy to read and accurate up to this depth.

The tube should be removed from the dial and cleaned out occasionally. This is especially true in salt water. Salt crystals can form inside the tube. If this happens, use a pipe cleaner to remove the crystals.

The bourdon tube depth gauge, shown in figure 1-104, is more expensive than the capillary type, but its dial is more readable and the accuracy extends down

Fig. 1-104 Bourdon Tube Gauge   Fig. 1-105 Liquid or Gas Filled Depth Gauge

to 200 feet. The bourdon tube is a curved, metal tube enclosed in a metal case. One end of the tube is open to surrounding water. When pressure increases, the curved tube tends to straighten out. This moves a pointer around the gauge dial.

The bourdon tube depth gauge requires careful maintenance and cleaning. Corrosion and salt can build up inside the tube, blocking the entrance of water, thus creating incorrect depth readings. Either rinse the gauge with warm, fresh water after every dive, or store it in liquid to keep salt crystals from forming inside the tube.

The liquid or gas-filled depth gauge is the most expensive and reliable gauge. This gauge (shown in figure 1-105) is completely sealed. The housing itself responds to pressure without admitting water. Since the housing is filled with oil or gas, corrosion or salt buildup is not a problem—maintenance consists of rinsing the gauge's exterior after each dive. Sealed gauges are extremely accurate below 20 feet.

COMPASS

The compass is important for both safety and convenience. A compass is the only way to maintain a sense of direction in murky or turbid water where visibility is poor. Night diving requires a compass for both underwater and surface orientation. In some coastal waters, it is not uncommon to descend under blue skies and surface in a thick fog. The compass indicates the way to shore and is a valuable navigation tool even when visibility is excellent. It is the only way to avoid repeated trips to the surface to check direction.

SELECTING A COMPASS

The simple watchband compass shown in figure 1-106, is the least expensive. It gives general direction but is not very accurate.

Fig. 1-106 Watchband Compass   Fig. 1-107 Side-Reading Wrist Compass

The larger side-reading wrist compass in figure 1-107, is more accurate and gives good directional information, but it does not have basic navigation features.

The most accurate compass is the top-reading navigation type shown in figure 1-108. It is designed for complete underwater navigation and has a movable face marked with desired course bracket lines that can be set for a specific course. The lubber line helps the diver maintain his course by giving him a sighting line. The movable face should be racheted, or notched, so it will not move accidently during a dive.

Fig. 1-108   Top-Reading Navigation Compass

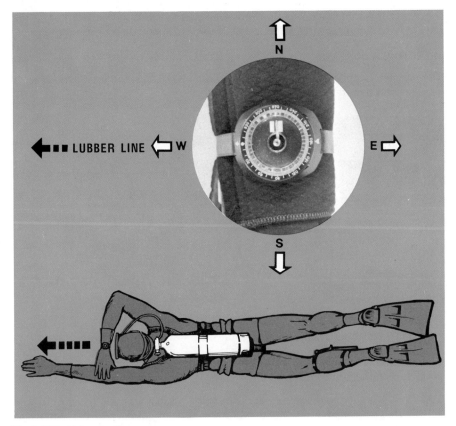

Fig. 1-109   Using the Compass

USING THE COMPASS

When using the compass to swim a certain course, hold the compass with the lubber line exactly parallel to the length of your body, as indicated in figure 1-109. If, for example, you want to swim straight west, set the movable face so the bracket lines are bracketing 270°. To maintain a 270° westerly course, simply keep the compass needle between the bracket lines.

DECOMPRESSION COMPUTER

Divers ordinarily use special tables together with a watch and depth gauge to calculate how long they can stay under water at certain depths. Sometimes, it is necessary to stop for decompression. (See Part II, Sections D and E for a discussion of decompression.) The decompression computer, shown on the right in figure 1-110, automatically makes these calculations and tells the diver when, and if, he should stop his ascent for decompression. The one on the left is designed to warn you in time to avoid decompression, but it does not compute decompression times.

When used properly, the decompression computer safely increases bottom times. It is much less complicated than the tables, depth gauge, and watch system for calculating decompression needs, but it should be used with the tables. Always keep track of your underwater depths and times as a double check against the computer.

To dive intelligently, you need a constant supply of correct information. To dive without the right instruments and gauges is to dive without knowing how much air is left or the time, depth, and direction of the dive. This is like driving a car on a dark night without the headlights. Information equipment gives you an essential orientation to the underwater environment, an orientation you need to make prompt decisions for a safe, fun dive.

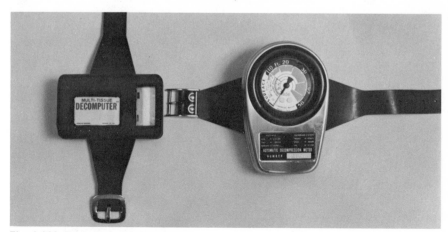

Fig. 1-110 Decompression Computers

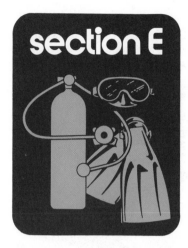

section E

tools and accessories

- FLOAT/FLAG, WHISTLE AND FLARE
- KNIFE AND LIGHT
- LOGBOOK AND SLATE
- REPAIR KIT
- GEAR BAG

SPECIAL EQUIPMENT AND TOOLS

People need special tools for most sports and jobs. A tool may be as simple as a baseball glove or as complicated as a computer, but whatever it is, it makes the task easier and safer. After skin diving and scuba diving began to grow in the 1950's, it didn't take long to develop waterproof and corrosion resistant tools. Now, the diver has tools to notify others of his location, to perform underwater tasks, to gather and record information, and to repair and protect equipment. Once you have fully adapted to the underwater environment, using tools becomes a big part of diving.

FLOAT AND FLAG

A boater on the surface cannot see an underwater diver. Even when buddy teams are at the surface, they are difficult to see from a fast-moving boat. This is why the diver's flag is an important safety tool. It protects the dive team by warning boats to stay clear. It means that divers are in the area—stay away.

Figure 1-111 shows the two diver's flags currently in use. The Sport Diver flag is red with a white diagonal stripe. The International Signal Code flag for the letter "A" (Alpha) is white and blue with a deep "V" cut into the outside edge. It means, "I have a diver down; keep well clear at slow speed." The diver's flag should be flown only when divers are actually in the water.

Fig. 1-111 Diver's Flags

The diver's flag hangs from a pole that can be attached to either a small buoy, inner tube, surf mat, surf board, or small boat. (See figure 1-112.) Floats can be resting stations during the dive, and larger floats are good places to store equipment. In emergencies, the floats quickly become helpful pieces of rescue equipment.

Fig. 1-112   Diving Floats

WHISTLE (Surface Signal)

Your buddy is your constant under-water companion; you should never leave your buddy, and the two of you should not stray far from the dive float or beach. A whistle effectively reunites divers who have strayed or separated accidentally. A simple whistle made out of plastic or some other noncorrosive material should be tied to the oral inflation tube on your buoyancy compensator. (Note figure 1-113.) A whistle is easier to hear over wind and waves and is less tiring than shouting or yelling.

Fig. 1-113   Emergency Diving Whistle

FLARE

A special day and night diving flare, pictured in figure 1-114, has a red smoke flare at one end and a red light at the other, for either day or night use. It should be taped to a belt or knife sheath. Even though the flare is waterproof, it will not ignite while submerged. Although available, flares are expensive and not in common use.

Fig. 1-114   Day and Night Flare   **Fig. 1-115   Chemical Glow Light**

For night diving, the chemical glow light, shown in figure 1-115, is an excellent safety device. It is a small glass container surrounded by a sealed plastic tube. To light the flare, simply bend the tube and break the glass container. When the two chemicals mix, they create a light-green glow that is extremely visible under water at night. Both buddies should activate their glow lights at the beginning of a night dive for easy location.

DIVE KNIFE

A knife is one of the most useful diving tools. The knife might be called the diver's primary tool. It is a hammer, saw, screwdriver, lever, pry bar, ruler, probe, and cutting tool. It is rarely, if ever, used as a weapon against underwater life. Trying to fight off a shark with a knife is not only ridiculous, it could also aggravate the situation.

The dive knife, shown in figure 1-116, should be made out of high-quality, noncorrosive steel that is strong enough for prying and hard enough to hold a sharp edge. The blade should extend all the way through an unbreakable handle. Divers pound with the hard steel butt at the end of the handle.

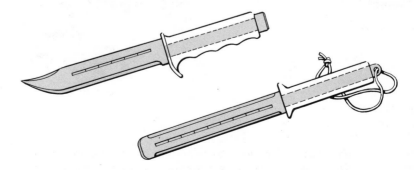

Fig. 1-116   Dive Knife and Tool

The knife sheath should have long, stretchable leg straps, strong buckles and a strong positive retainer to keep the knife in place.

For accessibility with both hands and to avoid snagging anything on the handle, wear the knife on the inside of the calf. Rinse and dry both knife and sheath after every dive.

UNDERWATER LIGHT

The underwater light makes night diving possible. It also adds a new dimension to daytime diving. Most colors are absorbed by water below 60 feet. The diving light restores vivid reds and yellows that would be lost without light.

There are three types of diving lights, as shown in figure 1-117. The first is basically a waterproof flashlight. The second light is much brighter. It uses more powerful dry cell batteries and sealed beam lamps. The sealed beam is like a waterproof automobile headlight with a built-in reflector and lens. The third type of underwater light uses a rechargeable battery. It comes with a separate charger and usually lasts from one to three hours before it needs recharging. Nonrechargeable battery lights often have a lower initial cost, but in the long run, they can be more expensive than rechargeable lights.

Fig. 1-117 Diving Lights

The diving light must, of course, be waterproof and pressure proof. If the battery fits into a plastic or metal case, be sure to store it separately from the housing and make sure everything is clean and dry before storing it.

LOGBOOK, THERMOMETER, AND SLATE

One of the diver's most important tools is information. It helps him understand his diving experiences and enables him to plan future dives intelligently. The logbook provides a record of good diving spots, depths, visibility, diving times, and total diving hours. Recording temperatures, for example, helps you anticipate wet suit needs for the next dive. Diving ability improves with experience, so the more information you can gather and record, the more experience you can bring to the next dive.

The logbook, thermometer, and underwater slate, all shown in figure 1-118, help you gather and record information. Like all diving instruments, the thermometer should be waterproof, pressure proof, and easy to read. It is not a necessary piece of equipment, but divers often find it useful.

The underwater slate can be made out of white plastic. If you sand the smooth surface with fine sandpaper, it will be rough enough to write on with an ordinary pencil. Use it to record times, depths, temperatures, and other observations that you will want to transfer to the logbook later. You can also use it to communicate with your buddy during the dive.

Fig. 1-118

Logbook, Thermometer, and Slate

SPARE PARTS AND REPAIR KIT

You may not realize the importance of each piece of diving equipment until you lose something as simple as a fin strap and are forced to bring the day's diving to an end. A simple repair kit with tools and spare parts is an excellent way to keep your gear working and you diving. Here are a few spare parts to take along:

1. Fin strap and buckle
2. Mask strap and buckle
3. "O" rings for tank valve
4. CO_2 cartridges
5. Snorkel-keeper
6. Regulator high pressure plug
7. Nylon line
8. Batteries
9. Silicone spray
10. Wet suit cement
11. Needle and thread
12. Mask lens
13. Silicone grease
14. Anti-fog solution
15. Waterproof plastic tape

Along with the spare parts, you should also have tools such as pliers, adjustable wrench, and screwdriver.

GEAR BAG

There are a number of different gear bags, packs, and containers to hold your gear and keep it organized, as shown in figure 1-119. Make certain it is large enough to hold all your gear except the tank and weight belt. Seams, handles, and zippers should be heavy duty and noncorrosive. Heavy cotton or nylon canvas, reinforced vinyl, or plastic are often used for gear bags.

When packing your gear bag, put the fins and other nonbreakable items on the bottom. Pack delicate instruments such as regulators, meters, gauges, compasses, and cameras in separate, rigid containers. Tanks are usually carried separately. Do not store anything in your gear bag unless it is perfectly clean and dry. The gear bag is both convenient and important when it comes to protecting equipment. Be sure it is strong enough to *withstand rough handling.*

Fig. 1-119   Gear Bags

The amazing growth of diving as a sport depended almost entirely on the development of diving equipment. It has enabled thousands of swimmers to experience the underwater world with comfort and freedom. Continuing advances in diving equipment are enabling divers to become more and more like fish. Someday, perhaps, your air supply will be unlimited and decompression will no longer be a concern, because artificial gills will let you exchange oxygen and carbon dioxide directly with the surrounding water.

The future of diving will be exciting, but so is the present. Diving equipment developed in the last two decades solved dozens of problems humans encountered when entering the underwater world. The diver who has the right equipment, knowledge, and skills can easily adapt.

PART II

the diver

introduction

Creatures that live on land and breathe air have always looked at water with mixed feelings. No one can deny the attraction of streams, waterfalls, ponds, and oceans. Everything from small summer cabins to giant cities seems to prefer locations near water.

Maybe this attraction to water is not so unusual. After all, living things and water have been together since the beginning. Approximately 70 percent of the human body is water; most of it is similar to ocean water. For years, scientists have found blood, sweat, and seawater to contain remarkably similar amounts of calcium, potassium, and sodium.

But man and seawater are not compatible in many ways. For example, man cannot drink seawater, he cannot water his crops with it, and he can drown in as little as a teaspoonful. He is attracted to water, but he is also threatened by it.

We are not, however, the only air-breathing mammals to challenge the sea. The otter and the sea lion have adapted amazingly well. Like man, they must *learn* how to swim and dive, but they don't have the advantage of higher understanding and technology that humans have. The sport diver, with equipment and knowledge, can easily adapt to water. More importantly, the diver can thoroughly understand this adaptation.

Knowing how your body and mind work below the surface, and understanding how water affects your body and mind, is a must for safe and enjoyable diving. With this understanding, you will come to know that water is a different, but very rewarding environment for the intelligent sport diver.

sensations

- **FLOATING**
- **SEEING**
- **HEARING**
- **EXPOSURE**

FLOATING, SEEING, HEARING, AND EXPOSURE

To jump into even shallow water is to be bombarded by new sensations. You see, hear, smell, taste, and feel differently in water than in air. To really grasp these differences, you need to know what water is and how it differs from air. This knowledge will help explain the various sensations and what you must do to adapt to them.

FLOATING

The feeling of buoyancy, or floating in water, is perhaps the most relaxing and pleasant of all the underwater sensations. Water gives most of us the only relief we will ever know from the constant pull of gravity. It is this weightlessness that gives divers almost complete freedom of movement in all three dimensions.

"Weightless" is a good word for floating, for most people, if they were to stand on a scale under water, would weigh next to nothing. Figure 2-1 is a graphic example. They may not float like a cork, but they don't sink like a rock either. The reason for this is that approximately 70 percent of the human body is water. Substances either slightly heavier or lighter than water make up the rest of the body. Fat, for example, isn't as heavy as muscle. So, to put a person into water is like placing a container of water into water—either one sinks very slowly or not at all.

Fig. 2-1 Underwater Buoyancy

BUOYANCY

The question of floating, or buoyancy, is an important one for divers. We know that most people float easily; that is, they have *positive buoyancy*. This is shown in figure 2-2. A very few are *negatively buoyant:* they tend to sink. Others are *neutrally buoyant:* they tend to neither float or sink. Here is the reason. People whose bodies are heavier than the same amount, or volume, of water displaced by them sink. People whose bodies are lighter than the same volume of water float.

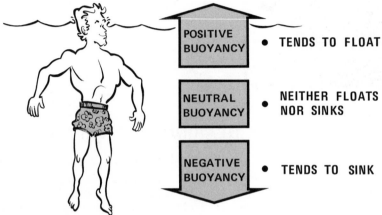

Fig. 2-2 Degrees of Buoyancy

No matter what it is, it sinks if it's heavier than water and floats if it isn't. A gallon of water, as shown in figure 2-3, weighs about eight pounds. A gallon of air is much lighter; it only weighs one-sixth of an ounce, so it floats. Similar volumes of wood and foam neoprene are also lighter than water and are positively buoyant. But similar volumes of lead, aluminum, and steel are heavier than water. They sink.

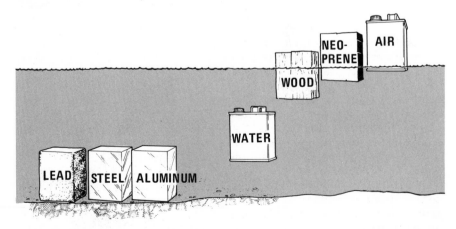

Fig. 2-3 Positive and Negative Buoyancy

Controlling Buoyancy

Fortunately for divers and swimmers, the human body has a built-in buoyancy mechanism that lets you adjust and control buoyancy in the water. The lungs hold about 1-1/2 gallons (five—six liters) of air when you inhale completely. This gives your body an extra 12 pounds of *buoyant force* in the water. In other words, 1-1/2 gallons of air will support 12 pounds above the surface of the water. When you inhale completely, your body has more than enough buoyancy to lift your face out of the water, as shown in figure 2-4.

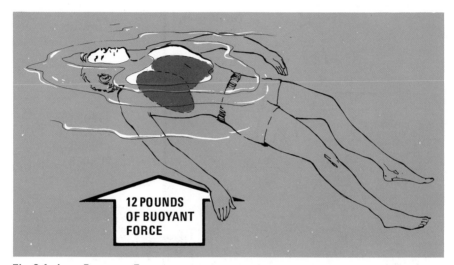

12 POUNDS OF BUOYANT FORCE

Fig. 2-4 Lung Buoyancy Force

By controlling the amount of air in your lungs, you can stay buoyant and relaxed at the surface without getting at all tired. It is important to remember, though, that the normal buoyancy of your body will only support a limited amount of weight above water. When resting on the surface, do not try to lift your head, shoulders, and arms out of the water. Stay as low as possible and keep your lungs as full as possible for maximum buoyancy.

Some people, depending on their body build, composition, and lung size, are more buoyant than others. Fat is not as heavy as muscle and bone, so obese people usually float better than thin people. However, even the skinniest diver can float with proper techniques, including inhaling as much air as possible and staying low in the water.

Changes In Buoyancy

Another thing that affects buoyancy is the weight, or density of water. Salt water, for example, is heavier than fresh water because it contains dissolved salts. The heavier the liquid, the greater the weight it will support. This is why it is easier to float in salt water than in fresh water. You will also be more buoyant in cold water than in warm. Cold water is more dense. The water molecules are closer together which makes the water heavier, or more dense, and more buoyant than warm water.

The laws of buoyancy were discovered by Archimedes. (See Appendix, Archimedes Principle.) He found that the amount of buoyancy an object has depends on how much water it *displaces*, or pushes away. To illustrate: if you put a box into water that displaces 64 pounds of water, then the box will be buoyed up with a force of 64 pounds, as shown in figure 2-5. The more water you displace, the more you will float. This is why wet suits and buoyancy compensators give buoyancy. They add very little weight to your body, but they cause you to displace much more water.

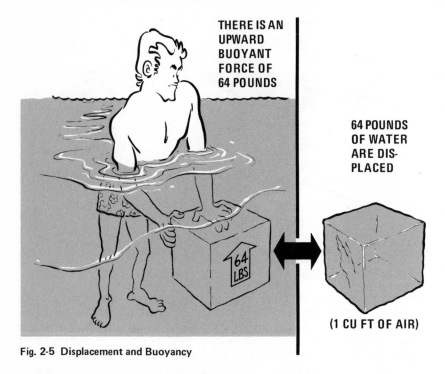

THERE IS AN UPWARD BUOYANT FORCE OF 64 POUNDS

64 POUNDS OF WATER ARE DIS-PLACED

(1 CU FT OF AIR)

Fig. 2-5 Displacement and Buoyancy

SEEING

The first time you opened your eyes under water without a mask was not only uncomfortable but also disappointing. The feeling of cold water directly touching the delicate tissues of your eyes was unexpected and unpleasant, especially if the water contained chlorine or salt. Everything was blurry and out of focus. Most of us can get used to the feeling of water, but the blurriness remains because of the way light travels in water.

LIGHT

The outer covering of the eye, surrounded by air, bends the light striking it at the exact angle necessary to focus it clearly on the back of the eye. Light meeting the eye directly from water must be bent at a greater angle to focus at the correct point. Both concepts are described in figure 2-6. Unfortunately, the eye is unable to adapt to this need, but the solution is fairly simple.

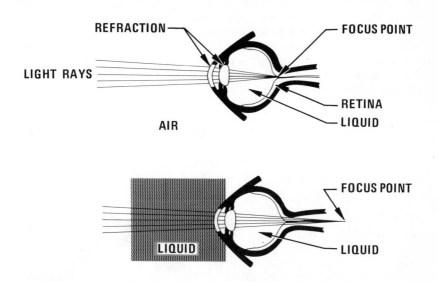

REFRACTION — FOCUS POINT

LIGHT RAYS

AIR

RETINA

LIQUID

FOCUS POINT

LIQUID

LIQUID

Fig. 2-6 Seeing on Land and Under Water

SEEING WITH A MASK

In theory, a special set of eyeglasses with the right lenses could correct the visual problem, but the face mask is a much more practical solution. The mask restores the necessary air space and also protects the eyes. Surprisingly, vision is one sense that, with the help of the face mask, actually improves under water. Figure 2-7 shows three underwater pictures of the same squirrel fish. The first shows what the fish looks like with water in direct contact with the eye: it is out of focus. The second picture shows what the fish looks like when seen through a mask. The third is the actual size of the fish.

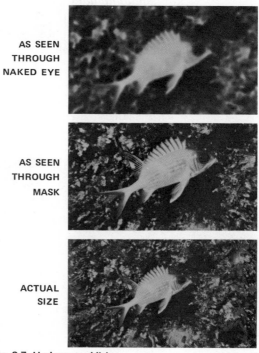

AS SEEN THROUGH NAKED EYE

AS SEEN THROUGH MASK

ACTUAL SIZE

Fig. 2-7 Underwater Vision

Notice that the squirrel fish seems about 25 percent bigger and 25 percent closer as seen through the mask. The reason for the magnifying effect of the mask is shown in figure 2-8. Light travels from the water, through the glass in the face mask, into the air space of the mask, and finally into the eye. Water, glass, and air all bend light to different degrees, so the light is refracted, or bent, twice instead of only once. It is this double bending of the light that causes magnification and actually improves vision.

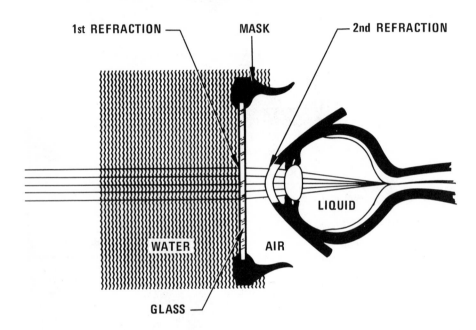

Fig. 2-8 Mask Magnification Underwater

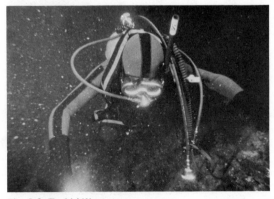

Fig. 2-9 Turbid Water

TURBIDITY

Even though your underwater vision improves somewhat, light does not move as well as it does in air. Light from the sun or from artificial lights is scattered or absorbed by particles suspended in the water, as shown in figure 2-9. Water that contains suspended particles is said to be *turbid*. Extremely turbid water can almost eliminate visibility.

COLOR

Even if the water is very clear and clean, however, it still absorbs light. Sunlight is a mixture of all colors. Water absorbs different colors at different rates. The chart in figure 2-10 illustrates this. Reds and oranges are absorbed in the first 30 feet. Yellows and greens disappear at about 60 feet, so below this depth, everything goes from a bluish color to completely gray. Artificial lights used for vision or photography will restore all natural colors no matter what the depth. Part IV, Section C gives information on this concept.

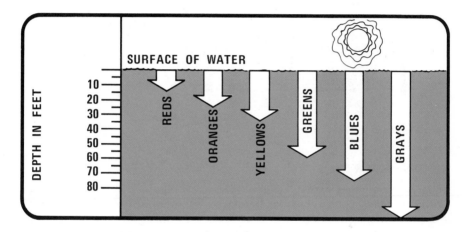

Fig. 2-10 Underwater Color

HEARING AND SPEAKING

Sound moves about four times faster under water than in air, but this does not improve your hearing. Ordinary speech is all but impossible below the surface, and it's very difficult to judge the direction of underwater sounds. In spite of this, the underwater world can be a noisy place. You can hear equipment clanking together, motorboats buzzing at the surface, bubbles leaving regulators, marine life, movement of rocks, and churning water.

The reason you cannot hear voices under water is that sound does not travel well from air into water, or from water into air. You can speak under water, but almost all the sound energy stays in your neck and mouth.

Judging the direction of sounds depends on a slight delay. For example, a noise made at your right side sends sound waves, as shown in figure 2-11. The sound hits your right ear first and your left ear a fraction of a second later which tells you from what direction the sound is coming. But because sound moves so much faster in water, this time delay is almost eliminated; the sound seems to be coming from every direction.

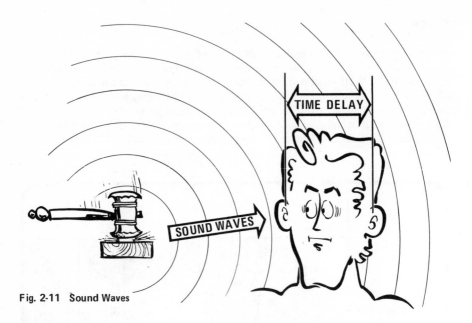

Fig. 2-11 Sound Waves

HAND SIGNALS

Underwater communication, especially between buddies, is extremely important. The diving community has developed a system of hand signals to meet this need. There are several different signaling systems, but the hand signals described in figure 2-12 are the most basic. Whatever system you use, make sure you and your buddy agree on the meanings to avoid confusion.

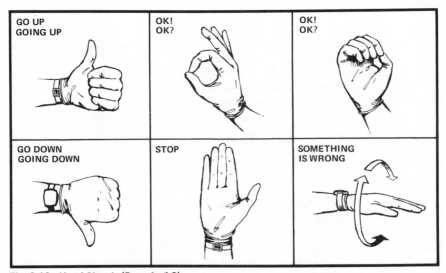

Fig. 2-12 Hand Signals (Page 1 of 2)

Fig. 2-12   Hand Signals (Page 2 of 2)

EXPOSURE

Most of us would agree that cold water produces an unpleasant sensation when you jump into it. The colder the water, the more unpleasant the sensation. Very cold water is not only unpleasant, it is also downright dangerous. It can cause unconsciousness and even death in extreme cases. (See Appendix for Water Temperature Protection Chart.)

MAINTAINING BODY TEMPERATURE

On land, the human body has an amazing ability to maintain a core temperature of 98.6° F. It cannot vary more than a few degrees without serious problems. The body can be thought of as a living heat machine. It generates heat constantly and controls its own temperature by regulating how much heat escapes into the surrounding air. The body's cooling systems, however, are designed for body heat passing into air, not water. Because of this, maintaining a constant body temperature in water is more difficult.

Conduction And Evaporation

Heat leaves your body in several different ways, but the two most important are *conduction* and *evaporation*. Conduction refers to heat passing from one thing into something else in direct contact with it. This is depicted in figure 2-13. When you put a pan of water on a flame, for example, the heat from the fire is conducted directly into the pan and from the pan directly into the water.

HEAT CONDUCTED
DIRECTLY FROM
FLAME, TO PAN,
TO WATER

Fig. 2-13 Heat Conduction

Evaporation occurs when a liquid changes into a gas. When this happens, the liquid absorbs heat as it changes into gas, as shown in figure 2-14. When you sweat, for example, perspiration absorbs heat as it evaporates. This is why it cools your body.

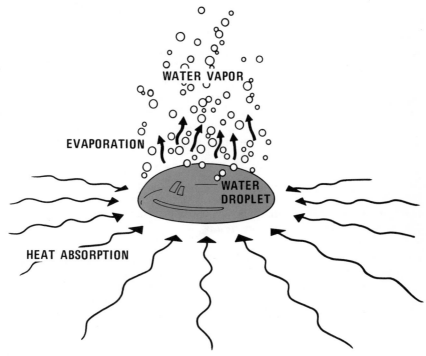

Fig. 2-14 Evaporation

When you jump into water, evaporation no longer works. Conduction is the main method of cooling the body in water but water conducts heat away from the body almost 25 times faster than air. This is why even relatively warm water feels cold when you first jump into it.

Maintaining Warmth

Your body, however, doesn't give up all that heat without a fight. Swimmers often talk about diving into "cold" water and then "getting used to it". What really happens when you get used to the cold is that certain changes take place in your body to prevent too much heat from passing into the water. The tiny blood vessels on the surface of the skin constrict automatically when plunged into colder temperatures. This reduces the amount of warm blood that flows to the cold surface of the body. As a result, less heat is conducted from the skin into the cold water.

If the reduced blood flow to the skin fails to keep the body warm, and if the skin temperature gets down to a certain level, then the body starts *shivering*. It takes muscular effort to shiver and this causes an increase in the body's production of heat. An extremely active diver stays warmer than a diver at rest for the same reason; he may be losing heat at the same rate, but the active diver produces enough to prevent a net heat loss. Physical activity can produce so much heat, in fact, that a diver in water warmer than 86°F (30°C) may have problems with *over*heating. Cold, however, is a much more common problem.

Effects Of Cold Water

The wet suit, by surrounding the body in a layer of air or gas bubbles, reduces the rate at which heat passes from the body into the water. But even with wet suit protection, heat loss still occurs, especially through the head, hands, and feet. When heat loss is extreme, it can cause a loss of strength, difficulty in handling equipment, muscle cramps, and a decrease in problem-solving ability. When the water temperature is close to freezing, a diver's lips can become too numb to inflate his buoyancy vest orally and his fingers can become too clumsy to activate mechanical inflators.

If you ever start shivering under water, stop diving. Your ability to move and to think decreases the longer you are cold. The discomfort that comes from being too hot or too cold is bad enough, but the effects of these two extremes on your mind and body are far more serious.

No other environment has a more profound effect on the body's five senses than the underwater environment. It changes your perceptions in every way. It creates a totally different set of experiences. Some sensations are enjoyable, others require adjustment by special techniques or equipment. In any case, there is no reason for underwater sensations to be unpleasant or uncomfortable. If they are unpleasant, you either need better equipment or more training.

section B

breathing

- RESPIRATION
- AVOIDING EXHAUSTION
- RESUSCITATION
- CLEAN AIR

RESPIRATION, GAS EXCHANGE, PANIC, RESUSCITATION, CLEAN AIR

Breathing is one of those things we ignore most of the time. We ordinarily breathe constantly, day and night, without giving it a thought. Swimming or diving under water, however, changes all this; the beginning swimmer quickly realizes that he cannot "breathe water." Since diving can change, stop, slow down, or speed up the breathing process, you should have a good understanding of what is going on in your body and mind when you breathe, both on land and in the water.

THE RESPIRATION PROCESS

Respiration refers not only to the simple act of inhaling and exhaling air, but also to the more complex processes of exchanging gases, making energy, and eliminating waste in order to keep the cells of all living creatures alive. Respiration, then, is the primary life process, a process that involves more than the lungs. The circulatory system, including the heart, blood, and vessels, and every living cell in the body are intimately connected with respiration.

LUNGS

Human lungs are built something like a spongy, upside down tree, as shown in figure 2-15. The trunk of the lung tree is the windpipe, a hollow tube about 4-1/2 inches long and one inch wide. The windpipe divides into two smaller branches called the *bronchi*, which continue to subdivide into smaller and smaller branches. The smallest twigs, or ducts, end in tiny clusters of air sacs called *alveoli*. Each cluster looks like a tiny bunch of grapes.

The alveoli are the leaves of the tree. They are extremely thin membranes where oxygen, carbon dioxide, and other gases pass into and out of the

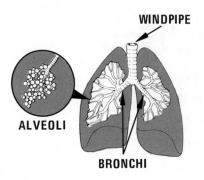

Fig. 2-15 Lungs

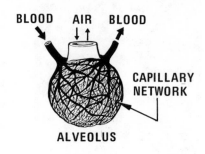

Fig. 2-16 Alveolus and Capillaries

bloodstream. The lungs contain about 600 million tiny alveoli. All of them make up an *alveolar* membrane with a surface area of about 600 square feet, or about 25 times the surface of the body. Each *alveolus* is surrounded by a network of tiny blood vessels, or capillaries. (See figure 2-16.)

The lungs are protected above and around the side by the rib cage. The diaphragm underneath is a powerful sheet of muscle. Figure 2-17 is an illustration of the diaphragm. When the diaphragm is flexed, it moves downward while the muscles around the rib cage lift the ribs up and out. Together, the action of the diaphragm and rib cage increases the size of the chest cavity. This is what pulls air down and into the lungs when you inhale.

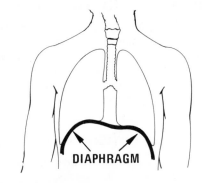

Fig. 2-17 Diaphragm

The alveolar membrane is elastic, so the air sacs have a tendency to contract and push air out of the lungs. When the diaphragm and muscles around the rib cage relax, air leaves the lungs. Ordinarily, this alternating contraction and relaxation of the muscles that control breathing is automatic. An average adult breathes between 14 and 20 times a minute. Small people and children usually breathe more often.

LUNG VOLUMES

An average pair of lungs can hold a total volume of 1.7 gallons (6.5 liters) of air. At rest, however, you only inhale and exhale a small fraction of this amount—a little over a pint (0.5 liters). This is called the *tidal volume*, as shown in figure 2-18.

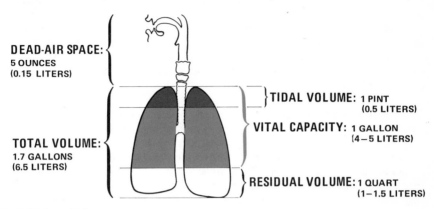

DEAD-AIR SPACE:
5 OUNCES
(0.15 LITERS)

TOTAL VOLUME:
1.7 GALLONS
(6.5 LITERS)

}**TIDAL VOLUME:** 1 PINT
(0.5 LITERS)

}**VITAL CAPACITY:** 1 GALLON
(4 – 5 LITERS)

}**RESIDUAL VOLUME:** 1 QUART
(1 – 1.5 LITERS)

Fig. 2-18 Lung Volumes

Exchanging the relatively small tidal volume of air is enough for a person sitting quietly in a chair reading a book, but the long-distance runner or the hard-working diver may need much more air. For example, after inhaling a pint of air during an ordinary breath, you can continue to inhale between two and three quarts (2.5 liters). After you exhale the pint of air in an ordinary breath, you can continue exhaling almost three-fourths of a quart (0.7 liters).

When you breathe as hard as you possibly can, you can exchange over a gallon (four – five liters) of air on any one breath. This amount is the *vital capacity* and it varies a great deal depending on the size and physical condition of the person. A small woman may have a vital capacity of only three quarts (2.8 liters) and a trained male athlete could have one larger than six quarts (6.5 liters).

No matter how hard you exhale, however, you still cannot force all the air out of your lungs. Over a quart (1.2 liters) of *residual* air remains in the lungs all the time. This is called the *residual volume*.

All the air you inhale, even during a very large breath, does not find its way to the lungs. Some of it, about five ounces (0.15 liters), fills up the windpipe, throat, and nose and is exhaled without ever touching the inside of an alveolus. This area is called the *dead-air space* because no gas exchange takes place inside it.

GAS EXCHANGE

The air you inhale is a mixture of about 78 percent nitrogen, 21 percent oxygen, 0.03 percent carbon dioxide, and small amounts of other gases. Nitrogen has very little effect on ordinary respiration. It is an inert (chemically inactive) gas that does not support life, but has an intoxicating effect under pressure. (See Part II, Section D.) Oxygen and carbon dioxide are the two gases that are exchanged during respiration.

The air you exhale has about the same amount of nitrogen, but the percentage of oxygen decreases from 21 to 16 percent, and the percentage of carbon dioxide increases from 0.03 percent to 5.6 percent. The body, in other words, produces an amount of carbon dioxide roughly equal to the amount of oxygen it absorbs. By maintaining this continuous exchange of gases, the blood and cells of the body maintain a certain minimum level of oxygen. This prevents an excessive buildup of carbon dioxide.

Because the body constantly uses oxygen and produces carbon dioxide, the levels of these two gases in the blood always change. When the carbon dioxide level reaches a certain level in the alveoli, it stimulates the *respiratory center*, a part of the brain that is sensitive to carbon dioxide. The respiratory center then stimulates the diaphragm and chest muscles to contract, which causes you to inhale. This, of course, lowers the carbon dioxide level in the alveoli. The respiratory center stops stimulating the diaphragm and chest muscles, the muscles relax, the alveoli naturally contract, and you exhale. As the carbon dioxide level builds up, the whole process involuntarily repeats itself.

CHANGING THE BREATHING RHYTHM

You can consciously override the involuntary control of breathing when, for example, you are talking or holding your breath. There are many ways to either slow down or accelerate the breathing rate, all of which have important effects on the exchange of oxygen and carbon dioxide. Changing the breathing rhythm is harmless as long as the balance of gas exchange stays within certain limits. But too much or too little of either gas can cause problems.

TOO MUCH CARBON DIOXIDE AND TOO LITTLE OXYGEN

Almost anything that interferes or hinders the normal breathing process can lead to a buildup of carbon dioxide in the blood. When you stop exhaling, the air in the dead-air space has a high level of carbon dioxide. When you start inhaling, you inhale this air first. The natural dead-air space in your windpipe, however, is small enough so carbon dioxide never builds up. An extremely long or large snorkel, however, can double or triple the size of this dead-air space. If you don't breathe deeper to maintain the right exchange of gases, carbon dioxide levels will climb.

A snorkel or regulator with a lot of breathing resistance will change your breathing and change the effort required to do the work of breathing. When this happens, the body might be producing more carbon dioxide than it can give off, so carbon dioxide gradually builds up.

Most of us have experienced carbon dioxide excess from swimming or running too fast. The "out-of-breath" feeling comes from the respiratory center working overtime in response to a large buildup of carbon dioxide. This can lead to shortness of breath and fatigue. On land, this isn't much of a problem, but, under water, it can be serious. If you feel unusually "hungry" for air and tired or weak from working too hard—stop, rest, and breathe deeply.

"Skip breathing" is a term that refers to a technique that used to be used to conserve air. Instead of breathing regularly, the diver "skips" every other breath or exhales twice on each breath. Unfortunately, the technique does *not* work and it can be dangerous. Skip breathing apparently uses only one-half the amount of air, but it really leads to a buildup of carbon dioxide. This, of course, eventually leads to a greater than normal breathing rate. Always avoid skip breathing or other so-called techniques of "conserving" air while using scuba.

Certain advanced and commercial breathing devices use gas mixtures and rebreathing systems instead of ordinary compressed air. Any breakdown or misuse of these systems can also lead to carbon dioxide buildup.

Many things that hinder or slow down the exchange of gases not only cause a buildup of carbon dioxide, but also cause a decrease in the amount of oxygen in the blood and cells of the body. This oxygen deficiency in the body's tissue is called *hypoxia*. Whether it comes from an equipment breakdown or improper breathing, the signs and symptoms of hypoxia are the same.

Both carbon dioxide excess and hypoxia can cause heavy breathing, headache, and unconsciousness. Hypoxia can also cause nausea. Carbon dioxide excess can cause muscular cramps and fatigue. The treatment for both is increased ventilation of the lungs and giving 100 percent oxygen if necessary.

CONTROLLED HYPERVENTILATION

Breath-hold divers have used *hyperventilation* for years to help them stay under water longer. By inhaling completely and exhaling completely three or four times before surface diving, you can "blow off" carbon dioxide. This lets you begin a breath-hold dive with very low carbon dioxide levels in the alveoli. Since the respiratory center in the brain is stimulated by a high carbon dioxide level, you will not feel the need to breathe as quickly after hyperventilation.

Hyperventilation must be very carefully controlled. Never hyperventilate more than three or four times before each surface dive. More than this can reduce the carbon dioxide level too much. Your body, during the surface dive, uses up oxygen. It is possible to use oxygen to the point of hypoxia before the carbon dioxide level gets to a level that tells you to breathe. This is called "shallow water blackout." When you feel the urge to breathe, head for the surface. Never ignore the need for air.

UNCONTROLLED HYPERVENTILATION

Simple anxiety and physical stress can cause a diver to hyperventilate whether he wants to or not. Unfamiliar equipment or a strange and unusual diving environment is sometimes enough to cause hyperventilation. Treating uncontrolled hyperventilation is easy—become aware of your breathing rate and slow it down if you find yourself breathing too fast and shallow. Holding your breath for a short time will help get the carbon dioxide level back to normal.

PANIC AND EXHAUSTION

Panic is defined as a sudden overpowering fear. You lose control, you cannot think, and you therefore take incorrect actions. You focus on one particular task or action that may or may not have anything to do with escaping the problem. No matter how well you are trained or experienced, you are not immune to panic. The best way to prevent panic is to understand it.

Fear is an ordinary, healthy response to danger. A fear of falling off a cliff is normal; stepping back from the edge of the cliff is a normal response. If the fear of falling becomes panic and causes you to freeze at the edge of the cliff, you have lost control. This is not a healthy response.

Avoiding panic, then, is largely a matter of controlling ordinary fear. If "something goes wrong" during a dive, you should accept the normal fear for what it is and do what has to be done to right the situation. Running out of air, difficulty with strong currents, unusually negative buoyancy from a full collecting bag, extreme cold, getting tangled in kelp, and equipment problems: these are all problems with sensible and logical solutions. To solve the problem, however, you must have your wits about you. Panic is never a solution.

A sure sign of panic in either yourself or your buddy is very rapid breathing. It may look like hyperventilation, but when the diver is panicking, breathing is rapid and *shallow*, not deep. This may eventually lead to a buildup of carbon dioxide and a decrease in oxygen in the blood and tissues. This soon causes exhaustion which makes everything worse. Panic increases and a vicious cycle ensues which can easily lead to disaster. Panic, in fact, is probably the leading cause of drowning and near drowning in sport diving and drowning is undoubtedly the greatest cause of fatal diving accidents.

If, at any time during a dive, you feel at all anxious or are having difficulty in any way, stop and think. Relax and breathe slowly and deeply until you have solved the problem and regained complete control. Know your physical limitations and don't exceed them when diving.

FIRST AID FOR DROWNING

When the exchange of oxygen and carbon dioxide completely breaks down, it is called *asphyxia*. When asphyxia occurs in water it is called drowning. A fatal drowning accident begins when the victim stops breathing and loses consciousness, often after panic and exhaustion have set in.

Whatever the cause, a drowning or near-drowning victim will have two definite symptoms: loss of consciousness and lack of breathing. His heart may or may not be beating. The most important element in first aid is time. Of all the cells in the body, brain cells are the most sensitive to a lack of oxygen. If heartbeat and breathing have stopped for more than four to six minutes, permanent brain damage is likely. It is extremely important to begin mouth-to-mouth artificial respiration *immediately*. Do not hesitate for any reason.

MOUTH-TO-MOUTH ARTIFICIAL RESPIRATION

Artificial respiration supplies oxygen to the victim's body until normal breathing resumes. Studies have shown that mouth-to-mouth or mouth-to-nose artificial respiration is by far superior to manual techniques. Specific procedures for the mouth-to-mouth method are basically the same, whether the victim is on land or in the water. Follow these steps, as shown in figure 2-19.

1. Start by placing the victim on his back and wiping away any visible foreign matter in his mouth.

2. Then, open the airway by tilting the victim's head back. Put one hand under the neck and lift; put the other hand on the forehead and push down. This extends the victim's neck and provides an open airway by moving the tongue away from the back of the throat.

3. To restore breathing, pinch the victim's nose with the thumb and forefinger of the hand on the victim's forehead. Pinching the nose prevents air from escaping; pressing on the forehead maintains the head-back position.

4. Next, open your mouth widely, take a deep breath, seal your mouth tightly around the victim's and, with your mouth forming a wide-open circle, blow into the victim's mouth 12 times per minute. For small children and infants, puff gently into both the nose and mouth about 20 times per minute.

5. Watch the victim's chest as it rises. After exhaling, raise your mouth, turn your head to the side, and listen for the victim to exhale. Watch his chest to see that it falls.

6. If the chest is not rising and falling, something is wrong. Check again for foreign matter stuck in the victim's mouth. Recheck the position of his head and jaw. If the stomach is bulging, turn the victim's head to the side and press down on the upper abdomen just below the rib cage.

7. If air still cannot pass in and out of the victim's lungs, turn him onto his side and administer sharp blows with the heel of your hand between the shoulder blades. The blows may jar any obstructions free.

Fig. 2-19 Mouth-to-Mouth Artificial Respiration

According to the American National Red Cross, mouth-to-mouth respiration should begin as quickly as possible in shallow water or while holding onto a boat or suitable buoyant aid. The wet suit and buoyancy compensator supply almost immediate buoyancy to both victim and rescuer when the weight belt is released. Once you establish buoyancy, it is easy to support the victim in the water with one hand under his neck, as shown in figure 2-20.

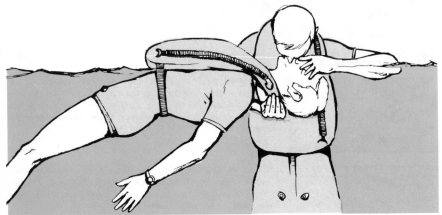

Fig. 2-20 Mouth-to-Mouth Artificial Respiration in Water

CARDIOPULMONARY RESUSCITATION

If the victim's heart has stopped beating, then blood circulation will also have to be restored. Cardiopulmonary resusitation (CPR) is a combination of mouth-to-mouth artificial respiration and external cardiac compression.

Cardiac compression is a relatively simple and mechanical method of compressing or pushing on the heart from outside the body, as shown in figure 2-21. When you press down on the lower breastbone, you squeeze the heart between

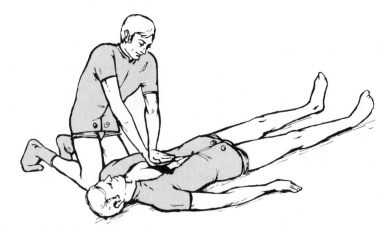

Fig. 2-21 External Cardiac Compression

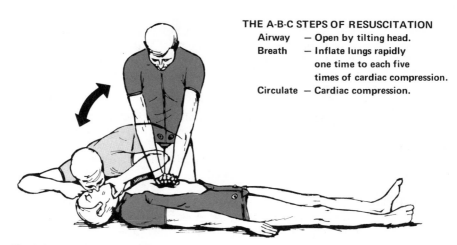

THE A-B-C STEPS OF RESUSCITATION

Airway   — Open by tilting head.

Breath   — Inflate lungs rapidly
one time to each five
times of cardiac compression.

Circulate — Cardiac compression.

Fig. 2-22 Cardiopulmonary Resuscitation

the breastbone and the backbone. This forces blood out of the heart and into the arteries. When you stop pressing, blood automatically refills the heart through incoming veins. Constant repetition of this squeeze-release process keeps the heart beating artificially.

When combined with mouth-to-mouth artificial respiration, one or two rescuers can perform both heart (cardio) and lung (pulmonary) resuscitation, as shown in figure 2-22.

Detailed directions for performing CPR are not provided here because the procedure requires special supplemental training in recognizing cardiac arrest. Instruction involves practice on manikins and performance of the skill both individually and as a team. Unless rescuers have repeated experiences performing CPR, they will need periodic training. Agencies such as the American Heart Association, the American Red Cross, and the YMCA offer courses in cardio-pulmonary resuscitation. Such instruction is highly recommended.

CLEAN AIR

Sport divers should never breathe anything but clean, dry, filtered air. It must be free from carbon monoxide, carbon dioxide, oil vapor, and other impurities. (See Appendix for Air Purity Standards Table.) Scuba tanks should never be filled with anything except ordinary air. Avoid other gases or gas mixtures.

From the time air is compressed by an air compressor until you inhale it from the regulator mouthpiece, there are a number of ways it can become contaminated. Here is a list of ways to prevent contamination:

1.   Make sure the compressor is located in a pollution-free area. Carbon monoxide from gasoline engine exhaust (automobile, electric generator,

boat, compressor engine, etc.) must not enter the compressor. Carbon monoxide gas combines with red blood cells 200 times more rapidly than oxygen. This prevents oxygen from getting to the body's tissues and also poisons living cells. Carbon monoxide poisoning can lead to unconsciousness and death.

2. Lubricate compressors and regulators only with special lubricants specified by the manufacturer. The wrong oil or grease used in the wrong place can find its way into the lungs and cause lipoid pneumonia, a lung infection caused by oil in air. Ordinary oils should never be used on a scuba regulator.

3. Before the air leaves the compressor, it must be filtered to remove any excess dangerous gases, water, oil, particles, and odor. Air compressors used in automobile filling stations do not have these filters and strict cleanliness requirements. This is why it is important to fill tanks only at reputable diving air stations.

4. High-pressure air from the compressors is often stored in special cylinders or storage tanks, as shown in figure 2-23. To prevent moisture or contaminants from entering the scuba cylinder, make sure the valve openings on both the storage system and the tank itself are clean and dry. Otherwise, moisture can be injected into the cylinder.

Fig. 2-23 High-Pressure Storage Cylinders

The act of breathing and the process of respiration do the work of supplying the cells of the body with life-giving fuel. Without fuel or with the wrong kind or amount of fuel, the body's machinery breaks down. It stops working. This is why divers have such a sensitive awareness of the breathing process. Make a point of developing this awareness, of understanding and appreciating all aspects of why and how people exchange oxygen and carbon dioxide on land and under water.

section C

descending and ascending

- EFFECTS OF PRESSURE CHANGE
- INCREASING PRESSURE
- DECREASING PRESSURE

EFFECTS OF INCREASING AND DECREASING PRESSURE

Even though people today live in a "pressurized" environment, pressure is rarely noticed until it changes. A customary change in pressure usually occurs while driving a car up or down steep hills. Most of us feel the change in our ears. Divers become aware of changes in both air and water pressure almost as soon as they enter the water. These changes are important, and to handle them effectively, you must understand how water pressure and air pressure affect each other, and how both affect the body.

AIR PRESSURE AND WATER PRESSURE

To say that air and water exert pressure is to say that they have weight. A cubic foot of air, for example, weighs a little over an ounce, and a cubic foot of salt water weighs 64 pounds. In the United States, pressure is usually measured in pounds per square inch, which is abbreviated "psi."

At sea level, ordinary air pressure exerts a force of 14.7 psi. A column of air, in other words, one inch by one inch wide extending as high up as the atmosphere (about 60 miles) "presses" toward the earth with a force, or weight, of 14.7 pounds, as shown in figure 2-24. This air pressure measurement of 14.7 psi is also called one *atmosphere* of pressure.

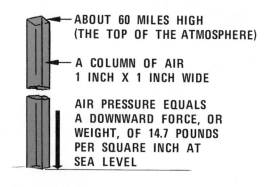

ABOUT 60 MILES HIGH
(THE TOP OF THE ATMOSPHERE)

A COLUMN OF AIR
1 INCH X 1 INCH WIDE

AIR PRESSURE EQUALS
A DOWNWARD FORCE, OR
WEIGHT, OF 14.7 POUNDS
PER SQUARE INCH AT
SEA LEVEL

Fig. 2-24 Air Pressure

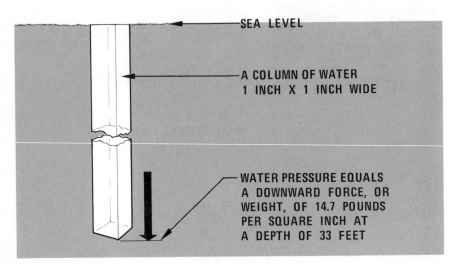

Fig. 2-25 Water Pressure

Salt water, because it is so much heavier than air, exerts one atmosphere of pressure in a mere 33 feet, as shown in figure 2-25. As you can see, a column of water one inch by one inch wide and 33 feet tall has a weight and exerts a pressure of 14.7 psi.

The amount of pressure depends on how much air and water is pressing down at any given time, as shown in figure 2-26. At an altitude of 18,000 feet, for example, there is only one-half the amount of air pressure that there is at sea level. Air pressure at this altitude is 7.35 psi, or one-half atmosphere. At an underwater depth of 66 feet, there are two atmospheres of water pressure (29.4 psi) and one atmosphere of air pressure (14.7 psi). Together, the water and air pressure exert a total of three atmospheres (44.1 psi).

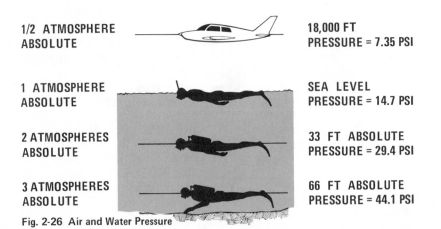

Fig. 2-26 Air and Water Pressure

Absolute pressure refers to a measurement of the *total* pressure exerted under water, including both water and air pressure. At 33 feet, for example, the absolute pressure would be two atmospheres absolute (one atmosphere of water and one atmosphere of air), or 29.4 psi absolute (14.7 psi of water and 14.7 psi of air). Unless indicated otherwise, pressure measurements given in pounds per square inch will usually refer to *absolute* pressure.

Ambient pressure is one way of saying surrounding pressure. It refers to the total or absolute water or air pressure surrounding a diver. At sea level, for example, the ambient pressure is 14.7 psi. At 33 feet under water, the ambient pressure surrounding a diver is 29.4 psi.

Gauge pressure refers to the measurement given by pressure gauges. They measure the difference between the surrounding air pressure and the pressure inside a scuba cylinder or air compressor. The zero mark on a pressure gauge, therefore, really represents air pressure at normal atmospheric pressure. At sea level this is 14.7 psi. On the pressure gauge, then, 500 psi refers to 500 psi over atmospheric air pressure.

INCREASING PRESSURE

When you descend below the surface, pressure increases by one atmosphere every 33 feet. The effects of this increasing pressure are easy to see. Take, for example, two standard, one-gallon containers, as shown in figure 2-27. If you fill one with water and one with air and carry them to 132 feet (five atmospheres absolute, 73.5 psi), the effects of increasing pressure are obvious. Nothing happens to the water-filled can, but the increasing pressure crushes the air-filled container.

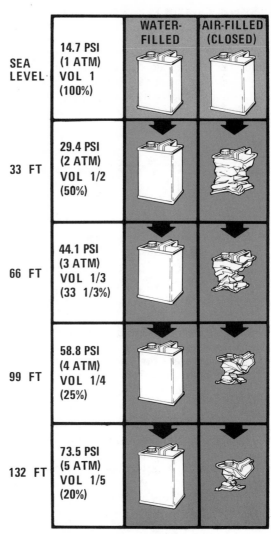

		WATER-FILLED	AIR-FILLED (CLOSED)
SEA LEVEL	14.7 PSI (1 ATM) VOL 1 (100%)		
33 FT	29.4 PSI (2 ATM) VOL 1/2 (50%)		
66 FT	44.1 PSI (3 ATM) VOL 1/3 (33 1/3%)		
99 FT	58.8 PSI (4 ATM) VOL 1/4 (25%)		
132 FT	73.5 PSI (5 ATM) VOL 1/5 (20%)		

Fig. 2-27 Effects of Increasing Pressure

The reason for this is that water is virtually incompressible. You can't "squeeze" it smaller or force it into a smaller space. Figure 2-28 illustrates how the increasing pressure is transmitted through the walls of the container directly into and through the water inside the container. No matter how great the pressure, the water stays the same size.

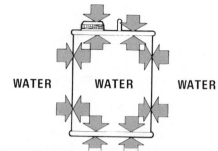

Fig. 2-28 Effect of Water Pressure on a Water-Filled Container

Air, or any gas for that matter, *is* compressible. Applied pressure squeezes it into a much smaller volume. As you can see in figure 2-29, the force of five atmospheres is enough to squeeze the air into a space that is one-fifth the original size of the container. The air inside the container is squeezed until the air pressure equals the surrounding water pressure. When the air in the container is *equalized* with the surrounding water pressure, the squeezing action stops.

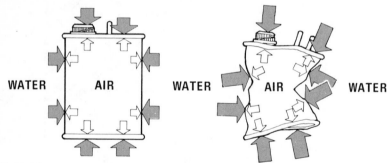

Fig. 2-29 Effect of Water Pressure on an Air-Filled Container

In 1610, Robert Boyle, a British physicist and chemist, noticed how pressure affects containers of air and other gases. He found the same thing happens in the same way every time, so he wrote what is now known as "Boyle's Law." It states that if the temperature stays the same, the volume of the gas gets smaller at the same rate that the surrounding pressure increases. (See Gas Laws in Appendix.)

Figure 2-30 shows how Boyle's Law works. If you take the one-gallon container, turn it upside down, and leave the cap off so water can enter the can freely, water will compress the air as pressure increases. When the absolute pressure doubles at 33 feet (two atmospheres absolute, 29.4 psi), the volume of air is cut in half as water fills one-half of the container. At 66 feet (three atmospheres absolute) the air is compressed to one-third of its original volume, at 99 feet (four atmospheres absolute) the air is squeezed to one-fourth its original volume, and so on as depth and pressure increase. When you return the container to the surface, the air expands to its original volume.

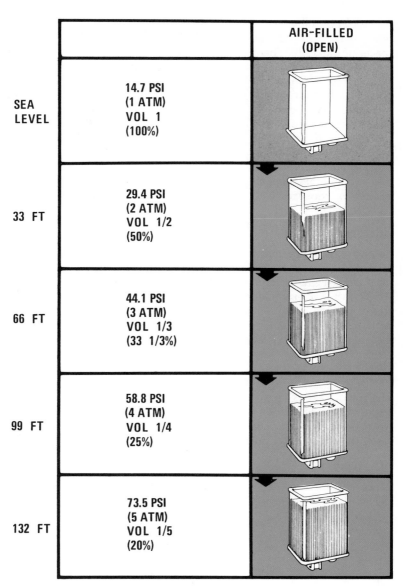

		AIR-FILLED (OPEN)
SEA LEVEL	14.7 PSI (1 ATM) VOL 1 (100%)	
33 FT	29.4 PSI (2 ATM) VOL 1/2 (50%)	
66 FT	44.1 PSI (3 ATM) VOL 1/3 (33 1/3%)	
99 FT	58.8 PSI (4 ATM) VOL 1/4 (25%)	
132 FT	73.5 PSI (5 ATM) VOL 1/5 (20%)	

Fig. 2-30 How Boyle's Law Works

Boyle's Law is significant for the diver in several ways. Most of your body can be thought of as a large liquid-filled "body balloon." Like the water-filled gasoline can, nothing happens during descent. Increasing pressure is simply transmitted into and through blood, bone, and solid tissue without damaging anything. No one knows exactly how much pressure the human body can withstand, but it is deeper than 1500 feet. This is far beyond any reasonable sport diving depth.

Boyle's Law really comes into play in the air spaces of the body. There are air-filled spaces in the ears, sinuses, lungs and airways, and stomach and intestines, as shown in figure 2-31. All of these spaces tend to respond to pressure in the same way the air-filled gallon container does—they are all subject to "squeezes."

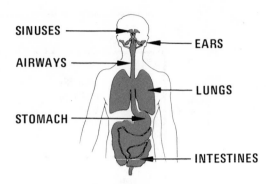

Fig. 2-31　Air-Filled Spaces in the Body

SQUEEZES

Boyle's Law states that air spaces will tend to equalize with the surrounding, or *ambient*, pressure. This equalization can take place in two ways. The space itself can get smaller or more air can be put into the space as pressure increases. At 33 feet, for example, the air-filled gallon container is either squeezed to a size of one-half gallon or it would hold two gallons of air in order to equalize with the ambient water pressure of two atmospheres. Your body uses both methods to equalize pressure and to prevent problems with squeezes.

Ear Squeeze

The middle ear is an air space connected to the back of your throat by the *eustachian tube*. (Note figure 2-32.) An ear squeeze occurs when increasing water pressure pushes against the eardrum without being equalized. In extreme cases, the pressure can break the eardrum.

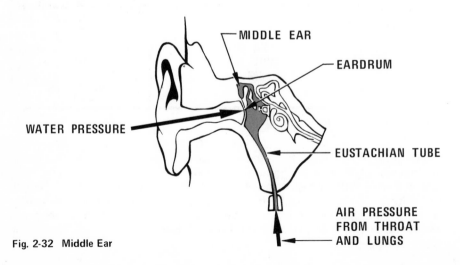

Fig. 2-32　Middle Ear

Putting more air into the middle ear space is the way to equalize pressure. Yawning or swallowing sometimes opens the eustachian tube enough to allow air to enter the middle ear. Usually, it is necessary to equalize the ears forcefully by holding your nose, closing your mouth, and gently blowing air from your throat, up the eustachian tubes, and into the middle ear. (See Part I, Section A.)

Anticipate ear squeeze. Start equalizing as soon as you feel any pressure change. Don't wait for pain to start; begin equalizing before and immediately after entering the water. Colds, allergic reactions, infections, and a number of other things can close the eustachian tube. This sometimes makes it impossible to equalize, so if you ever have trouble equalizing, don't continue the dive.

Sinus Squeeze

Another set of air spaces is located in the nose and forehead area, as shown in figure 2-33. These spaces, or sinuses, are surrounded by bone and lined with a membrane connected to the nasal cavity. Like the middle ear, they must be filled with extra air during descent to prevent a painful sinus squeeze.

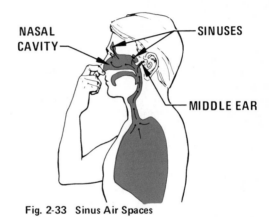

Fig. 2-33 Sinus Air Spaces

Usually, when you equalize your ears, air will also pass from your nasal cavity into the sinuses. Colds, allergies, and infections, however, sometimes swell the nose and sinus membranes which prevents air from passing into the sinuses.

Some divers use decongestants, nose drops, sprays, or pills to open the sinus passages. Problems can result, however, if the decongestant effect wears off too soon. Also, some decongestants contain antihistamines which make some people drowsy. In any case, if you have trouble with your sinuses, it is better to postpone diving activities than to use decongestants.

Lung Squeeze

Compared to the middle ear and sinus cavities, the lungs are flexible. When you descend, the increasing water pressure ordinarily reduces the size of the lungs and compresses the air inside until it is automatically equalized with ambient pressure.

A lung squeeze might occur, however, at great depths during a *breath-hold dive.* When the water pressure is great enough to compress lung volumes smaller than the residual air volume, then the lungs and rib cage become a semi-rigid air space. With scuba equipment on, the lungs are constantly replenished with adequate air which eliminates the possibility of lung squeeze.

Stomach and Intestine Squeeze

Digesting food often produces gas in the stomach and intestines. Air spaces or air pockets in the stomach and intestines are "squeezed" harmlessly during descent because they are surrounded by flexible tissue. If gas continues to form at depth, however, it will expand when you return to the surface. This can be painful and may call for a slow ascent. To prevent this kind of a squeeze, stay away from gas-producing foods before diving.

Equipment Squeezes

Artificial air spaces next to the body can cause squeezes the same way internal air spaces can. The mask squeeze, for example, can damage tissues around and in the eyes. A preoccupied diver might not notice the pain caused by the mask squeeze until the damage has been done. It's important, therefore, to make a point of exhaling through your nose into the mask to equalize pressure during descent. (See Part I, Section A.)

Never wear goggles or earplugs while scuba or skin diving. The air spaces created by these devices cannot be equalized, so the eye tissues or eardrums can be easily damaged.

DECREASING PRESSURE

During ascent, when pressure decreases, air naturally expands. Figure 2-34 shows what happens to two one-gallon containers filled with air from a scuba tank at a depth of 132 feet (five atmospheres absolute, 73.4 psi). Since air at this depth is compressed to only one-fifth of its sea level volume, the gallon containers hold five gallons of sea level air. As the cans ascend, the air expands to five gallons.

The first container in figure 2-34 is left open, so that expanding air escapes into the surrounding environment during ascent. The second container is sealed at 132 feet after being filled with scuba air. As it ascends, the container begins to bulge until finally a seam breaks to allow the expanding air to escape. The ears, sinuses, mask, and lungs usually do the same thing that container number one does—the expanding air simply escapes into the surrounding water during ascent. But if the air spaces are closed off like the second container, surrounding tissues can be damaged. Normal breathing during ascents will prevent closing off the lungs and eliminate the possibility of ill effects.

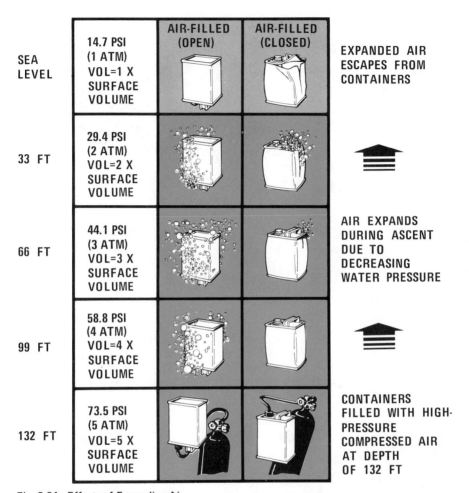

		AIR-FILLED (OPEN)	AIR-FILLED (CLOSED)	
SEA LEVEL	14.7 PSI (1 ATM) VOL=1 X SURFACE VOLUME			EXPANDED AIR ESCAPES FROM CONTAINERS
33 FT	29.4 PSI (2 ATM) VOL=2 X SURFACE VOLUME			
66 FT	44.1 PSI (3 ATM) VOL=3 X SURFACE VOLUME			AIR EXPANDS DURING ASCENT DUE TO DECREASING WATER PRESSURE
99 FT	58.8 PSI (4 ATM) VOL=4 X SURFACE VOLUME			
132 FT	73.5 PSI (5 ATM) VOL=5 X SURFACE VOLUME			CONTAINERS FILLED WITH HIGH-PRESSURE COMPRESSED AIR AT DEPTH OF 132 FT

Fig. 2-34 Effects of Expanding Air

AIR EMBOLISM

The largest air spaces in the body are also the easiest to close. When you hold your breath, the lungs are shut tight to the outside world. During a scuba diving ascent, unvented lungs can rupture from the expanding air they contain. There are several different ways air can escape. If the air escapes from the alveoli directly into the pulmonary veins, the bubbles may find their way directly into the heart, as shown in figure 2-35. From the heart, they travel up the carotid arteries in the neck and eventually find their way into the small arteries and capillaries of the brain. Embolism comes from the word *embolus*, which means "plug." Sooner or later, the air bubble or bubbles will get stuck in a small artery or capillary and will form a "plug," which cuts off the blood supply to brain tissue. This can be extremely serious, leading to unconsciousness and death.

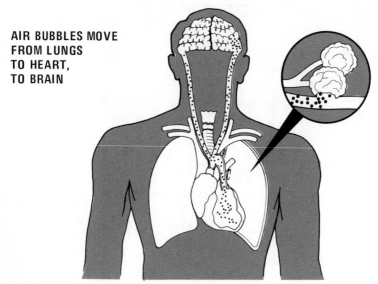

AIR BUBBLES MOVE
FROM LUNGS
TO HEART,
TO BRAIN

Fig. 2-35 Air Embolism

The only treatment for an air embolism is *immediate* recompression in a chamber, as shown in figure 2-36. Here, air pressure is increased quickly to reduce the size of the air bubbles so they won't stop the flow of blood. Then the pressure is decreased very slowly to prevent bubbles and embolisms from forming.

Fig. 2-36 Recompression Chambers

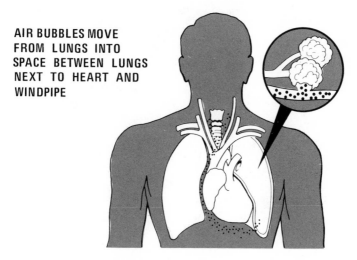

AIR BUBBLES MOVE
FROM LUNGS INTO
SPACE BETWEEN LUNGS
NEXT TO HEART AND
WINDPIPE

Fig. 2-37 Mediastinal Emphysema

Air can also pass out of the alveoli altogether and into the *mediastinum*, or the space between the lungs near the heart and along the windpipe, as shown in figure 2-37. Air in the mediastinum can cause mediastinal emphysema, a problem that brings about chest pain, breathing difficulties, and faintness because of air pressure against the heart.

From the mediastinum area, the air bubbles can travel up along the neck and under the skin in the neck and upper chest region, as shown in figure 2-38. This is called *subcutaneous emphysema*, which may also cause breathing difficulties along with swelling and even changes in voice.

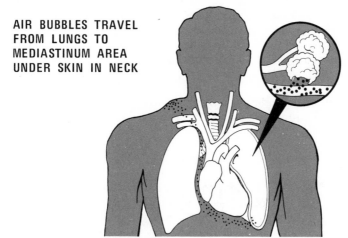

AIR BUBBLES TRAVEL
FROM LUNGS TO
MEDIASTINUM AREA
UNDER SKIN IN NECK

Fig. 2-38 Subcutaneous Emphysema

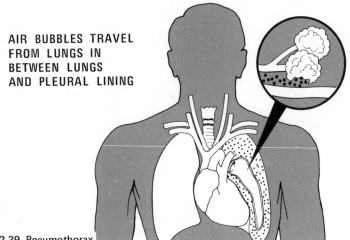

AIR BUBBLES TRAVEL
FROM LUNGS IN
BETWEEN LUNGS
AND PLEURAL LINING

Fig. 2-39 Pneumothorax

Between the lungs and rib cage is a moist membrane called the pleural lining. If air escapes from the alveoli in between the lungs and the *pleural lining*, it could expand and cause the lung or lungs to collapse, as shown in figure 2-39. This is called *pneumothorax*, a rare but serious medical problem. The expanding air in the pleural space not only collapses the lung, but also may press against the heart and affect circulation. Again, chest pain and breathing difficulties occur.

First Aid for Embolism and Emphysema

Symptoms of air embolism occur in a matter of seconds after the diver surfaces and may even occur during ascent. Before losing consciousness, an embolism victim may experience weakness, dizziness, paralysis, changes in vision, chest pain, blood in the mouth, convulsions, and cessation of breathing.

Whenever there is the least suspicion that a diver could have experienced a lung-expansion injury, take the following first aid measures and get him to a recompression chamber as soon as possible. Do not try to recompress a possible embolism victim in the water. The symptoms are too severe to allow for adequate underwater treatment. (See Appendix for reference of Hyperbaric, or recompression, Chambers.)

1. Lay the victim down on left side with head lower than the rest of the body.
2. Give mouth-to-mouth resuscitation if necessary.
3. Administer oxygen.
4. Treat victim for shock.
5. Immediately take the victim to the nearest recompression chamber.

As in all diving accidents, prevention is much more effective than a cure. Anything that could possibly prevent air from escaping naturally from the lungs should be carefully examined. Such things as pneumonia, asthma, lung scars, and even smoking can block the free flow of air out of alveoli and can contribute to the causes of embolism.

It's important to remember that the greatest pressure changes occur in shallow water. Pressure increases by 50 percent in the first 33 feet. In the next 33 feet, from 33 to 66 feet, pressure increases by 17 percent—less than half the pressure increase of the first 33 feet. From 66 to 99 feet gives a pressure increase of only 8 percent. The deeper you go, the smaller the rate of change in pressure. The danger of embolism, then, is greater in shallower water where the most dramatic changes in pressure exist; cases have occurred in water as shallow as 12 feet.

The most common cause of air embolism is breath holding. It is entirely natural for an air-breathing creature to hold its breath under water. In an emergency or panic situation, holding your breath is a powerfully strong instinct. It's important to fight this natural tendency whenever you scuba dive. Never hold your breath when scuba diving. Always breathe naturally or exhale continuously on ascent.

ASCENT PROCEDURES

The purpose of learning specific diving procedures is to establish safe habits. You will develop habits whether you want to or not, so it's important to develop good habits from the beginning. Every ascent should follow these steps:

1. Check with your buddy to make sure you both know the dive is over and that it is time to ascend.
2. Check your watch and note the time.
3. Inflate your buoyancy vest until you have a slight positive buoyancy.
4. Put your head back, lift one arm straight up, look toward the surface, and ascend at a rate of 60 feet per minute (about the speed of medium-size bubbles) while turning around slowly to assure no obstructions are in the ascent area.
5. Breathe regularly and continuously all the way to the surface and let expanding air escape from your buoyancy vest to maintain an ascent rate of no more than 60 feet per minute, as shown in figure 2-40.

Fig. 2-40 Ascent Procedures

When you reach the surface, inflate your vest completely and switch from regulator to snorkel. As always, be ready to help your buddy in any way. This is especially important at the end of the dive when both divers are tired and when the air supply is at its lowest point.

EMERGENCY ASCENTS

If you should ever lose your air supply under water, you will have two basic methods of returning to the surface safely: you can ascend by yourself or with the help of your buddy. The best method of ascent depends on the situation.

An emergency ascent is similar to an ordinary ascent. The main difference is that the diver ascends by himself instead of with his buddy. In an emergency, there may not be time to check with your buddy. It is much faster to simply ascend, exhaling continuously on the way up to prevent overexpansion of the lungs.

The emergency ascent should begin immediately when the need is recognized. Ditch your weight belt at once. Flip the weight belt buckle and throw the belt well away from your body. Take your regulator out of your mouth as the air stoppage may be equipment malfunction rather than low air supply. Leaving your regulator in your mouth will make you prone to inhale or hold your breath as you ascend. It is critical to remember to exhale continuously. You will become buoyant the minute you ditch the weight belt and your ascent rate will accelerate rapidly. Look up and raise one arm above your head, and turn around slowly as you rise.

If your vest is operated from a CO_2 cartridge, or a separate air bottle, you may wish to also use that. If you convert your emergency swimming ascent into a buoyant ascent, be prepared for the high rate of speed at which you will start to ascend and flare out at about 15 feet to slow down. This is done by throwing your feet forward, your shoulders backwards and arching your back. This creates a great deal of drag and slows you down in that most crucial area where embolism is most likely.

Emergency Buddy Breathing Ascent

Buddy breathing is explained in Part I, Section C. It is perhaps the most controlled method of getting to the surface as long as both buddies are thoroughly trained, experienced, and close together.

At sport diving depths as great as 80 or 90 feet, buoyancy becomes a critical matter. An ordinary buddy breathing ascent from deep water can easily exhaust a buddy team if they are not positively buoyant. A good way for both divers to establish buoyancy while buddy breathing is for each to exhale into his vest when not inhaling from the regulator, as shown in figure 2-41.

The "donor" holds the regulator in the right hand and holds the vest inflator with the left hand. The "needer" grabs onto the "donor's" right hand and

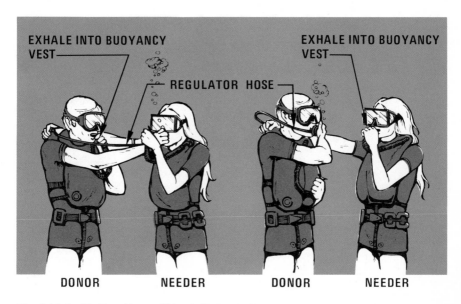

Fig. 2-41 Buddy Breathing and Vest Inflation Ascent

regulator, and holds the vest inflator with the left hand. One buddy inhales from the regulator two times, while the other slowly exhales into the vest inflator. The buddy team continues this procedure until both vests are adequately inflated.

It is important for you and your buddy to practice this skill repeatedly. Buddy breathing requires a highly coordinated series of actions between buddies. It involves a lot of concentration. It's easy to lose track of your rate of ascent and it is especially tempting to hold your breath when the regulator is not in your mouth. Again, never hold your breath when using scuba gear. When buddy breathing, make sure both you and your buddy exhale continuously when not inhaling.

The effects of pressure on the human body can be severe. We could withstand changes in pressure much more easily without middle ears, sinuses, lungs, and other air spaces. A totally liquid and solid human body would make for a much more efficient sport diver when it comes to confronting increasing and decreasing pressures. The air spaces, however, are here to stay. Until we find a way to either remove them or fill them with water, sport divers will have to use knowledge and skill to handle pressure changes effectively.

section D

depth and time limits

- ● SPORT DIVING LIMITS
- ● THE BENDS
- ● PREVENTING THE BENDS

EFFECTS OF DIVING TOO DEEP AND TOO LONG

The direct effects of increased pressure on the air spaces inside and outside the diver's body are obvious. Spaces get bigger and smaller almost immediately, and you can either see or feel the changes while they occur. There are, however, less obvious changes. Pressure affects gases and gas mixtures in the body in definite ways, but the effects on the mind and body are sometimes less direct. Even though you may not see or feel these changes as easily, they are equally profound and demand a thorough understanding.

Fortunately, the direct and indirect effects of breathing air under water are measurable and predictable. Because they are predictable, certain depth and time limits can be set for sport divers. Staying within these limits is an easy and sure way to prevent problems resulting from effects of pressure.

It is suggested that sport divers limit diving to depths of less than 100 feet. Deeper diving requires extensive training and more sophisticated equipment than a certified sport diver may have.

The 100-foot limit may sound restrictive, but not really. Many sport divers, in fact, usually dive in waters shallower than 30 feet; they prefer the warmer water and better visibility usually found closer to the surface.

NITROGEN NARCOSIS

What makes 100 feet the suggested limit? Ordinarily, inert gases like nitrogen (or helium) are more or less inactive. They are not consumed or used by the body, and they have no effect on your mind. Under pressure, however, they can become "narcotic." Your ability to think and perceive is altered. At depths greater than 100 feet, scuba divers have been known to do strange things as a result of breathing air at a pressure of four or more atmospheres.

SYMPTOMS AND PREVENTION

Beyond 100 feet, nitrogen narcosis can affect your ability to think and make judgments; at 150 feet, you may become somewhat dizzy. Between 200 and 250 feet, you may be unable to communicate or perform simple motor or mental tasks, and below 250 feet, the average diver is more or less useless and becomes a safety menace to himself and others. (Note figure 2-42.)

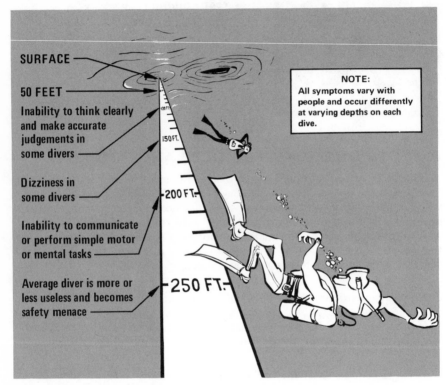

Fig. 2-42 Nitrogen Narcosis Symptoms

Several things lower resistance to nitrogen narcosis. Alcohol, hangover, fatigue, excess carbon dioxide, inexperience, and anxiety tend to reduce a diver's tolerance to high-pressure nitrogen. Also, nitrogen narcosis affects different people in different ways, and any one diver may experience a variety of symptoms inconsistently. But whatever the symptoms, returning to shallower depths is the easiest way to both prevent and treat nitrogen narcosis.

OXYGEN POISONING

Living things need oxygen for survival. An excess of oxygen, however, is just as bad as too little. If you breathe an excess of oxygen for an extended period of time, the outcome can be harmful. Excess oxygen can injure lung tissues and can adversely affect the central nervous system.

PARTIAL PRESSURES

How much oxygen is too much? This depends on three things: the amount, its pressure, and the exposure time. Ordinarily, we breathe a mixture of 78 percent nitrogen and 21 percent oxygen at atmospheric pressure (14.7 psi). Dalton's Law states that the total pressure of a gas mixture equals the sum of the *partial* pressures that make up the mixture. In other words, the sea level partial pressure of nitrogen equals 78 percent of 14.7 psi, or 11.6 psi. The partial pressure of oxygen is 21 percent of 14.7 psi, or 3.09 psi.

Now, oxygen poisoning can occur when the partial pressure of pure oxygen equals two atmospheres absolute, or 29.4 psi (two times 14.7 psi). This could happen if you were breathing pure oxygen (not air) at a depth of 33 feet. It could also happen by breathing ordinary air at a depth of 297 feet, or 10 atmospheres (10 times 3.09 psi). (See figure 2-43.)

**100% OXYGEN AT 33 FT.
(2 ATMOSPHERES)**

**AIR AT 297 FT.
(10 ATMOSPHERES)**

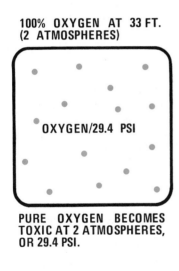

OXYGEN/29.4 PSI

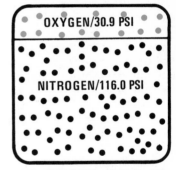

OXYGEN/30.9 PSI

NITROGEN/116.0 PSI

PURE OXYGEN BECOMES
TOXIC AT 2 ATMOSPHERES,
OR 29.4 PSI.

AIR BECOMES TOXIC AT
10 ATMOSPHERES BECAUSE
THE PARTIAL PRESSURE OF
OXYGEN EQUALS ABOUT
2 ATMOSPHERES, OR 30.9
PSI.

Fig. 2-43 Oxygen Poisoning

Oxygen poisoning will never be a problem to the sport diver as long as he uses clean, dry, filtered air *only* and stays within the 100-foot depth limit for sport diving.

Early symptoms of oxygen poisoning are muscular twitching, nausea, vision and hearing problems, breathing difficulty, anxiety, confusion, unusual fatigue, and clumsiness. These symptoms stop as soon as the partial pressure of oxygen is reduced to below 14.7 psi either by decreasing ambient pressure or by reducing the concentration of oxygen in the breathing mixture.

THE BENDS

"The bends," or decompression sickness, is certainly the most famous of diving illnesses. The story of a diver crippled and bent over with the bends and saved in the nick of time by a recompression chamber, has provided suspense and drama to more than one diving movie. Decompression sickness is a serious diving ailment, but if you never go below 33 feet you can dive for as long as you wish.

Decompression sickness was "discovered" in the 19th century by laborers who worked in tunnels beneath rivers. The tunnels were pressurized to keep water from flowing into the working areas. At the end of the day's work, the workers returned to an ordinary atmospheric pressure. Many of the workers developed pain in their joints and some became paralyzed. The malady became known as "caisson disease."

The disease of the tunnel workers remained a mystery and a problem until 1907 when Dr. J. S. Haldane determined a method of "stage decompression" to prevent decompression sickness. By bringing anyone who has been in a high-pressure environment back to a normal atmospheric pressure in gradual stages, decompression sickness does not occur.

A slow decompression eliminates the bends by preventing the formation of small pockets of nitrogen in the blood and tissues. According to Henry's Law, gases will enter into a liquid in proportion to the partial pressure of the gas. If you double the partial pressure of nitrogen, for example, the amount of nitrogen that can be dissolved in the blood and tissues of the body also doubles. If you triple the pressure, blood and tissues will hold three times the amount of nitrogen.

Nitrogen dissolved in the body is harmless as long as it stays dissolved. Nitrogen, oxygen, carbon dioxide, and other gases transfer into and out of the bloodstream in the lungs constantly whether you are diving or not. But if you reduce the ambient pressure too quickly, the dissolved nitrogen can come out of solution and form tiny bubbles in the blood and tissues of the body.

The classic example of dissolved gas coming out of solution is a soda pop bottle, shown in figure 2-44. With the cap on, no bubbles are visible because the liquid is under pressure and the "carbonation" bubbles (carbon dioxide gas) are too minute to be seen. When you take the cap off, the pressure is suddenly reduced. The soda pop bubbles. The bubbles seem to come from nowhere. They will

Fig. 2-44 Gas Coming Out of Solution

continue to expand until the soda pop "goes flat." A "flat" bottle of soda does not bubble because the partial pressure of the carbon dioxide gas dissolved in the liquid equals the partial pressure of the gas at ambient pressure in the air surrounding the liquid.

A bubbling, carbonated beverage decompresses in much the same way liquids and tissues of the body decompress during the bends. The symptoms of decompression sickness vary, depending on where the bubbles form in the body, as shown in figure 2-45. Symptoms begin within an hour in most cases, but may not begin for six or more hours.

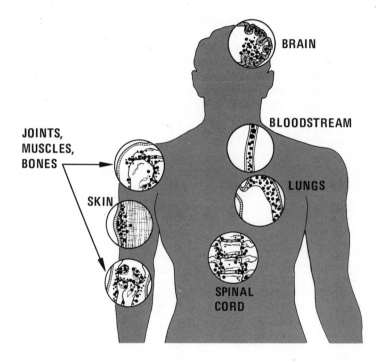

Fig. 2-45 Bubble Formation

Blindness, dizziness, paralysis, unconsciousness, and convulsions are evidence of bubble formation in the brain. Pain is experienced if bubbles form in the joints, muscles, or bones; the bloodstream is affected with blocked circulation. Paralysis and loss of feeling in the spinal cord means decompression sickness is occurring there. Asphyxia and choking are signs of lung decompression sickness, while the skin will itch or break out in a rash if bubble formation takes place there.

Inadequate decompression is the immediate cause of decompression sickness, but several factors help contribute to the formation of bubbles. Anything that reduces or hinders blood circulation can prevent nitrogen from quickly entering and leaving the blood, such as, age, extreme fatigue, alcoholic intoxication, old injuries, extremely hot or cold water, and dehydration.

Obesity presents a special problem with decompression sickness. Fat absorbs about 5 times more nitrogen than blood or other tissues of the body. It takes longer for fatty tissues to become saturated with nitrogen, and it also takes longer for the nitrogen to leave these tissues during decompression.

PREVENTION

To prevent decompression sickness, stay within the depth and time limits put forth in the U.S. Navy Decompression Tables. (See Appendix.) The first two vertical columns of the No-Decompression Limits Table show the number of minutes you can dive at certain maximum depths. (See figure 2-46.) At depths of 30 feet or less, you can scuba dive for as long as you wish; there are no no-decompression limits. At 35 feet, however, you must return to the surface before 310 minutes have passed to avoid stage decompression. At 60 feet, your no-decompression limit is 60 minutes. You can dive to 90 feet for only 30 minutes; then you must ascend directly to the surface to avoid decompression stops on the way up.

NO-DECOMPRESSION LIMITS AND REPETITIVE GROUP DESIGNATION TABLE FOR NO-DECOMPRESSION AIR DIVES

Depth (feet)	No-decom-pression limits (min)	A	B	C	D	E	F	G	H	I	J	K	L	M	N	O
10		60	120	210	300											
15		35	70	110	160	225	350									
20		25	50	75	100	135	180	240	325							
25		20	35	55	75	100	125	160	195	245	315					
30		15	30	45	60	75	95	120	145	170	205	250	310			
35	310	5	15	25	40	50	60	80	100	120	140	160	190	220	270	310
40	200	5	15	25	30	40	50	70	80	100	110	130	150	170	200	
50	100		10	15	25	30	40	50	60	70	80	90	100			
60	60		10	15	20	25	30	40	50	60						
70	50	5	10	15	20	30	35	40	45	50						
80	40	5	10	15	20	25	30	35	40							
90	30	5	10	12	15	20	25	30								
100	25	5	7	10	15	20	22	25								
110	20		5	10	13	15	20									
120	15		5	10	12	15										
130	10		5	8	10											
140	10		5	7	10											
150	5		5													
160	5				5											
170	5				5											
180	5				5											
190	5				5											

Fig. 2-46 No-Decompression Limits

Ascent Rate

The U.S. Navy Standard Air Decompression Tables are based on an ascent rate of 60 feet per minute. The smaller exhaled bubbles ascend at about this rate, so always stay below your smallest exhalation bubbles to avoid too fast an ascent, as shown in figure 2-47.

Bottom Time

The no-decompression limits are given in minutes of bottom time. You are technically "on the bottom" from the time you begin your descent until the time you begin your ascent directly to the surface, as illustrated in figure 2-48. For example, you descend to 25 feet for 10 minutes. Then you descend deeper to 50 feet for 15 minutes. After this, you ascend back to 25 feet for five minutes, and then ascend directly to the surface.

After a dive like this, your "bottom time" is 30 minutes at 50 feet, even though you actually spend only 15 minutes at 50 feet. Bottom time, in other words, refers to the *total* time of the dive from the beginning of the descent to the beginning of the direct ascent. The depth of the dive always refers to the deepest point of the dive, no matter how briefly you stay at that depth. Bottom time and depth are also defined in Part II, Section E.

Fig. 2-47 Ascent Rates

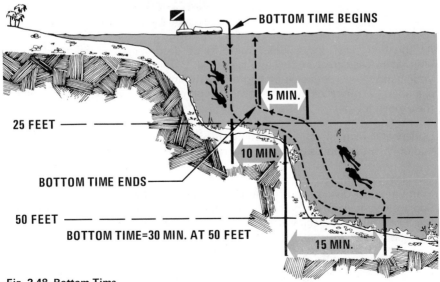

BOTTOM TIME BEGINS

5 MIN.

25 FEET

10 MIN.

BOTTOM TIME ENDS

50 FEET

BOTTOM TIME=30 MIN. AT 50 FEET

15 MIN.

Fig. 2-48 Bottom Time

HIGH ALTITUDE DIVING

Diving in mountain lakes or other high altitude waters increases the possibility of decompression sickness. When you ascend from a dive at a high altitude location, the atmospheric pressure is lower than it is at sea level. This results in a greater difference between water pressures at depth and air pressures at the surface. Because of this, decompression computors and depth gauges are inaccurate above sea level. Also, the U.S. Navy Decompression Tables are inaccurate either above sea level or in fresh water. If you plan to dive at high altitudes, be sure to consult local divers for corrections to the tables. Use a capillary depth gauge and make only shallow, single, no-decompression dives.

FLYING AFTER DIVING

The decompression tables are designed for use at sea level during and after the dive. Airplanes, however, are rarely pressurized to sea level pressures. Flying in pressurized commercial airliners can cause serious decompression problems to a diver partially saturated with nitrogen in his blood and tissues. To prevent decompression sickness, always wait at least 12 hours after diving before flying.

The only effective treatment of decompression sickness is immediate recompression in a recompression chamber. Figure 2-49 is an illustration of one. Recompression reduces the size of the nitrogen bubbles and forces them back into solution. Then, the pressure is slowly reduced inside the chamber according to the U.S. Navy Standard Air or Oxygen Treatment Tables to allow the diver to decompress gradually.

Fig. 2-49 Recompression Chamber

At the first sign of possible symptoms of decompression sickness, do not hesitate to seek treatment. Time is critical. Before diving, make sure you and your buddy know the location and phone number of the nearest recompression chamber. A reference to help locate recompression chambers is provided in the Appendix.

Underwater recompression should be considered only in an extreme emergency and only if it is impossible to get to a recompression chamber.

The indirect effects of pressure can be easily avoided. The depth and time limits of sport diving need not inhibit even the most adventurous buddy team. Sport divers have little reason to go beyond reasonable limits. Most underwater life lives well within the warm and lighted depths above 100 feet. This is where diving is most enjoyable, interesting, and safe.

section E

repetitive dives

● BOTTOM TIME, DEPTH AND SURFACE TIME
● REPETITIVE DIVE TABLES
● DIVE PLANNING

RESIDUAL NITROGEN, MORE THAN ONE DIVE, DECOMPRESSION DIVING, AND DIVE PLANNING

Your body normally contains a certain amount of nitrogen dissolved in the blood and tissues. Whenever you dive, your body absorbs more nitrogen because of increased pressure underwater. The blood and tissues can continue to absorb nitrogen for about 24 hours under pressure. After 24 hours, the body is said to be "saturated" with nitrogen—it cannot hold any more, so absorption stops. When you return to a lower pressure at the surface, the nitrogen slowly leaves the blood and tissues through alveoli in the lungs. The body continues to give off nitrogen until the gas dissolved in blood and tissues returns to normal.

RESIDUAL NITROGEN

The extra nitrogen that stays in your body after the dive is called "residual nitrogen." According to the theory Dr. J. S. Haldane developed in 1907, this residual nitrogen in the body is harmless at the surface as long as the amount stays less than twice the normal surface amount.

Dr. Haldane's ratio of 2 to 1 (underwater partial pressure to surface partial pressure) has been somewhat changed by later studies, experience, and hundreds of test dives, but the basic principle is the same. The U.S. Navy Decompression Tables are more or less based on the simple fact that nitrogen will stay in solution and will not form bubbles as long as the partial pressure of nitrogen is not immediately reduced more than one-half.

The no-decompression time limits at depths from above 33 feet down are all designed to keep you within this 2 to 1 ratio. At 60 feet, for example, your no-decompression limit is 60 minutes. This means it will take 60 minutes for the partial pressure of nitrogen in the blood and tissues of your body to double. The deeper you go, the faster your body absorbs nitrogen. At 150 feet, it only takes five minutes for the partial pressure of nitrogen to almost double.

MORE THAN ONE DIVE

The No-Decompression Limits and Repetitive Group Designation Table for No-Decompression Air Dives (see Appendix) tells you how long you can stay at certain depths in salt water and return to the surface without decompression stops. But what if you want to make another dive soon after the first one? Your body contains a certain amount of residual nitrogen from the first dive, so you will have to take this into consideration on your second dive. The U.S. Navy uses two tables (see Appendix), to let you account for residual nitrogen in two or more dives in salt water.

The No-Decompression Limits and Repetitive Group Designation Table and the Residual Nitrogen Timetable for Repetitive Air Dives have instructions and examples to help you use them. Let's examine a typical sport diving situation in which a buddy team uses the tables to make two dives in one day.

A TYPICAL REPETITIVE DIVE

Figure 2-50 is a diagram of the two dives. The buddy team plans to make one dive in the morning and one after lunch. They descend at 11 a.m. to a maximum depth of 73 feet and swim along the bottom toward shore. The bottom gets slightly shallower as they swim until they run into a vertical, underwater cliff. They ascend along the face of the cliff until they discover an underwater ledge at about 55 feet.

After finding the ledge, they agree, as planned, to ascend. They both look at their watches and note the time and begin a direct ascent to the surface at 11:22 a.m.

After eating lunch and refilling tanks, the buddy team begins their descent at 1:07 p.m. They explore the underwater ledge at a depth of 55 feet for one-half hour. Their ascent from 55 feet to the surface begins at 1:37 p.m.

Before, during, and after these two dives, the buddy team used the U.S. Navy Tables to plan and recheck both the time and depth of each dive. To use and understand the tables, you must become familiar with several important terms:

> *Bottom time* refers to the total elapsed time starting from when the buddy team begins their descent until they begin a direct ascent to the surface. (See also Part II, Section D.)

> *Depth* is the deepest point reached during a dive. (Also mentioned in Part II, Section D.)

> *Surface interval time* is the time a buddy team spends on the surface between dives.

> *Repetitive Dive* refers to any dive that begins within 12 hours of surfacing from an earlier dive. If the surface interval between dives, however, is 10 minutes or less, then consider both dives as one long dive with a bottom time equal to the total bottom times of both dives.

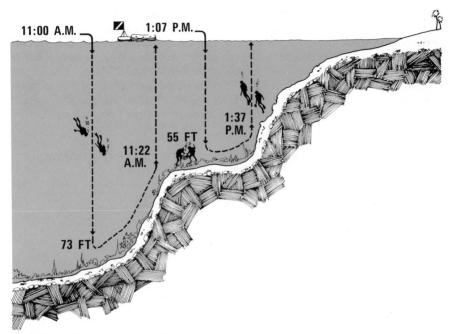

Fig. 2-50 A Typical Repetitive Dive

THE DIVE PROFILE

To plan and analyze repetitive dives, the buddy team sketches a dive profile, as shown in figure 2-51. It is a simple diagram of one or more dives and a convenient way to record time, depth, and information from the decompression tables. The profile shown here is the one the buddy team uses for the dive illustrated in figure 2-50.

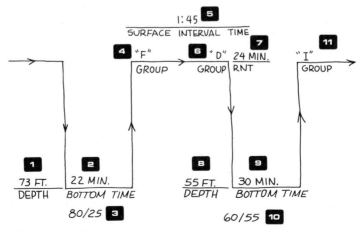

Fig. 2-51 The Dive Profile

The buddy team knows, before arriving at the dive site, that the maximum depth of this particular location is about 75 feet. In order to stay within the no-decompression limits, they consult the No-Decompression Limits and Repetitive Group Designation Table, as shown in figure 2-52. Looking at the first two columns, they find that any dive between 70 and 80 feet is considered a dive to 80 feet (item 1) with a maximum bottom time of 40 minutes (item 2). If they went to the maximum depth, in other words, they would have to ascend within 40 minutes. They agree to end the first dive well before this time limit is up.

NO-DECOMPRESSION LIMITS AND REPETITIVE GROUP DESIGNATION TABLE FOR NO-DECOMPRESSION AIR DIVES

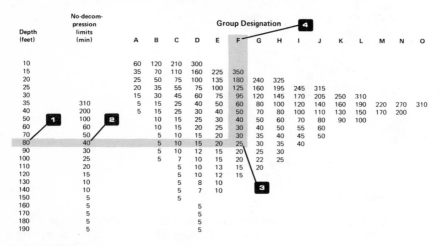

Depth (feet)	No-decompression limits (min)	A	B	C	D	E	F	G	H	I	J	K	L	M	N	O
10		60	120	210	300											
15		35	70	110	160	225	350									
20		25	50	75	100	135	180	240	325							
25		20	35	55	75	100	125	160	195	245	315					
30		15	30	45	60	75	95	120	145	170	205	250	310			
35	310	5	15	25	40	50	60	80	100	120	140	160	190	220	270	310
40	200	5	15	25	30	40	50	70	80	100	110	130	150	170	200	
50	100		10	15	25	30	40	50	60	70	80	90	100			
60	60		10	15	20	25	30	40	50	55	60					
70	50		5	10	15	20	30	35	40	45	50					
80	40		5	10	15	20	25	30	35	40						
90	30		5	10	12	15	20	25	30							
100	25		5	7	10	15	20	22	25							
110	20			5	10	13	15	20								
120	15			5	10	12	15									
130	10			5	8	10										
140	10			5	7	10										
150	5			5												
160	5				5											
170	5				5											
180	5				5											
190	5				5											

Fig. 2-52 No-Decompression Limits Table

Since the actual depth and bottom time of the first dive is 73 feet for 22 minutes, they enter this information on the dive profile (items 1 and 2 in figure 2-51). Returning to the No-Decompression Table for the 80-foot depth, they find that the *exact or next greater* time, over 22 minutes, is 25 minutes (item 3). They next enter this information in the profile: "80/25" (Fig. 2-51, item 3).

The shaded area in figure 2-52 (No-Decompression Table) illustrates that a dive to 80 feet for 25 minutes puts the dive team in repetitive group "F" (item 4). They enter this information in the dive profile (Fig. 2-51, item 4). The repetitive groups "A" through "O" actually represent a system for cataloging how much residual nitrogen a diver contains in his body after a no-decompression dive. An "A" diver, for example, has very little residual nitrogen, while an "O" diver has a great amount.

The surface interval time between dives is one hour and 45 minutes. They enter this time on the dive profile (Fig. 2-51, item 5). While the buddy team is on the surface, they are constantly giving off nitrogen. When they begin the repetitive dive, therefore, their bodies contain less residual nitrogen than they did at the end of dive one. To get credit for this decrease in residual nitrogen, they turn to the second table, the Residual Nitrogen Timetable for Repetitive Air Dives, as shown in figure 2-53.

Since the dive team ended dive one as "F" divers, they enter the Residual Nitrogen Timetable at "F" on the slanted left-hand side of the table. The paired numbers, to the right, refer to minimum and maximum surface interval times.

RESIDUAL NITROGEN TIMETABLE FOR REPETITIVE AIR DIVES

*Dives following surface intervals of more than 12 hours are not repetitive dives. Use actual bottom times in the Standard Air Decompression Tables to compute decompression for such dives.

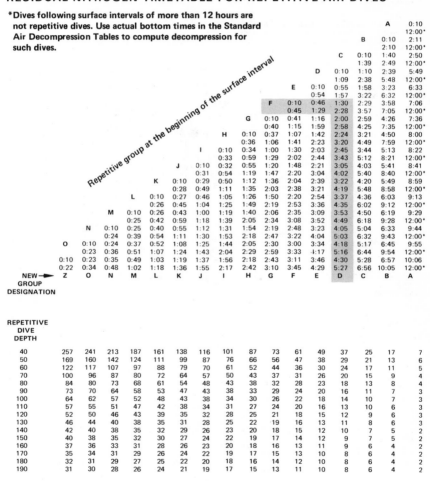

RESIDUAL NITROGEN TIMES (MINUTES)

Fig. 2-53 Residual Nitrogen Timetable

Reading from left to right (Fig. 2-54), they find that their time, one hour and 45 minutes, puts them in the fourth column from the right side of the table, or the box containing 1:30 (minimum time in that designation) and 2:28 (maximum time). Following the column downward, the buddies find they have given off residual nitrogen to move from the "F" group designation to the "D" group designation.

The buddy team has less residual nitrogen in their bodies, but they still have some nitrogen that must be taken into account for the second dive. The new

RESIDUAL NITROGEN TIMETABLE FOR REPETITIVE AIR DIVES

*Dives following surface intervals of more than 12 hours are not repetitive dives. Use actual bottom times in the Standard Air Decompression Tables to compute decompression for such dives.

Repetitive group at the beginning of the surface interval

Designation	Surface interval ranges (top = minimum, bottom = maximum)
A	0:10 – 12:00*
B	0:10/2:10 2:11/12:00*
C	0:10/1:39 1:40/2:49 2:50/12:00*
D	0:10/1:09 1:10/2:38 2:39/5:48 5:49/12:00*
E	0:10/0:54 0:55/1:57 1:58/3:22 3:23/6:32 6:33/12:00*
F	0:10/0:45 0:46/1:29 1:30/2:28 2:29/3:57 3:58/7:05 7:06/12:00*
G	0:10/0:40 0:41/1:15 1:16/1:59 2:00/2:58 2:59/4:25 4:26/7:35 7:36/12:00*
H	0:10/0:36 0:37/1:06 1:07/1:41 1:42/2:23 2:24/3:20 3:21/4:49 4:50/7:59 8:00/12:00*
I	0:10/0:33 0:34/0:59 1:00/1:29 1:30/2:02 2:03/2:44 2:45/3:43 3:44/5:12 5:13/8:21 8:22/12:00*
J	0:10/0:31 0:32/0:54 0:55/1:19 1:20/1:47 1:48/2:20 2:21/3:04 3:05/4:02 4:03/5:40 5:41/8:40 8:41/12:00*
K	0:10/0:28 0:29/0:49 0:50/1:11 1:12/1:35 1:36/2:03 2:04/2:38 2:39/3:21 3:22/4:19 4:20/5:48 5:49/8:58 8:59/12:00*
L	0:10/0:26 0:27/0:45 0:46/1:04 1:05/1:25 1:26/1:49 1:50/2:19 2:20/2:53 2:54/3:36 3:37/4:35 4:36/6:02 6:03/9:12 9:13/12:00*
M	0:10/0:25 0:26/0:42 0:43/0:59 1:00/1:18 1:19/1:39 1:40/2:05 2:06/2:34 2:35/3:08 3:09/3:52 3:53/4:49 4:50/6:18 6:19/9:28 9:29/12:00*
N	0:10/0:24 0:25/0:39 0:40/0:54 0:55/1:11 1:12/1:30 1:31/1:53 1:54/2:18 2:19/2:47 2:48/3:22 3:23/4:04 4:05/5:03 5:04/6:32 6:33/9:43 9:44/12:00*
O	0:10/0:23 0:24/0:36 0:37/0:51 0:52/1:07 1:08/1:24 1:25/1:43 1:44/2:04 2:05/2:29 2:30/2:59 3:00/3:33 3:34/4:17 4:18/5:16 5:17/6:44 6:45/9:54 9:55/12:00*
Z	0:10/0:22 0:23/0:34 0:35/0:48 0:49/1:02 1:03/1:18 1:19/1:36 1:37/1:55 1:56/2:17 2:18/2:42 2:43/3:10 3:11/3:45 3:46/4:29 4:30/5:27 5:28/6:56 6:57/10:05 10:06/12:00*

NEW → GROUP DESIGNATION: Z O N M L K J I H G F E D C B A

REPETITIVE DIVE DEPTH

DEPTH	Z	O	N	M	L	K	J	I	H	G	F	E	D	C	B	A
40	257	241	213	187	161	138	116	101	87	73	61	49	37	25	17	7
50	169	160	142	124	111	99	87	76	66	56	47	38	29	21	13	6
60	122	117	107	97	88	79	70	61	52	44	36	30	24	17	11	5
70	100	96	87	80	72	64	57	50	43	37	31	26	20	15	9	4
80	84	80	73	68	61	54	48	43	38	32	28	23	18	13	8	4
90	73	70	64	58	53	47	43	38	33	29	24	20	16	11	7	3
100	64	62	57	52	48	43	38	34	30	26	22	18	14	10	7	3
110	57	55	51	47	42	38	34	31	27	24	20	16	13	10	6	3
120	52	50	46	43	39	35	32	28	25	21	18	15	12	9	6	3
130	46	44	40	38	35	31	28	25	22	19	16	13	11	8	6	3
140	42	40	38	35	32	29	26	23	20	18	15	12	10	7	5	2
150	40	38	35	32	30	27	24	22	19	17	14	12	9	7	5	2
160	37	36	33	31	28	26	23	20	18	16	13	11	9	6	4	2
170	35	34	31	29	26	24	22	19	17	15	13	10	8	6	4	2
180	32	31	29	27	25	22	20	18	16	14	12	10	8	6	4	2
190	31	30	28	26	24	21	19	17	15	13	11	10	8	6	4	2

RESIDUAL NITROGEN TIMES (MINUTES)

Fig. 2-54 Residual Nitrogen Timetable

group designation letter "D" is added to the dive profile (item 6, Fig. 2-51). Then, they turn to the lower half of the Residual Nitrogen Timetable, as shown in figure 2-54. The purpose of this part of the table is to convert the group letter and the depth of the next repetitive dive into minutes of residual nitrogen time that the buddy team must consider that they have already spent on the bottom *before* they begin the next repetitive dive. Depths for the next dive are listed on the far left-hand column.

The shaded area in figure 2-54 shows that a "D" diver going to a repetitive dive depth of 60 feet will have a residual nitrogen time of 24 minutes. The residual nitrogen time (RNT) is added to the dive profile (item 7 Fig. 2-51). This means that our buddy team must *start* their second dive at 55 feet as though they had already been at this depth for 24 minutes.

Now, to make sure that they don't go beyond the no-decompression limits, they go back to the No-Decompression Limits Table (Figure 2-55) and find that a dive to 60 feet (55 actual feet) will have a maximum bottom time of 60 minutes.

NO-DECOMPRESSION LIMITS AND REPETITIVE GROUP DESIGNATION TABLE FOR NO-DECOMPRESSION AIR DIVES

Depth (feet)	No-decompression limits (min)	A	B	C	D	E	F	G	H	I	J	K	L	M	N	O
10		60	120	210	300											
15		35	70	110	160	225	350									
20		25	50	75	100	135	180	240	325							
25		20	35	55	75	100	125	160	195	245	315					
30		15	30	45	60	75	95	120	145	170	205	250	310			
35	310	5	15	25	40	50	60	80	100	120	140	160	190	220	270	310
40	200	5	15	25	30	40	50	70	80	100	110	130	150	170	200	
50	100		10	15	25	30	40	50	60	70	80	90	100			
60	60		10	15	20	25	30	40	50	55	60					
70	50		5	10	15	20	30	35	40	45	50					
80	40		5	10	15	20	25	30	35	40						
90	30		5	10	12	15	20	25	30							
100	25		5	7	10	15	20	22	25							
110	20			5	10	13	15	20								
120	15			5	10	12	15									
130	10			5	8	10										
140	10			5	7	10										
150	5			5												
160	5				5											
170	5				5											
180	5				5											
190	5				5											

Fig. 2-55 No-Decompression Limits Table

In order to stay well within the no-decompression limits, the buddy team decides to limit their actual bottom time to 30 minutes (item 9, Fig. 2-51). Since they are beginning the repetitive dive with a residual nitrogen time of 24 minutes, their total bottom time will be 30 plus 24 minutes, or 54 minutes—6 minutes short of the 60 minute no-decompression limit.

At the end of the repetitive dive, the two divers use the No-Decompression Limits Table to find their repetitive group designation, as shown in figure 2-55.

The shaded area in the table shows that their second dive of the day was to 60 feet for 55 minutes (55 actual feet and 54 actual minutes) which makes them "I" divers. The "I" repetitive group designation is entered on the profile at the appropriate place and would be used for another repetitive dive if they decided to make one (item 11, Fig. 2-51).

DECOMPRESSION DIVING

The sample repetitive dive situation, just described, illustrates two dives made *within* the no-decompression depth and time limits. But what if a buddy team wants to go beyond the no-decompression limits? If, for example, the buddy team wants to dive to 73 feet for a total bottom time of 48 minutes, they must make a stage decompression stop during their ascent to prevent nitrogen bubbles from forming in their bodies.

The U.S. Navy Standard Air Decompression Table gives the depths and times of decompression stops during ascent. This table is used whenever a buddy team goes beyond the depth and time limits of the No-Decompression Limits Table. A decompression stop may be anywhere from 50 to 10 feet deep for a period of one minute to over an hour. Figure 2-56 shows a dive profile for a typical stage decompression dive.

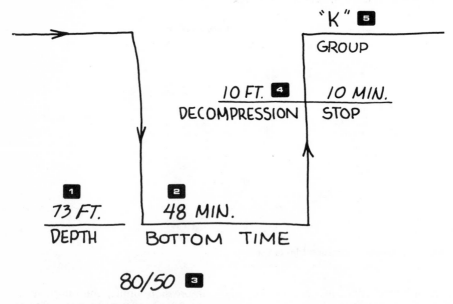

Fig. 2-56 A Typical Decompression Dive Profile

The actual depth and bottom time of the dive are 73 feet for 48 minutes. This is entered on the dive profile (items 1 and 2, Fig. 2-56). Turning to the Decompression Table in figure 2-57, the buddy team finds that the exact or next greater depth and time for this dive is 80 feet for 50 minutes. Entering the table from the left side at this depth and time (80/50), they find it will take one minute and 10 seconds to ascend to the first decompression stop at 10 feet. When they reach a depth of 10 feet, they have to stay there with the chest area at that exact depth for 10 minutes before making a direct ascent to the surface. At the far right-hand side of the table is the repetitive group designation. In this case, the buddies will be "K" divers when they surface. The ascent time (at a rate of 60 feet per minute) is not considered as part of the decompression stop time. This information is then entered in the dive profile (Fig. 2-56, items 3 through 5).

U.S. NAVY STANDARD AIR DECOMPRESSION TABLE

Depth (feet)	Bottom time (min)	Time first stop (min:sec)	50	40	30	20	10	Total ascent (min:sec)	Repetitive group
40	200						0	0:40	*
	210	0:30					2	2:40	N
	230	0:30					7	7:40	N
	250	0:30					11	11:40	O
	270	0:30					15	15:40	O
	300	0:30					19	19:40	Z
	360	0:30					23	23:40	**
	480	0:30					41	41:40	**
	720	0:30					69	69:40	**
80	40						0	1:20	*
	50	1:10					10	11:20	K
	60	1:10					17	18:20	L
	70	1:10					23	24:20	M
	80	1:00				2	31	34:20	N
	90	1:00				7	39	47:20	N
	100	1:00				11	46	58:20	O
	110	1:00				13	53	67:20	O
	120	1:00				17	56	74:20	Z
	130	1:00				19	63	83:20	Z
	140	1:00				26	69	96:20	Z
	150	1:00				32	77	110:20	Z
	180	1:00				35	85	121:20	**
	240	0:50			6	52	120	179:20	**
	360	0:50			29	90	160	280:20	**
	480	0:50			59	107	187	354:20	**
	720	0:40		17	108	142	187	455:20	**

Fig. 2-57 Standard Air Decompression Table

DIVE PLANNING

Every scuba dive must be carefully planned. Before entering the water, make sure you and your buddy consult the No-Decompression Limits Table and firmly plan the depth, time, and direction of the dive. You should decide on a maximum depth and agree not to go deeper under any circumstances. Decide, to the minute, how long your maximum bottom time will be. You should know the exact location of the nearest recompression chamber before starting the dive.

What you do on the bottom should also be planned. If you are hunting, taking pictures, or just exploring, agree on a general direction for the dive. Whatever the purpose of the dive, you and your buddy should plan the steps and procedures you will be taking to achieve that purpose.

Decompression diving requires very careful advance planning. Extra tanks and regulators must be tied off on a descent line at the appropriate decompression stops. Safety divers and surface personnel are also necessary for dives beyond the no-decompression limits.

Good planning and intelligent use of the decompression tables should almost eliminate the need for decompression in the water. No-decompression diving is safer and more enjoyable; stage decompression, at its best, is not fun.

Sport diving gives human beings a marked admiration for fish. Few creatures are more completely adapted to their environment than fish.

Sport divers, on the other hand, need equipment, skills, knowledge, procedures, and intelligence to adapt to both their natural and underwater environment. You must know how your body works in both air and water to really understand physical sensations, breathing, and the direct and indirect effects of underwater pressure.

As human beings, we have certain limitations when it comes to entering the underwater environment. Our intelligence not only allows us to overcome and work within these limitations, but also gives us the much greater advantage of appreciating and enjoying our adaptation. No fish, in spite of its almost total adaptation, can possibly appreciate its own home as well as a trained and knowledgeable sport diver can.

PART III the environment

introduction

The seas may be earth's last frontier. They cover most of the planet's surface and offer a source of recreation without peer.

To the diver, the challenge of the water is strong. Where else so close to home can you enter a world no human may have been before. For the ocean diver, the chain of life, from the smallest organisms to the earth's largest creatures, can be observed and studied. The freshwater diver can observe the ecosystem, which includes creatures that depend on the water, as well as those that live in the water.

Figure 3-1.

Once you have grasped a total understanding of the equipment required to safely enter the underwater world, and know how your body reacts to pressure and temperature changes, you must learn about the new environment itself. Learn how the movement of water can be a friend when you understand it and how it can be an awesome adversary when you don't. Learn about its creatures: which ones are friendly and which ones are not. Just as important is learning how to understand the delicate balance of nature, how to maintain and protect it so the waters can continue to provide food and recreation for generations to come.

section A

the worlds of diving

- FORMATION OF LAND AND SEA
- BEGINNING OF LIFE
- VARIATIONS WITHIN THE ENVIRONMENT

ORIGIN OF EARTH AND LIFE; TEMPERATURE EFFECTS

FORMATION OF LAND AND SEA

No one really knows about the beginnings of the earth and heavens, but it is estimated that earth originated billions of years ago and that it was a molten mass hurtling through the dark reaches of space. As the earth cooled, the heaviest materials settled in the center, as shown in figure 3-2. Theoretically, the core of the earth today is liquid iron with lighter elements lying in successive layers outward toward the crust. The intermediate layer is supposedly semi-hard basalt, while the outer shell or crust is solid basalt and granite.

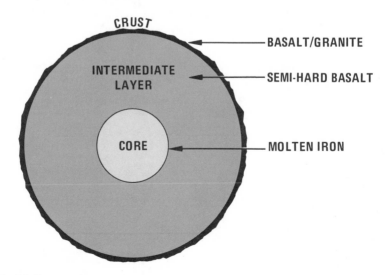

Fig. 3-2 Earth's Construction

The moon had its beginning at approximately the same time that earth was forming. One theory, as imagined in figure 3-3, holds that it was originally a part of earth while this planet was still in a molten state. It then was torn away and hurtled into space. This theory is supported by the fact that the largest hole in the earth is the Pacific Ocean basin and its bottom is basalt; while the rest of the ocean bottoms are granite. If correct, this theory could explain continental drift.

Fig. 3-3 Moon Formation Theory

The general shape of the continents today indicates that at one time they may have been interconnected. If, in fact, the moon derived from the Pacific Ocean area, it would have caused cracks in the semi-hard crust which floated on the molten core. (Note figure 3-4.) The spinning of the earth could have separated the cracks and allowed the continents, as we now know them, to literally "drift" into the relative positions they now occupy.

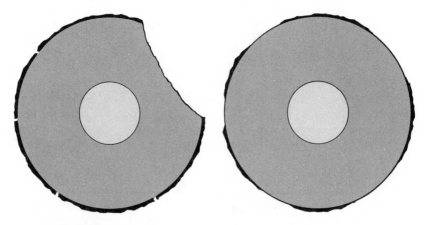

Fig. 3-4 Continental Drift

As the earth cooled, the gases condensed and became clouds. Eventually the clouds produced enough rain to fill the basins which are today's oceans. The dissolving of rocks and minerals through land erosion has created the salinity of the oceans.

BEGINNING OF LIFE

Life on the earth may have begun with the smallest microorganism. Down through the centuries, the stream of life grew and became more complex, developing from small one-celled creatures to the more sophisticated animals with specialized cell structure.

The warm seas acted like an incubator for all life forms; they grew with great speed. Simple aquatic life forms such as sponge and coral animals appeared first. Jellyfish, worms, and starfish probably came along at about the same time, followed by the hard-shelled creatures with jointed legs. Simultaneously, plants resembling seaweed must have begun to develop; and truly the chain of life had commenced.

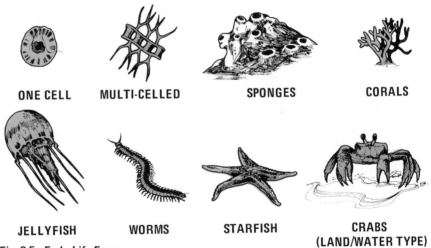

ONE CELL   MULTI-CELLED   SPONGES   CORALS

JELLYFISH   WORMS   STARFISH   CRABS
(LAND/WATER TYPE)

Fig. 3-5   Early Life Forms

A fossil record of sorts has been kept for the last 500 million years. Prior to that time, the animals must have had soft shells, for they left no traces. However, creatures did not appear on land until approximately 350 million years ago, and it is theorized that the first land creature was a member of the phylum which includes crabs, lobsters, and insects. Fish appeared at approximately the same time. The first record of amphibians is approximately 320 million years ago.

After about 50 million years on land, approximately 170 million years ago, some reptiles reentered the sea. It is further estimated that possibly 50 million years ago some mammals returned to the sea. Their descendants are today's sea lions, seals, sea elephants, and whales.

Fig. 3-6   Sea Mammals

The evolution of land creatures was remarkable. It was almost as though the sea creatures had ceased to develop, while the land creatures had to adapt in order to survive. They developed not only in physical capability but also in mental capability. The past one million years have brought about the transformation and development of more intelligent life.

THE EFFECTS OF TEMPERATURE ON SEA LIFE

Just as temperature affected the initial growth of life on land and sea, it affects life today in many ways. Temperature affects the salinity of the water. The Red Sea is the planet's warmest sea; it has 40 parts per million of salt compared to the polar cap with the least parts per million. The North Atlantic, for example, contains 33 parts per million, while the waters of Florida have 36 parts per million. The water temperatures of the earth vary from 28°F (-2°C) in the Arctic to 90°F (32°C) in the Persian Gulf. Thermoclines, which are abrupt changes in water temperature within a column of water, may be found anywhere.

Life in the warm seas varies greatly from life in the cold seas. The differences are quite complex, but at the same time amazingly simple. The warm seas produce large numbers of different species, whereas the cold waters produce profuse quantities of only a few different species.

The cold water produces greater surface life. Consequently there is more food available for pelagic fish, and as a result, there is greater bird life. This can be seen clearly throughout the earth's cold water currents. Plant life also varies from cold to warm water. There is a great deal of plant life in the colder waters whereas the warm waters have considerably less plant life. The plant life is small, like the turtle grass found in the Caribbean, as compared to the giant kelp found in the colder northern California waters, as shown in figure 3-8.

Fig. 3-7 Cold Water Surface Life

Fig. 3-8 Kelp

Fig. 3-9 Coral Reef

Coral reefs develop in the warm waters. They support their particular dependent life forms, while kelp beds and rock formations in the colder water support an entirely different type of life. Each serves its own special function within the ecosystem, each supporting some other form of life that adds to the overall chain of life not only in the oceans but on land as well. The diver must carefully consider the delicate balance of nature as it affects the chain of life. His presence is that of a foreigner in the water environment and he must learn to respect it and adapt to it. Above all, the privilege must not be abused.

section B

water movement

● WAVES
● TIDES AND CURRENTS

WAVES, CURRENTS, AND THEIR EFFECT ON DIVING

For centuries man has observed the waters of the world with awe. The waters have been a source of inspiration and fear for all who view them. Fresh water is, for the most part, more stable and predictable than the oceans, and because most freshwater bodies are smaller, they lack the ocean's potential destructive force. Only the Great Lakes of the United States and Canada approach the oceans in terms of potential power from water movement.

Lack of understanding about the mechanics of water movement is what creates and sustains fear of the oceans. Although the seas do have great destructive power, once you understand the cause and effect of water movement, fear is replaced by respect, and anxiety is replaced by excitement and enjoyment.

This section will help you understand how the sea can be your friend, and how you can use water movement to your advantage. The formation and types of waves, and how they affect you as the diver will be explained. Tides, currents, and their corresponding effects on the diver also will be presented.

WAVES

Waves form in essentially two ways: they are either generated by wind or by some geologic disturbance beneath the surface of the water. Wind waves are also of two basic types: the stable waves that approach the coast in even sets, and the unstable waves that form as the result of wind in the immediate vicinity.

WIND WAVES

Three things determine the size of a wave: how hard the wind is blowing (velocity), how long the wind blows (time), and how far the wind blows (distance).

The beginnings of a wave are the same no matter where it happens—in the middle of the ocean or on the surface of a small pond. First the wind disturbs the surface, as shown in figure 3-10. When the surface is disturbed, ripples appear. The ripples, though small, resist the wind. The wind pushes against the ripple until it becomes a small wave. Now we begin to see the effects of velocity. The harder the wind blows, the more quickly it disturbs the water and begins to form waves. The newly-formed wave presents a larger surface for the wind to blow against, and the result is an even larger wave. The longer and harder the wind blows, the larger the wave becomes.

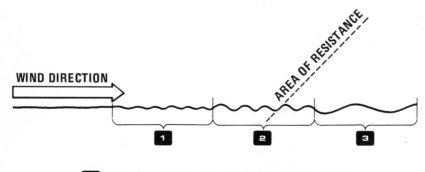

1 WIND DISTURBS SURFACE OF SMOOTH WATER
2 DISTURBED WATER PRESENTS AREA OF
       RESISTANCE FOR WIND TO BLOW AGAINST
3 BEGINNING OF WAVES

Fig. 3-10 Wave Formation

The wind literally blows the water into a pile. With time, the pile can become quite large, but the crest can never reach an angle of less than 120° without breaking, as illustrated in figure 3-11. So a wave is limited as to just how big it can grow in open water. The white foam on the crest of a wave is nothing more than the top of the wave being blown off by the wind, or perhaps the angle of the wave has dropped below 120° and is simply spilling over.

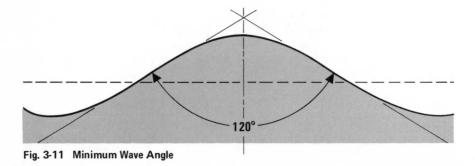

Fig. 3-11 Minimum Wave Angle

Because the wind pushes the water for a short distance, the water in a given wave appears to be moving. The water itself actually moves a very short distance. It rises and falls, as illustrated by figure 3-12. The water follows a figure eight pattern that is extended by the size of the wave. The energy from the waves can travel almost indefinitely if unobstructed. This principle is often difficult to understand and can be best explained with the aid of a length of rope, as shown in figure 3-13. If you hold one end of a rope extended outward in a straight line along the ground, and then flip the rope several times, it will send a series of "waves" along the rope. The rope remains in the same place; only the energy moves to the other end.

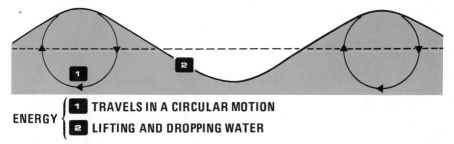

ENERGY { 1 TRAVELS IN A CIRCULAR MOTION
2 LIFTING AND DROPPING WATER

Fig. 3-12   Energy Motion

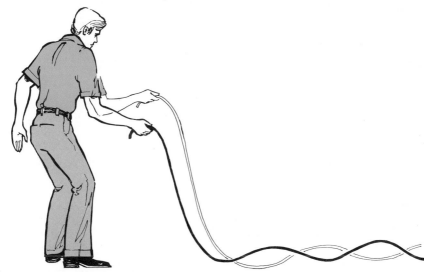

Fig. 3-13   Energy Waves

The same thing happens in water. The wind pushes the water into a pile which lifts and then falls back into place. The energy thus created works with the wind to form larger waves. In this way the water seems to move, but the movement is really the flow of energy.

Stable Waves

If left unobstructed, waves can grow to enormous proportions, often reaching 40 feet or more in height. The height of a wave is measured from the trough to the crest. The length is measured from crest to crest. (See figure 3-14.) Once the wind stops blowing, the energy will keep going until it reaches shore. Depending on how far offshore the waves were created, they will tend to stabilize themselves into even sets. A set of waves is a series of waves of similar size followed by one or more larger waves. Every so many sets, there will be either a particularly large wave or set of waves. Shore entries and exits should be timed to coincide with the smaller waves.

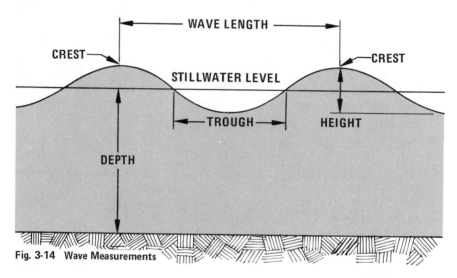

Fig. 3-14 Wave Measurements

The waves created by offshore storms may eventually flatten to the point where waves are no longer visible. But the energy is still moving: as it approaches shore, the energy is compressed by the resistance of the bottom coming up to meet the surface. Once again it begins to form waves. (See figure 3-15.) Waves formed in this manner are surfing waves and may be quite large, depending on the amount of energy behind them.

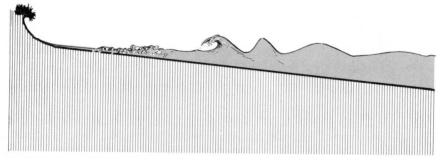

Fig. 3-15 Ocean Floor Resistance

Unstable Waves

Waves formed as a result of wind in the immediate vicinity have little or no pattern, and are considered *unstable.* The meeting of stable and unstable waves moving in different directions can be an uncomfortable and unpleasant experience for boat passengers.

For the diver, wave action is of prime importance when making entries or exits from shore where surf is present. Large waves breaking against the beach can be dangerous. People have been injured as a result of underestimating the power of surf. However, you can pass in and out of surf safely if the proper techniques are employed, you have a good understanding of what is happening and you use good judgement.

Beach Entries

The primary problem with the surf is the weight of large quantities of water tumbling from the top of the wave to the shore. There can be tons of water in the breaking crest of large waves, as figure 3-16 shows. Once the wave has rushed up onto the beach, it must return to the sea. As it rushes back, it can catch an unwary diver, pull his feet out from under him, and then wash him down into the path of another crashing wave. Being knocked down in the path of breaking waves can pose a real problem.

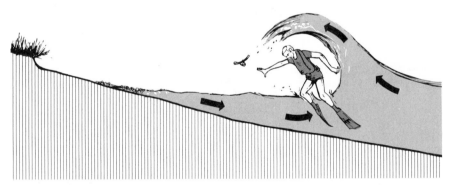

Fig. 3-16 Breaking Wave Crest

To avoid danger while entering surf, several procedures must be followed quite carefully:

1. Put on your fins *before* you enter the water. It is difficult enough to stand up in surf on two feet without attempting to do it on one.
2. Inflate your buoyancy control device. If you should be swept from your feet, the weight of the equipment makes it almost impossible to stand up. If you are buoyant, you will float instead of being held on the bottom, and it will give you an opportunity to regain your feet.
3. If high, or rough surf indicates a possible need for stabilization, use your buddy. Walk hand in hand *backwards* into the water until you are deep enough to swim.

4.   When you are deep enough to swim, turn around and swim out through the surf with your regulator *in your mouth*. The surf disturbs a great deal of sand; your regulator will be filled with sand if it hangs loose. (See figure 3-17.)

5.   The power of a wave is concentrated in the surface area, as illustrated in figure 3-18. To avoid fighting that power, simply swim through or under the wave, not over it. Swim as low as possible, next to the bottom, to pick up the back current to help you.

WALK IN BACKWARD

UNTIL DEEP ENOUGH TO SWIM

TURN AROUND AND SWIM OUT

Fig. 3-17   Entering Surf

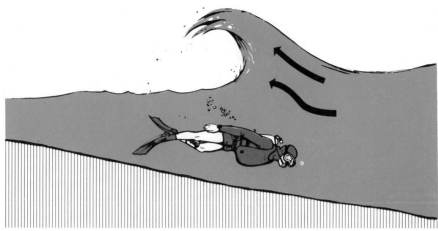

Fig. 3-18 Swim Under Waves

Once you are past the surfline, you and your buddy should rejoin and rest by inflating your buoyancy compensator before proceeding. Any items such as spearguns, and so forth, should be tied to a float and *pulled* through the surf rather than pushed. You should *push* the float when you return to exit so it won't hit you.

Returning to shore is easier than entering. You should watch the waves, and swim in with the smaller ones. Once you can touch bottom, don't stand up. Let the water carry you as far up on shore as possible. Lie on the beach and relax until you are certain you are up as far as the water will carry you. When the water rushes back and leaves you on dry ground, *crawl* out of reach of the water, then stand up.

Freshwater entries are essentially the same as for the ocean, but there is a noticeable lack of heavy surf, although it is possible to have large unstable waves which require the similar techniques.

SEISMIC WAVES (TSUNAMIS)

Wind waves are the ones the diver deals with day-to-day, so they are of primary interest. However, there is another kind of wave which can have a dramatic effect on people and property along any coastal region—the seismic wave, known around the world as the tsunami or tidal wave. These waves have created legends, and with good reason. A full-blown tsunami wave has a destructive power unlike any natural force known on earth.

The tsunami is formed as the result of a disturbance beneath the sea, such as a volcanic eruption or shift in the earth's surface. When these things happen beneath the ocean, the resulting energy is overwhelming. If a split in the floor of the ocean should occur, it leaves a void which must be filled. When the water rushes in to fill the void, it sets off an energy flow. (See figure 3-19.)

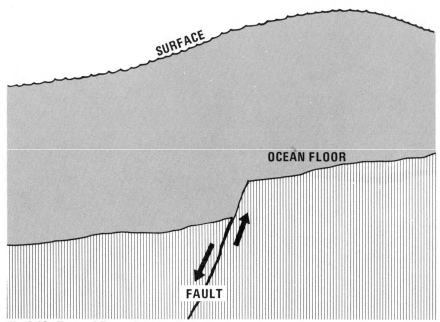

Fig. 3-19 Tsunami Formation

If left undisturbed in the open ocean, the energy moves at amazing speeds—often in excess of 1720 kilometers (450 miles) per hour. In deep water, the energy creates a small wave approximately 18 inches high. A tsunami with all its power can pass undetected beneath a ship in open water.

As the wave nears shore, and the ocean bottom begins to cause resistance, the wave is slowed and great quantities of water begin to pile up behind the energy front. At the same time, the water from shore is pulled away to join the oncoming front. This pulling away has the appearance of an extreme tidal drop, and many unfortunate persons often rush out to where the water once was—only to be caught by the onrushing wave. (Note figure 3-20.)

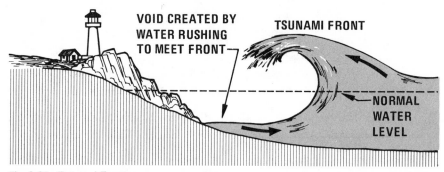

Fig. 3-20 Tsunami Front

Tsunami waves represent the greatest natural disaster force known to modern man. They have been known to reach heights of 60 meters (200 feet), and build up enough water behind them to inundate low-lying coastal areas several miles inland. As a result of a number of unfortunate disasters from tsunamis, an early warning system now exists throughout the Pacific Ocean, where most large waves develop. Thousands of lives have been saved because of this system.

CURRENTS

Waves are only part of the mechanics of water motion. There is constant movement of water in some form all over the world. Movement of water is referred to as a current. Currents vary in speed, width, depth, and duration. Some temporary currents are caused by wind in the area; others are the result of tidal changes, and while they occur regularly each day, they last only a short while. Other currents flow continuously.

RIVERS IN THE SEA

Let us examine the currents which flow constantly. There are six major whirlpool effects on the earth's surface, as shown in figure 3-21. One is in each hemisphere of the Pacific, Atlantic, and Indian Oceans. Currents which flow away from the equator are warm; those which flow toward the equator are cold. These rivers in the sea may have several names. They may be known as currents, streams, or drifts. All are the same thing, except that drifts are currents which flow in the direction of the prevailing westerlies. Drifts are slower and wider than other rivers in the sea. The Gulf Stream, for example, is the name given to a particular current in the Atlantic Ocean that runs northward along the Florida coast.

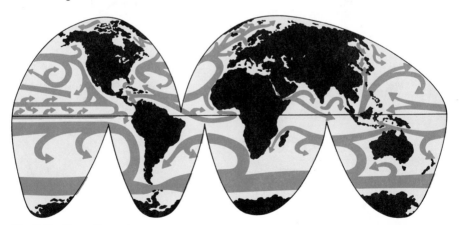

Fig. 3-21 Ocean Currents

The rivers of the sea result from temperature change. As seawater freezes in the polar regions, the salt is squeezed out of the ice and deposited in the unfrozen water. This cold, salty water is much heavier and falls into the deeper warmer waters. It pushes the warmer water out of the way and the result is a movement of water into and away from the warmer deep water, so that the water is constantly warmed near the equator and cooled as it returns to the polar regions. This creates a never-ending whirlpool effect over all the earth.

TIDES

Another predictable type of current is created by the tides, a daily rise and fall of water. Tides vary in intensity, depending on the distance between the moon and the earth and in their relation to the equator. Many parts of the world experience two tidal changes each day, while others have only one. The number of tidal changes varies according to the size and shape of the tidal basin.

Tides are caused by the gravitional pull of the moon and sun on the water. The moon exerts a much stronger influence on the water than the sun. Only this influence will be discussed.

As the earth turns on its axis, the gravitional pull of the moon causes the waters to bulge in its direction. At the same time, on the opposite side of the earth, a similar bulge is created by the centrifugal force by the moon and the earth revolving around a common center between them. As the bulge approaches a given coastline, the water level rises (high tide), and as it moves away, the level drops (low tide). (See figure 3-22.) The amount of tidal change can vary from a few centimeters in the Mediterranean to as much as 12 meters (40 feet) in the Bay of Fundy, New Brunswick. It may also vary within a very small geographical area, depending on the configuration of the coastline. Deep, narrow estuaries (inlets or arms of the sea) show a more pronounced change than straight beaches.

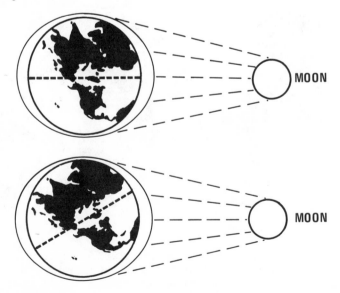

Fig. 3-22 Tidal Action

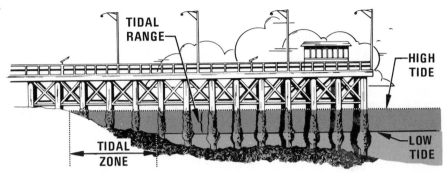

Fig. 3-23 Tide Differentials

You must pay close attention to tides in order to use them to your advantage. Dives should begin as the tides are coming in (flooding) rather than going out (ebbing). An ebbing tide can be impossible to swim against and can literally wash a diver to sea. Select an entry point that will permit an easy exit somewhere downcurrent, and then allow the current to carry you along. It should be noted that a clear and total understanding of the times and currents involved are vital to using the tides and avoiding problems.

WIND CURRENTS

Constant currents are more predictable. They make it possible to plan the time, location, and conditions that will be encountered on a dive. Such is not the case with currents produced by wind. These currents seem to spring from nowhere and can vary greatly in speed, depth, and duration. Wind currents normally affect only the top few feet of water, and then only for a short period of time. They have a much greater effect on the shore diver than on the boat diver, but both must understand what they are and how to use them.

Learning to read the ocean is not complex, but does take experience to enhance your enjoyment as well as your safety. Depending on the configuration of the shoreline and the bottom, and the direction of current flow, you can learn to estimate the depth of the water and the general shape of the bottom. You can also determine the best places to enter and exit. When you learn to do this, the ocean truly becomes your friend and ally.

RIP CURRENTS AND OTHER CURRENTS

All parents who raise their children around water fear that the children might somehow fall into the water and drown. In an effort to avoid this, many parents go to the extreme of frightening their children with terrible stories of the water's dangers. As a result, several names have cropped up through the years, which instantly strike terror into the hearts of those whose parents, teachers, or well-meaning friends have related the evils of such things, as rip currents, riptides, and undertows. While there is little question that these are a potential hazard, they also can be beneficial forces. Understanding how they operate is another step toward eliminating fear, gaining respect, and having fun in the water.

RIP CURRENT

Wherever people surf, they look for rip currents. Rip currents are used to carry the surfer out beyond the breaker line where he simply paddles out of it, turns around, and rides the surf back in. Remember, when the water moves toward the shore it can't continue to go on, so it must stop and return to the open water. In doing this, it takes the course of least resistance. In the shore configuration shown in figure 3-24, the direction of current is from left to right toward shore. As it reaches the point on the right, it is turned in toward the center. As it approaches the cove's bank, its flow changes to the left. When the two forces meet, they must return to open water. At that point a rip current is formed. It's nothing more than a current running back out to sea.

Depending on the amount of water flowing in, the rip current may run for a few feet or it may run for some distance, but it dissipates rather rapidly for two reasons. First, it lacks sufficient power to keep it going and, second, the meeting with the oncoming waves or current helps dissipate it. Normally, the current will spread to the right and left, so a swimmer, rather than swimming against it, should move to either side. In the case of figure 3-24, he would move to the right side of the current and then catch the incoming current and ride it back into shore. Accidents that occur as a result of rip currents happen because people try to swim against them. Even very good swimmers are only able to maintain a maximum pace of less than one knot, and swimming against a current of more than one knot is a losing battle. It makes sense to swim to the side of the current and then catch the current coming back.

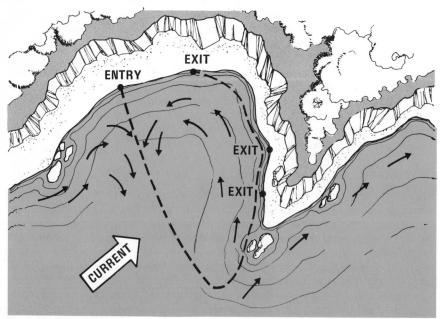

Fig. 3-24   Point Rip Current

When the current moves in along a long straight beach, as shown in figure 3-25, rip currents may appear in several places. Normally this occurs because a trough is formed and the water will be slightly deeper at the point of the rip current. Even along the straight beaches, there must be a point where the water returns to the open sea.

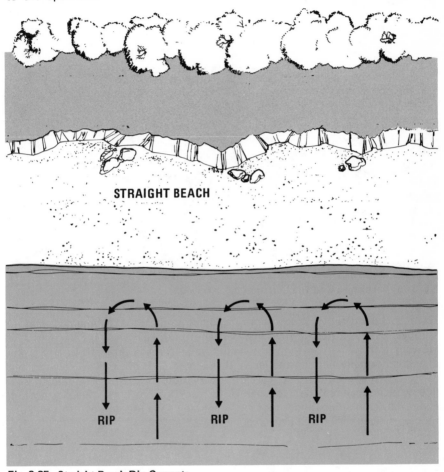

Fig. 3-25 Straight Beach Rip Currents

The illustration in figure 3-26 shows the water moving in past two submerged obstacles. As the water moves in around them and then begins to move back out to sea, it will be channeled with some velocity through the opening in the two reefs. It could be very dangerous if this channel is narrow and passes through a coral reef. As the flow of water is concentrated in that small channel, it picks up speed and could exceed four or five knots. A diver caught in this could be badly injured. You should swim directly to the inside of the cove so you are in the protection of the bar; the water will turn and carry you back into shore.

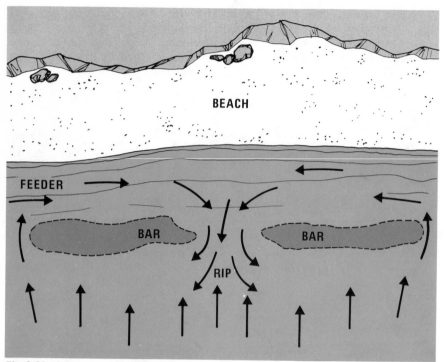

Fig. 3-26 Submerged Reef Rip Current

Waves breaking away from shore generally indicate a submerged reef or sandbar, as illustrated in figure 3-28. The outer reef may be a reef that is growing from a flat bottom or it could be an outside dropoff. In any event, diving is normally best on the leeward side of a reef; however, it can also be a dangerous place to dive, so careful observation should be maintained. It is highly recommended that you gain information from local divers as to best diving times, locations, points of entry, and local sea life, so you can avoid any problems when diving in a new area.

Fig. 3-27 Rip Current from Height

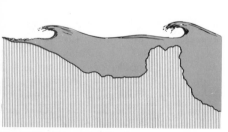

Fig. 3-28 Submerged Reef

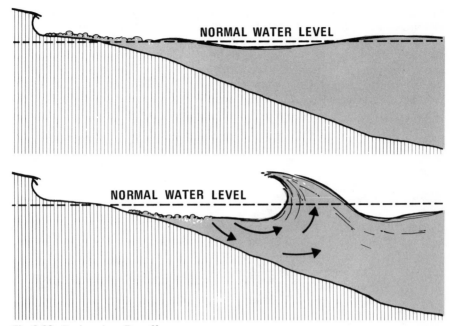

NORMAL WATER LEVEL

NORMAL WATER LEVEL

Fig. 3-29 Backwash or Runoff

BACKWASH OR RUNOFF

As the energy from waves moves toward shore, two things happen: the surface water begins to pile up, and the shore water rushes out to meet it, as illustrated in figure 3-29.

The water rushing out to meet the oncoming wave is called backwash or runoff and may be rather extensive, depending on the size of the incoming waves and the configuration of the bottom. It usually doesn't last too long or go out too far. In the rare instance of a tidal wave or tsunami, the current could be extreme, ranging out many hundreds of feet and being quite strong; however, this is rare. The normal current extends no further than the crest of the wave or to the base of the trough, and because the water moves in a circular motion, it doesn't hold you down, but rather, lifts you back up and carries you back toward shore. The problem results from being caught in the path of the next wave.

As you can see by the illustrations, knowing the currents cannot only make your dive more safe, but also more enjoyable. By utilizing the currents to carry you to your dive, and then returning to shore by the incoming currents, you use less energy and make the dive more pleasant.

EFFECT OF CURRENTS ON BOAT DIVERS

When diving from a boat, you will notice that many currents tend to run parallel to the shore. When you are diving offshore of an island, you normally have one of two conditions: a current running parallel to the shore or no current at all on the lee of the island. When the boat is anchored, it tends to swing into the current, as illustrated in figure 3-30. Before entering the water, the diver should watch the current and estimate its strength. If the current looks strong (greater than one knot) diving should not be considered. If it is not too strong, or if you can determine that it is a surface current, diving can be conducted quite safely, *if* proper procedures are observed.

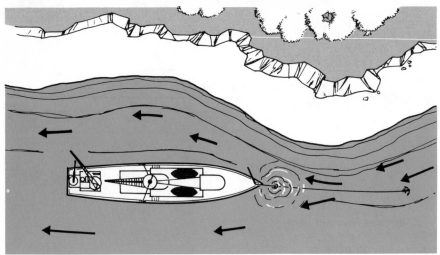

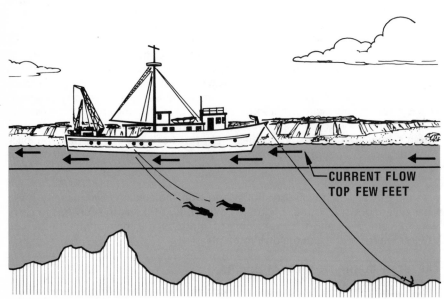

CURRENT FLOW
TOP FEW FEET

Fig. 3-30 Current Action

You should always dive *into* the current at the beginning of a dive. You can go to the bottom, pull yourself over the rocks and away from the boat while you are still fresh and have plenty of strength. It would be a mistake to allow yourself to go downcurrent only to be faced with the problem of returning to the boat into the current when you are tired. If you move into the current to begin with, you may simply return to the surface and let the current carry you back to the boat.

Certain safety precautions should be taken in the event that you may be carried downcurrent. A good buoyancy compensation device should be worn so that if you get caught in the current, you can maintain yourself for long periods of time. You should use a whistle to attract the attention of the people on the boat. Whistles can be heard for a great distance above water and they can be blown for long periods of time with little effort.

While some of these examples are extreme, it is always best to be prepared for the unexpected. You must always remember—the greatest problem comes from fear and its resulting panic. You should possess the proper equipment and training to insure your safety under any condition.

section C

ocean life

- BOTTOM AND REEF FORMATION
- REEF INHABITANTS
- DANGEROUS MARINE LIFE

REEFS AND THEIR INHABITANTS, DANGEROUS MARINE ANIMALS

The ocean depths are a sightseer's dream. Their panorama is so vast, that quite often the inexperienced diver sees very little of it. Life dwells on every rock, however, and unless you familiarize yourself with these life forms, you might miss the most enjoyable part of the dive.

Another thing to consider is—despite their beauty and fascination, some creatures present potential hazards. The diver must study his new surroundings so that he might appreciate and understand them well enough to avoid harm during his underwater explorations.

Underwater animals have one thing in common with their untamed relatives on land—they are wild. Water creatures are neither aggressive nor friendly. They are more or less indifferent to strange invaders in their domain. While some may be a little curious, most are nervous when they see a diver, and you should remember that some are capable of inflicting serious injury when molested. Most injury, however, is the result of accidentally disturbing a sea creature and does not stem from aggression. Because some wounds can be serious, it is important to know exactly which animals you can touch, and which ones to avoid.

This section is designed as a brief introduction to the marine environment: to explain the development of the ocean floors; to make you aware of a few of the creatures there; and to help you avoid the hazardous ones.

REEF DEVELOPMENT

CORALS

Corals are members of the phylum Coelenterata. They are found in both hard and soft forms, as shown in figure 3-31. The hard corals (Scleractinia) are the foundation for the reefs. The soft gorgonian corals (hydroids) are also large contributors to the reef formation.

Corals are bisexual and divide themselves. The way in which they divide determines the formation of the coral. New colonies develop when the coral releases seeds which float along with the current toward shallower water. They settle to the bottom of the shallow water and attach themselves to anything solid. Due to several factors, including water movement, sunlight, and the availability of solid objects, coral is limited to the relatively shallow depths. Some are too delicate to survive in areas of violent water action. Others grow right up to the low tide level and even protrude slightly out of the water.

Corals protect the reef inhabitants. They are also a symbiotic home for the zooxanthellae, an algae which lives in the coral polyps and provides oxygen for the coral animal, which in turn supplies carbon dioxide for the algae. This algae gives coloration in most corals and furnishes the chemistry for the actual formation of the coral structure.

Corals are a source of food for many creatures, and as the animals eat the coral, the pulverized residue becomes sand. Corals are an important part, if not the entire basis for the ecosystem in warm waters, especially where no rocks exist. The reefs provide shelter, food, and protection from its inhabitants' enemies. It is difficult to conceive of oceans without coral reefs.

Numerous coral growths exist; every reef contains a wide variety. There are corals that simply spread themselves over an area of the reef. For sake of simplicity, they can be referred to as blanket corals, an accurate, if not entirely scientific, description. For identification purposes, the corals of interest in this section are those that form recognizable clumps or formations. The following examples illustrate many of the corals that contribute to the general reef makeup. This includes hard and soft corals, and sponges.

Hard Corals

The magnificent elkhorn coral, shown in figure 3-32, grows very fast and forms a large portion of the reefs, particularly in the Caribbean. It is razor sharp and can cause severe cuts. You should immediately attend to cuts or scratches caused by coral, for they often become infected and do not heal easily.

Figure 3-33 shows examples of staghorn coral, some growing and some dead. This coral serves as a home for many small fishes.

The young star coral, as shown in figure 3-34, illustrates the early stages of most coral. Shown in an extreme closeup, the growth is approximately one inch across. Although it appears soft, it is quite hard and abrasive.

You can find many other less spectacular but equally beautiful corals all along the reef, such as, brain coral (figure 3-35), star coral (figure 3-36), and fire coral (figure 3-37). Fire coral demands respect because it has a nematocyst or stinger long enough to penetrate human skin and toxic enough to cause a reaction. The sting feels like a burn—hence the name, fire coral. Its effect varies from a minor rash lasting a few minutes, to large, slow-healing sores.

Fig. 3-31   Hard and Soft Coral

Fig. 3-32   Elkhorn Coral

Fig. 3-33   Staghorn Coral

Fig. 3-34   Star Coral

Fig. 3-35   Brain Coral

Fig. 3-36   Star Coral

Fig. 3-37   Fire Coral

Fig. 3-38   Black Coral

Fig. 3-39   Sea Fan

Fig. 3-40   Deepwater Sea Fan

Fig. 3-41   Tube Sponge

Fig. 3-42   Basket Sponge

Fig. 3-43   Tube Sponge

Fig. 3-44   Basket Sponge

Fig. 3-45   Coral Reef Formation

Soft Corals

The hydroids, or soft gorgonian coral, form another part of the reef-building process. These soft corals are flexible and appear to be a plant form rather than an animal form. There are many soft corals, including the famous black coral, shown in figure 3-38. Hydroids remain flexible while alive, but when they are removed from water, the skeletons become hard and rigid. The sea fan, shown in figure 3-39, is found at all depths and in various forms. Its height ranges from 12 to 24 inches. Collectors have taken and displayed them for many years, however these beautiful creatures grow very slowly and it is unfortunate when they are destroyed for no reason. Coral is much more beautiful in the sea than on a shelf.

The deepwater sea fan, illustrated in figure 3-40, is a huge specimen found in depths over 100 feet. Despite their flexibility, sea fans are delicate. Very large specimens normally are not found in shallow water.

SPONGES

Another large contributor to reef building is the sponge (Porifera). They come in every size, shape, color, and texture. The sponge is animal, not plant, and the forms humans see are sponge skeletons. The actual animal lives inside. Sponges are not edible, but some varieties are used for washing and other household chores. The varieties of sponges are shown in figures 3-41 through 3-44.

REEF FORMATION AND DEPTHS

Three distinct reef formations are illustrated in figure 3-46: the deep reef found at 80 to 100 feet deep; the midreef found in the 20 to 40 foot range; and the shallow reef found from 15 feet up to sea level.

Development of the deep reefs can be seen by first observing the shallow and then the midreef. It appears that the surface of the oceans was once near the level of the deeper reef. The midreef formed as the waters rose. The water then continued to rise to its present level; now we are seeing the development of the shallow reef.

Small individual clumps of one or more coral animal colonies live in shallower waters. In the midreef area, corals have had time to grow together and form larger overlapping clumps. These look like small islands; many are as large as 50 to 75 feet, but they remain as separate and distinct coral clumps. (See figure 3-45 on page 3-30.) In the deep reef, the clumps or small islands have had an

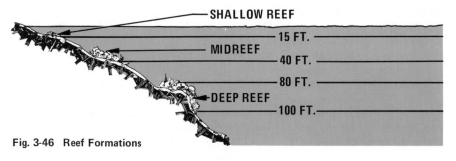

Fig. 3-46 Reef Formations

opportunity to grow together, forming one continuous reef cut intermittently by ravines, and a series of large and small caves created partly by worms. The worms eat into the coral and weaken it, causing breakage. The reefs become honeycombed because the various corals grow and overlap. The resulting effect appears to be solid rock, but, in reality, it is a network of caves and passageways. (Note figure 3-47.)

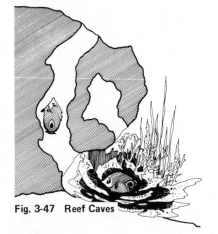

Water temperature also limits the area in which coral can flourish. It requires temperatures above 75° F (24° C). This restricts coral to an area 30° north and 30° south of the equator. Interestingly enough, coral reefs are only found on the eastern shores of the continents. This is thought to be due in part to the upwelling of cold water from the currents on the western side of the continents.

Fig. 3-47   Reef Caves

BOTTOM FORMATION IN COLD WATERS

In the cold water areas which lack the warmth to produce hard corals, bottom formations are comprised primarily of rock, and in some areas, the coastline is protected by kelp beds.

Rocks and kelp provide the same kind of protection for sea animals in cold water regions that coral provides in warmer waters. While cold waters normally don't produce the profusion of different individuals that the warm waters do, the population in terms of numbers of animals in cold water is more intense, especially in the kelp forest.

Kelp has very strong roots and kelp stocks grow from the bottom to the surface in as much as 50 to 75 feet of water. Kelp strands are normally several feet apart, but when they reach the surface, the strands lay in a mat. (See figure 3-48.) They resemble a forest with the leaf-covered branches of the trees intertwining and shutting out the sun in many places. Kelp is a wonderful place to dive. It contains more sea life than one might imagine possible.

There have been stories of divers becoming entangled in kelp. While this is a possibility, it is not probable. The broad flat leaves of the kelp are capable of entangling a diver who struggles, but a diver who remains calm can use a kelp crawl to move through the forest with the greatest of ease. When you move across kelp, push it down with your forearm and crawl on your hands and knees, as shown in figure 3-49.

Giant kelp beds can be found along the cold water coasts of the North Pacific, the islands of Japan, around the Aleutian Islands extending to Alaska, and along the coast of California.

Fig. 3-48   Kelp Mat

Fig. 3-49   Passage Across Kelp

REEF INHABITANTS

The reef makeup is extremely complex. It ranges from the smallest microorganism in coral to the sponges, shellfish, crustaceans, and the fish and plant life. Large free-swimming pelagic fish that use the reef as a source of food and as a breeding area, also live within the reef's ecosystem. Each animal serves its special function within this underwater environment.

By watching the reef for a period of time, you can clearly see the existing territorial system. In every reef system, a big fish presides over an entire section of the reef. This fish is the reef master. Under its control, the reef is divided into territories. The size of the territory depends upon the size of the fish, extending down to the smallest fish that inhabits no more than a few square inches.

To the new diver, the most apparent reef inhabitants are fish. Reef fish can be divided into two categories: edible and inedible. What is edible in one part of the world may not be edible in another part. To be certain, check with the local residents.

EDIBLE REEF FISH

Pictured in figures 3-50 through 3-55 are the common edible fish found on most reefs. It must be realized that the variety of life along the reefs and in the oceans staggers the imagination. It is not the purpose of this text to identify each variety. However, it is possible to point out a few of the most common and easily recognizable fish in each category.

Parrot fish, as seen in figure 3-50, are one of (if not the most) important contributors to the reef. They eat the living coral animals and in so doing, bite off pieces of coral growth and grind it up, making sand. They also eat algae and are the most efficient and unwasteful eaters on the reef. In terms of collective pounds, they are the biggest reef inhabitants. There are over 30 varieties of parrot fish in every conceivable color. They are considered edible, but, depending on their diet, they may be poisonous in some areas.

Members of the porgy tribe have a similar appearance, differing mostly in color. They weigh between two and four pounds and are found throughout the Caribbean. The most outstanding example of the porgy tribe is the blue, yellow, and black porkfish, shown in figure 3-51.

The grouper, as shown in figure 3-52, is very common, but it is highly prized for its food value. It grows to great size, but is harmless to divers. Large groupers are found in deeper water and are quite shy. The grouper has two cousins, the black sea bass and the jewfish which are even larger, weighing 800 or more pounds.

The squirrel fish is aptly named. Its big brown eyes give it an almost comic look, as seen in figure 3-53. Although they are edible, they are not a very good source of food, because they are quite small (8 to 10 inches long) and very bony.

Fig. 3-50   Parrot Fish

Fig. 3-51   Porkfish

Fig. 3-52   Grouper

Fig. 3-53   Squirrel Fish

Fig. 3-54   Red Snapper

Fig. 3-55   Amber Jack

Snapper can be found in many varieties including the red snapper, dog snapper, mangrove snapper, and yellowtail snapper, to name a few. The fish shown in figure 3-54 is a red snapper. They range in size from quite small up to over 100 pounds and are usually edible.

The jack family forms a large part of the pelagic free-swimming fish that skirt the reefs. They are characterized by the amber jack, shown in figure 3-55. They are large and powerful, reaching weights up to 100 pounds. They may be several feet in length. Jacks normally travel in schools and while they are edible and quite delicious, it is unlikely that a diver would ever have the opportunity to spear one.

Fig. 3-56   Puerto Rican Butterfly   Fig. 3-57   Spot Fin Butterfly

Fig. 3-58   French Angel   Fig. 3-59   Gray Angel

Fig. 3-60   Queen Angel   Fig. 3-61   Pisaster Star

Fig. 3-62   Yellow Feather Star   Fig. 3-63   Sea Urchin

INEDIBLE REEF FISH

The variety of inedible reef fish seems endless. The warm seas of the Caribbean and South Pacific provide a breeding ground for fish of every conceivable shape, size, and color.

The butterfly and angel fish are two of the friendly reef fish that are often confused. The Puerto Rican butterfly, shown in figure 3-56, is also known as the banded butterfly. It is from five to seven inches long. Reef fish of this type are quite tame and appear to have very few, if any, natural enemies. The same is true of the spot fin butterfly, shown in figure 3-57.

The angel fish are among the most beautiful on the reef and are certainly the most graceful. The French angel, shown in figure 3-58, is black with bright yellow scales. This fish almost glows in its brilliance, and like the butterfly fish, it is quite tame. A cousin, the gray angel, shown in figure 3-59, has almost no fear of man and can be touched occasionally. If left undisturbed, this angel fish will swim around oblivious to divers. The queen angel, shown in figure 3-60, is the most beautiful of the angel fish. It is extremely graceful and brilliant. Its dazzling colors change with each shift of light.

INVERTEBRATES

Fish are the reef inhabitants the diver sees first, but they comprise only a small part of the total population. Another common reef inhabitant is the starfish. The pisaster star, shown in figure 3-61, is one of the most common. They are bottom dwellers, found clinging to rocks or crawling across the bottom. Their main food is shellfish and barnacles. While the pisaster star is what you normally think of, a starfish may have up to 20 arms, like the yellow feather star, shown in figure 3-62. Its skeleton is a loose meshwork of calcareous plates or rods. When it dies, the skeleton becomes rigid and can be preserved—making it a natural for collectors.

Another large reef contributor, the sea urchin, is shown in figure 3-63. The sea urchin is nature's pin cushion, because it has needlelike spines that protrude from its body in all directions. Beneath the spines is a small globular shell containing ova, which is considered a delicacy. However, this food must come from the correct species. Some urchins will cause illness, although it isn't known if it is caused by poison, bacteria, or an allergenic reaction.

There are two layers of spines; the largest of the poison spines serve to protect and feed the urchin. Near the body, down between the long spines are the pedicellariae, small pincer-like organs that keep away larvae and minute creatures. There are many varieties of urchins which vary in color, size, and appearance. Sea urchins are normally found tucked away in the cracks and crevices of reefs and along the rocks in shallow water.

The sea anemone is a colorful marine animal that looks like a plant. It is in the same phylum as coral, jellyfish, and hydroids. They range in size from a fraction of an inch to over one foot in diameter. Many are brightly colored and look like flowers, as shown in figure 3-64, but they contain a nematocyst and poison capable of killing small fish.

Featherduster worms, shown in figure 3-65, are further evidence in the overlap of appearance between plant and animal. The dusters' flowerlike plumage is used to breathe and attract food. They are less than eight inches high and many are barely visible. They are found on the bottom in sand or growing in coral and appear to be more plentiful in shallow water. As you might imagine, they are quite fragile and retract at the slightest touch. Another example is the spiral Christmas tree worm, shown in figure 3-66.

Crustaceans

Careful observation in the little nooks and crannies of the reef will expose many creatures like the coral shrimp pictured in figure 3-67. This tiny coral shrimp is only about one inch long and is nearly transparent. This animal contributes little to the reef—except as food for others. They are primarily nocturnal and their transparency helps protect them from enemies.

The hermit crab, shown in figure 3-68, is considered a long-tail crustacean, but the tail lacks the skeletal protection of its relatives, the lobster and shrimp. For protection, it adopts the discarded shell of other marine animals. The hermit may begin life in the smallest of shells and as it grows, will try many shells until one is found that fits properly. The largest hermits can be found in huge conch shells.

Figure 3-69 shows a California spiny lobster. It differs from the Maine lobster, shown in figure 3-70, in that it has no large front claws and a larger tail. The spiny lobster grows to over 20 pounds, although 12 pounds is considered large.

It is known that lobsters shed their shells periodically but nothing is known about their growth rate, and commercial incubation attempts have been futile. The fine taste of lobster has created such a demand that the supply is dwindling. They are increasingly more difficult to find, and most coastal fish and game departments are controlling the number taken. Commercial fisherman make the greatest catches with their highly efficient traps.

Shellfish

The contribution of shellfish to the marine ecosystem is significant. Among the most common are the scallops and oysters. (See figure 3-71.) They are a good food source and are commercially cultivated.

The conch, as shown in figure 3-72, is also an excellent food source and can be found crawling along the bottom in warm water areas of the world. Abalone, as shown in figure 3-73, is another commercially desired food source. It thrives in the colder water regions and is found clinging to rocks in the cracks and crevices along the shore.

Fig. 3-64   Sea Anemone

Fig. 3-65   Featherduster Worms

Fig. 3-66   Christmas Tree Worm

Fig. 3-67   Coral Shrimp

Fig. 3-68   Hermit Crab

Fig. 3-69   Spiny Lobster

Fig. 3-70   Maine Lobster

Fig. 3-71   Scallops

Fig. 3-72　Conch

Fig. 3-73　Abalone

Fig. 3-74　Sculpin

Fig. 3-75　Stonefish

Fig. 3-76　Lionfish

DANGEROUS MARINE ANIMALS

It has been noted that while some fish are capable of inflicting serious wounds, there are very few that are aggressive. Although some of the more exotic and dangerous animals don't frequent the American coastline, there are common ones you should learn to recognize and avoid.

The California sculpin (Scorpaena guttata), pictured in figure 3-74, is an extremely timid poisonous fish found along the west coast of the United States and in many other parts of the world. The sculpin is also known by a variety of names, including: scorpionfish, rockfish, sea pig, bullroute, waspfish, bullhead, and blob. It hides under rocks most of the time—the only way you can see one is to watch carefully. The sting is not fatal, but if you are stung, the best first aid is to apply hot water directly to the wound.

The stonefish (Synanceja), shown in figure 3-75, resembles the sculpin, but it is much more dangerous. Like sculpins, they are shy and use their poison only for defense. They are not a problem to divers along United States coasts, however, because they live mostly in the South Pacific.

When handled and released, the stonefish will simply sink to the bottom, but if you molest it, the fish will tend to move its dorsal fin toward you. Again, the best first aid is to quickly apply extremely hot water and an injection of Emetine Hydrochloride directly into the wound within 30 minutes.

The lionfish (Dendrochirus zebra) is beautiful and carries a powerful sting. (Note figure 3-76.) Fortunately, lionfish are shy and brightly colored, which makes them easy to avoid. First aid procedures are the same as for the sculpin.

Stingray (Dasyatis americana) is the name generally given to the butterfly ray, bat ray, round ray, and to the true stingray. Some variety of each of these rays may be found in American waters. Rays live in the bottom and remain camouflaged.

Only the bat ray, shown in figure 3-77, is considered a free swimmer. Rays differ mostly in shape. They all have a flat body with winglike fins and a long tail. The stinger rests along the top of the tail, as shown in figure 3-78. If

Fig. 3-77 Bat Ray

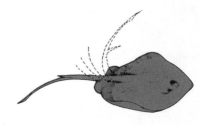

Fig. 3-78 Tail Stinger

molested, the tail is looped over the top of the body causing the stinger to point forward. In this position, it may be driven into the intruder. The greatest danger from stingrays lies in the fact that they camouflage themselves on the bottom. When you move on the bottom, it is wise to look carefully and make sure nothing is there. First aid includes soaking the wound in hot water.

The puffer (Diodon holocanthus), shown in figure 3-79, isn't poisonous unless you eat it. Every part of the world has fish which are dangerous if eaten, but only the puffer is universally considered poisonous.

The appearance of the barracuda (Sphyraenidae) causes its terrible reputation. It may reach a size of six feet and exceed 100 pounds, as shown in figure 3-80. It moves with lightning speed and has razor-sharp teeth, but there have been very few authenticated reports of attacks on humans. The real danger of barracuda exists while spearfishing. They are attracted by water motion and blood. Barracuda meat is considered excellent, but it can be poisonous.

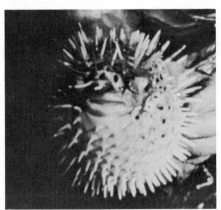

Fig. 3-79 Puffer   Fig. 3-80 Barracuda

Fig. 3-81 Moray

There are over 10 species of morays, three are common in United States waters. The moray is nocturnal—only a small percentage are ever seen. Their length varies greatly among the different species, but they may reach six feet and weigh 25 to 35 pounds. The moray's appearance is ferocious because of its needlelike teeth and the way it opens and closes its jaws. (See figure 3-81.) The jaw movement is a breathing process and while morays could bite if molested, they are quite shy and want nothing to do with divers.

The shark (Selachii) is the most feared fish in the sea and with good cause. They are fast, strong, and they are nature's garbage disposal. They eat constantly—anything in the water is a potential dinner. There are so many small easy things to eat, that larger aggressive animals (like humans) are not normally on their menu. The shark is really quite cowardly, despite its strength and continuous feeding habits. In fact, sudden movement in their direction will generally send them away. Sharks seem to be attracted to low frequency vibrations, the kind emitted by weak or sick fish. A human swimming on the surface emits the same frequency and for that reason, surface swimmers are in the greatest danger.

The white shark is the most dangerous of all sharks. It is quite rare. The most common are the blacktipped bull, hammerhead, lemon, mako, nurse, reef, requiem, sand, sharp nose, tiger, and white tip, some of which are shown in figure 3-82.

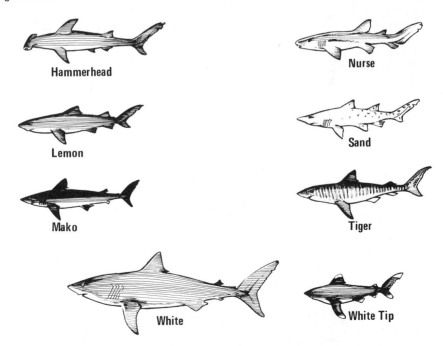

Hammerhead

Nurse

Lemon

Sand

Mako

Tiger

White

White Tip

Fig. 3-82 Sharks

The phylum Coelenterata includes three classes: Hydrozoa, Scyphozoa, and Anthozoa. These classes contain familiar names like jellyfish, sea wasps, Portuguese-man-of-war, sea anemones, and coral. They are known as cnidarians because of their ability to sting. All members of the phylum contain a poisonous stinging mechanism and are capable of inflicting various degrees of discomfort.

The stinger is known as a nematocyst. When you touch animals containing a nematocyst, the sharp, whiplike stinger releases and forces poison into the victim. Only a very few have a nematocyst long or strong enough to penetrate human skin. Of those that do, only two or three are capable of any discomfort. The Portuguese-man-of-war (Hydrozoa Physalia physalis), shown in figure 3-83, has a bad reputation and is considered dangerous due primarily to its great numbers.

The creature is completely at the mercy of the wind and its float serves to support thousands of individual cells joined in the appendages trailing below. Each cell contains a nematocyst and contact produces hundreds of little stings, resulting in a burning sensation. The best first aid is baking soda scraped off after 30 minutes.

There are 9,000 varieties of jellyfish (Schyphozoa). All contain the same nematocyst system found throughout this phylum. Unlike the Portuguese-man-of-war, the jellyfish, as shown in figure 3-84, are swimmers. They propel themselves by alternately sucking in and expelling water, much like the opening and closing of an umbrella, creating a jet effect. The true jellyfish also contains a central digestive system and forms tissue and organs. The first aid is the same as for the man-of-war.

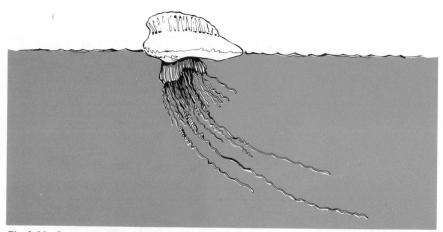

Fig. 3-83 Portuguese Man-of-War

Fig. 3-84 Jellyfish

One final animal to avoid is the cone shells (Gastropoda), as shown in figure 3-85. Cone shells are dangerous to man because they possess a powerful stinger and are poisonous. However, they don't attack and being stung is a result of careless handling. The shell is cone-shaped and varies in size from three to five inches.

Fig. 3-85 Cone Shell

Fig. 3-86 Cone Shell Stingers

VENOM DUCT

PROBOSCIS

VENOM BULB

RADULA

Figure 3-86 shows the stinging mechanism of the cone shell. There is a venom bulb and a venom duct which is connected to and extends through the stinger. The radula is a small sack which contains teeth. The teeth are needlelike and are actually forced through the stinger into the victim in the manner of a small dart.

When unsure of a shell, pick it up by the large end and always wear heavy leather gloves.

Ocean life is fascinating, and sometimes mysterious, to mankind who will continue to unlock their endless array of secrets. By constantly learning more about the oceans, we will be able to enjoy and use them without exploiting them, or their inhabitants.

section D

fresh waters

- ● LAKES, RIVERS, QUARRIES, AND CAVES
- ● FRESHWATER LIFE

DIVING AREAS AND FRESHWATER ANIMALS

When you mention freshwater diving, you are likely to find any number of reactions. For some reason, most people only associate diving with oceans. The nondiver finds it hard to imagine where you would dive inland and the saltwater diver tends to look upon the freshwater diver with disdain.

Since many divers in the United States live inland, most of their diving naturally takes place in fresh water. Simply because you live inland doesn't mean that freshwater diving is less challenging or exciting than its saltwater counterpart.

DIVING AREAS

Fresh water offers a great variety of locations for diving. There are lakes, rivers, sandpits, quarries, caves, sinkholes, springs, and even swamps. In fact, any place where there is water means possible diving to the real diver.

Fresh water provides an array of places to dive, and the activities can be just as varied and in some cases, more varied than in the oceans. Exploring can be very rewarding; some rivers and streams offer the diver an opportunity for prospecting. Spearfishing can be excellent in fresh waters where it is permitted and the collecting potential is outstanding. Photography, too, can be rewarding in most fresh waters, and of course, many of the marine sciences can be applied to fresh water.

Freshwater divers should never feel inferior to ocean divers. Their skills must be just as, if not more finely developed than saltwater diving skills. Activities like cave and ice diving require a degree of capability and training that many ocean divers never find necessary. (See Part IV, Section D.)

While it is true that fresh water lacks the sea's variety of colorful life, a wide assortment of fish, crustaceans, and shellfish do live there. A nearly endless variety of diving sites is also found in fresh water. Every small stream and pond is a new and different environment; each demands and deserves your attention as a diver.

LAKES

Lakes are the largest source of inland diving, ranging in size from a few acres to the huge freshwater seas in the northern part of the United States, the Great Lakes.

Fig. 3-87 Lakes

Artificial lakes of every size are being developed all over the United States. These lakes or reservoirs are generally built by damming rivers. As the lakes form, a whole new ecosystem evolves. The diver exploring reservoirs can witness a chain of life that differs from natural lakes.

Because of the relative newness of manmade lakes, most of the diving activities there involve exploring, spearfishing, and photography. You find very few artifacts in manmade lakes, although there is normally a great deal of aquatic life. You may discover "treasures" in the form of lost boats, motors, and fishing tackle. This type of diving is not only fun, but also can be financially rewarding.

Natural lakes offer the greatest diving potential. They are normally clear and, depending on their location, offer the greatest potential for finding old relics. With the constant desire for memorabilia and antiques, there is hardly a better place to look than in natural lakes. The early settlers used the lakes as a handy disposal and because fresh water doesn't rust metals like salt water does, most metal items can be salvaged in nearly their original condition.

Wherever railroads were built over natural waters, there is increased potential for finding artifacts. The railroaders had a habit of throwing waste such as old bottles into the water. You may be able to chance upon items lost during the construction of railroad bridges across lakes and rivers. Fresh water gives the diver an opportunity to find long forgotten items in good condition. It is rumored more than one Colorado mountain lake contains gold from old wrecked trains.

The Great Lakes are large enough to handle oceangoing vessels and there are countless numbers of wrecks containing valuable artifacts and treasure.

RIVERS

Rivers can be a lot of fun. No matter where you live in the United States, there is probably a river near you. While not all rivers are deep or clear enough to justify diving, many offer good diving potential.

Fig. 3-88 Rivers

In the areas where gold is possible, like the Rocky Mountains and the California mountain ranges, gold dredging is an exciting and sometimes rewarding hobby. You can also come across artifacts, because the rivers have long been dumping places for man's waste.

Photography is another fascinating sport in the rivers. Rivers offer an opportunity for unusual photographs of life that is not normally seen in the lakes. Freshwater sciences (limnology) can be applied in the rivers in many forms and there is also the pure recreational potential of rivers.

Quiet river pools are deep and offer the best diving. The less turbulent areas beneath waterfalls should not be neglected, however, because they are the most likely spot for gold and artifacts to settle. In many cases, they have the clearest water.

SANDPITS AND QUARRIES

A sandpit or quarry is a small pond artificially formed by removing its natural deposits. Actual rock quarries contain large pieces of mined rock, and the bottom is usually rock, covered with a fine silt. Rock quarries are generally clear, and they may be quite deep. Spearfishing and general exploring can be quite exciting in quarries with fish life.

Fig. 3-89 Quarries

Sandpits are formed when sand is removed from a small existing spring area; the bottoms are normally sand, covered with a light layer of silt. Sandpits offer possibilities for photography, spearfishing, and occasional fossil hunting.

One thing that should be remembered about freshwater lakes and rivers is that the land animals in the area depend on that water for sustenance and because of the broad range of land animals, amphibians, and fish life that depend on the waters, nature can be observed at every level, much more readily than at the ocean. In fact, a complete land/water ecosystem can be seen, particularly in the dry land areas where water is more of a rarity.

NATURAL CAVES

Natural caves are normally above water and speleologists are the people who explore caves. They occasionally run into water which, depending on the cave's formation, may block an entrance to another part of the cave. The surfacing of an underground river may also block an entrance, but in any event, it is quite often worth exploring. So, for the speleologist who wishes to explore the additional cave area, diving is essential.

Fig. 3-90 Caves

SINKHOLES

Sinkholes can be extremely deep and long. They quite often contain fossils and artifacts and offer excellent opportunities for photography. A number of the sinkholes in Florida contain actual bones and remnants, such as sharks' teeth; however, they are rather dangerous to dive in and require a great amount of special training.

SPRINGS

Springs are like sinkholes and they, too, may contain fossils, artifacts, and some unusual life. In both springs and sinkholes, the water is normally quite clear and warm, having a constant temperature of 72°F (23°C). In some areas, like the mountains of Wyoming and Colorado, there are springs which have a high mineral content and extremely warm water, sometimes over 100°F (38°C).

MINES

Abandoned mines can provide exciting diving and are quite often very clear. Many contain relics which makes exploring and photography a natural activity. Because of high mineral content, there may be no animal life. Mines are normally deep and at the base of the open pit, there is often a mine shaft. Depending on the condition and size of the shaft, it may offer interesting, exciting diving.

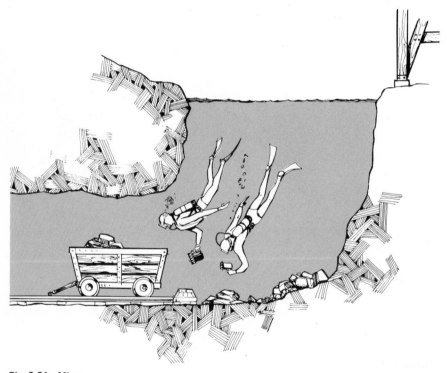

Fig. 3-91 Mines

COMMON FRESHWATER ANIMALS

The fresh waters of the United States lack the immense variety of fish found in the oceans. Depending on the location and water temperature, however, you can find a considerable variety in fresh water.

Fresh water, like salt water, contains edible and inedible fish. In most cases, the fish are edible, but due to their eating habits or water conditions, are not desirable. Undesirable fish are referred to as nongame or scrap fish. Whether or not a fish is a scrap or game fish depends partly on the area of the country. What is considered a scrap fish in one place may be considered a game fish in another.

The purpose of this section is to allow the new diver to identify the inhabitants of his new environment. For that reason, the text will be limited to the fish that might normally be seen by a diver. There are, of course, many fish, like trout, that may exist in great numbers in the lakes where you dive, but which are never seen.

GAME FISH

Largemouth Bass

The largemouth, as illustrated in figure 3-92, is found in almost every state in the United States, in Canada, and Mexico. It can change color according to its surroundings; this color may range from a light brown to almost black. The largemouth is frequently confused with the smallmouth, but it differs, in that the jaw point of the largemouth extends back beyond the eye, while the smallmouth's jaw ends directly beneath the eye. The average size of largemouth bass caught in cold waters is from one to two pounds. In warmer waters the fish may run as large as one to six pounds with a 9 or 10-pounder being possible.

Smallmouth Bass

You can also find smallmouth bass in almost every state, as well as Canada and into Mexico. Like the largemouth, the color of the smallmouth varies according to the terrain. The dorsal fin of the smallmouth appears to be one long fin instead of the two fins of the largemouth. The smallmouth, as shown in figure 3-93, is smaller than its cousin and averages about 1 to 1-1/2 pounds. Five pounds is common, but it is rare to find a smallmouth bass weighing over 10 pounds.

Smallmouth cling close to rocks in lakes and are found around partially submerged boulders and pools in streams.

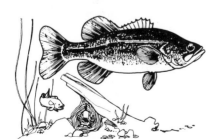

Fig. 3-92 Largemouth Bass

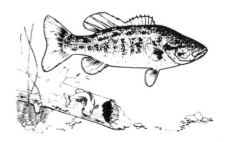

Fig. 3-93 Smallmouth Bass

White and Black Crappie

White and black crappie, as illustrated in figure 3-94, are found in nearly every state in the United States. The white crappie is more numerous in the south and the black crappie is more prevalent in the north.

Both fish are spotted and have vertical stripes. The black crappie is heavier than a white crappie of the same length. The black has seven or more dorsal spines while the white has seven or less. They average 1 to 1-1/2 pounds, although some may be two pounds, with the largest reaching five pounds.

Crappies are primarily lake fish. They run in schools, close to shore along the points. They can be seen occasionally around weeds and in the open water.

Walleye

Walleye are excellent sport fish and are commonly known as walleyed pike, even though they are members of the perch family.

Walleye are found in almost every state, with the exception of the far west and extreme south. Their color varies, but it usually runs from gray-green to almost white. The walleye is different from the true pike in that it has two separate dorsal fins and exceptionally large eyes. (See figure 3-95.) It has strong canine teeth and an upper jaw which extends to a point beneath the rear margin of the eye.

Walleye range in size from an average of two to five pounds, up to 22 pounds. They tend to be a school fish and are normally found around the thermocline. They may swim in water a few inches deep. They are primarily nocturnal and prefer the sandy bottoms near dropoffs in clear waters.

Yellow Perch

Yellow perch are found from southern Canada to the Carolinas. In recent years they have been introduced on the Pacific coast and elsewhere.

Perch are distinguished by six to eight prominent vertical bands. They have a humpback appearance and the two dorsal fins are distinctly divided as shown in figure 3-96. Perch normally weigh less than one pound but may range as high as four pounds. They are normally found in great numbers in schools, and while they are considered lake fish, they may be found in streams and rivers.

Northern Pike

The long, streamlined northern pike is sometimes referred to as freshwater barracuda, primarily because of its appearance. It is a voracious eater, and has canine teeth. (See figure 3-97.)

Pike are found throughout the world, but they prevail in the northern part of the United States. Their color runs from olive gray to almost white; it also varies according to the terrain.

Fig. 3-94 White and Black Crappie

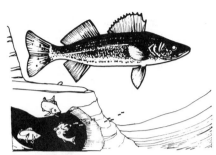

Fig. 3-95 Walleye

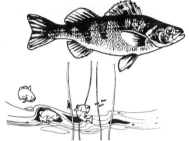

Fig. 3-96 Yellow Perch

Fig. 3-97 Northern Pike

Northerns average from two to four pounds, but may run as high as 46 pounds. There are unauthenticated reports of northern pike weighing over 100 pounds. The pike is a solitary fish which hides along weed beds around logs and other places.

Muskellunge

The muskellunge, or muskie, the largest member of the pike family, is found mostly in the northern part of the United States, Canada, and as far north as Alaska. (Note figure 3-98.) Its color ranges from dark slate gray to a greenish brown. The general appearance is similar to the northern pike, but it can be distinguished by scales on the upper half of the cheeks and gill covers.

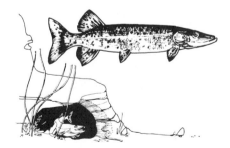

Fig. 3-98 Muskellunge

The average muskellunge weighs 15 to 25 pounds. Fish of 75 pounds have been reported and it is believed some could weigh 100 pounds. Like a northern pike, the muskie is a solitary fish which lays in concealed spots along weeded areas next to logs. Both the northern and muskellunge have been known to eat water fowl and small animals that live around the water.

Pickerel

Pickerel, though similar to muskellunge and northern pike, are much smaller. (Note figure 3-99.) They may be found in the south, even in Florida, and they flourish in streams and rivers as well as lakes. Their feeding habits are much like the northern's.

Channel Cat

The catfish family contains over 1,000 species, but channel cat is considered the sportiest member.

The channel cat, shown in figure 3-100, is found from Canada to Florida, to the gulf states, and into northern Mexico. Their color is slate gray with a slight silvery gray along the sides. None of the catfish have scales. The single spine of the dorsal and pectoral fins is extremely tough and sharp and has the ability to lock in place, which makes catfish dangerous to handle. The whiskers on a channel cat are quite long and the tail fin is very forked. They range from one to two pounds in weight. However, 10-pounders are fairly common and the largest known is 55 pounds.

Channel cat may be found in slow-moving muddy bottom waters, but they normally prefer clean, swift-moving streams and rivers. They are primarily nocturnal feeders and hide under rocks during the day.

Blue Catfish

The blue cat, illustrated in figure 3-101, is the largest catfish in the United States and is found from southern Canada, down to the Appalachians, and into the gulf states. It is also very populous in the Mississippi and its tributaries. The coloring is a solid dark blue-grey fading into silver-white on the belly. The average size is from two to five pounds, although 10 to 20-pounders are common in certain waters. Blue catfish as large as 160 pounds have been reported.

The blue cat prefers larger lakes and rivers and slow-moving quiet waters. Mostly bottom feeders, they feed at night like the other members of the family. During the day they can be found tucked away under rocks in lakes or under the ledges of deeper river pools.

Flathead Catfish

The flathead, as shown in figure 3-102, is found from South Dakota to Pennsylvania and down through Texas and Alabama. Like the blue catfish, it grows to a very large size with 30 to 50-pounders being fairly common. Specimens of 100 pounds have been reported. It differs from the blue catfish because the tail is rounded rather than forked.

Trout

Trout are by far the most beautiful and colorful of the freshwater fish. They range in size from the small brook trout of a few ounces, up to the huge lake

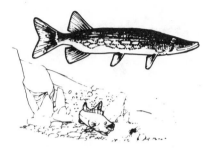

Fig. 3-99 Pickerel

Fig. 3-100 Channel Catfish

Fig. 3-101 Blue Catfish

Fig. 3-102 Flathead Catfish

trout that may weigh as much as 100 pounds. They are found in virtually all waters of the United States and while they prefer and grow larger in colder waters, they swim in the deeper waters of warmer lakes and streams.

There is a great variety of trout, including the rainbow, brown, cutthroat, lake, brookie, golden trout, and the mackinaw. They are illustrated in figures 3-103 through 3-109. Trout are rarely seen by divers. They free swim in open water and are extremely shy and wary. It is a rare and fortunate diver who is privileged to see one of these beautiful fish.

Fig. 3-103 Rainbow Trout

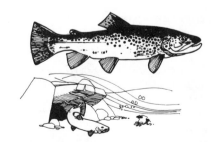

Fig. 3-104 Brown Trout

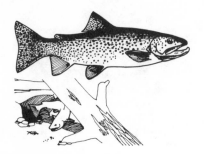

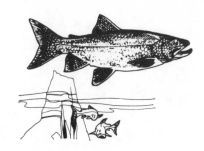

Fig. 3-105 Cutthroat Trout   Fig. 3-106 Lake Trout

Fig. 3-107 Brook Trout

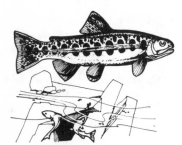

Fig. 3-108 Golden Trout   Fig. 3-109 Steel Head Trout

NONGAME FISH

Carp

The extremely hardy carp are originally natives of Asia. They were transplanted here from Europe. They are not generally considered a game fish, but they are edible. Carp can be quite delicious if they are prepared properly, but they are an extremely bony, tough fish. Several varieties exist. One is the mirror carp, shown in figure 3-110. The standard carp in figure 3-111 is a rich golden color and is very streamlined. The mirror carp has the appearance of having lost a number of its scales.

Fig. 3-110 Mirror Carp

Fig. 3-111 Standard Carp

They average from one to six pounds, but may go as high as 55 pounds. They feed on the bottom of streams, rivers, and lakes and must be carefully controlled or they will totally overcome a small body of water and force out the game fish.

Suckers

There are many members of the sucker family, but the white sucker, illustrated in figure 3-112, is the best known. This sucker is found in virtually every state in the United States. Its size ranges from one to two pounds; four pounds is the maximum. It ranges in color from creamy white to silver. Those with a rather pinkish stripe are sometimes referred to as rainbow suckers.

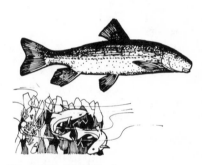

Fig. 3-112 White Sucker

The sucker has a suction-type mouth for bottom feeding. They are found in streams, rivers, ponds, and lakes, and prefer cleaner water. Like carp, they must be controlled.

Gar

Gar are most plentiful in the southern states, but they thrive as far north as southern Canada. Their coloring is an olive green to brown. They are long and thin with alligator-like mouths that contain sharp needlelike teeth.

Garfish grow to a huge size; sometimes they measure as much as seven or eight feet and weigh over 125 pounds. The gar will eat almost anything and are extremely destructive to less vicious fish. They prefer warm sluggish pools and muddy bottoms, but they can be found in rivers and slow-moving streams. There are four common varieties of gar: the alligator, the longnose, the shortnose, and the spotted gar, as shown in figures 3-113 through 3-116.

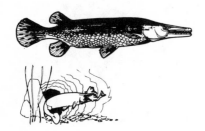

Fig. 3-113 Alligator Gar

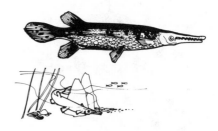

Fig. 3-114 Longnose Gar

Fig. 3-115 Shortnose Gar

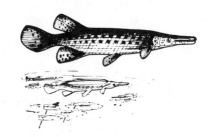

Fig. 3-116 Spotted Gar

While there are many other varieties of freshwater fish, those illustrated are the animals most likely to be seen by divers in the waters of the United States.

CRUSTACEANS

The crayfish is the only noteworthy freshwater crustacean. (See figure 3-117.) The crayfish resembles a lobster, but is much smaller, ranging in size from a few millimeters to eight inches. They are found in almost any type of fresh water, but they prefer clear shallow water. Crayfish are nocturnal. At night they crawl along the water's edge, which makes them fair game for fish and land animals. Crayfish are considered edible and are quite good, but they have limited food value because of their size.

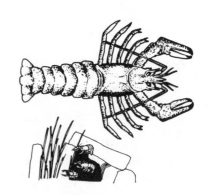

Fig. 3-117 Freshwater Crayfish (Crawdad)

SHELLFISH

Several varieties of freshwater shellfish exist, but only one is of interest—the freshwater clam, as shown in figure 3-118. This three-to-five inch clam lives throughout the United States. Its meat is very good but tough.

Clams found in clear fresh water are the only ones recommended for eating. If you can open them with your bare hands, the clams are probably sick and should not be eaten.

Like their saltwater cousins, freshwater clams bury themselves in the bottom of lakes and ponds. They protrude only enough to breathe and eat. Clams can't hide

Fig. 3-118 Freshwater Clam

from the observant diver because they leave a trail along the bottom when they move from place to place.

As a freshwater diver, you are blessed with a variety of diving locations and activities. You have the rare opportunity to see unexplored places within a few miles of your home and to observe nature on its most fundamental level. The chain of life, from the tiniest water creature to the land animal that depends on the water for its life, is yours to experience.

There is an exceptional and exciting opportunity for the diver to find and recover antique relics and to reward himself intellectually, along with the continuing probability of rewarding himself financially as well.

Fresh water may lack the publicity and glamour of the oceans but it is by no means second best. It rivals and equals the oceans in every sense of the word.

section E

ecology

- THE DELICATE BALANCE OF NATURE
- POLLUTION PROBLEMS
- POLLUTION SOLUTIONS

SOURCES OF PROBLEMS

The balance of nature is really a very simple thing. Every creature, in order to live, must have food. If you remove its source of food, the creature dies. In nature there is a chain of life wherein every living thing, be it plant or animal, provides either food or shelter for every other living thing.

Fig. 3-119 Chain of Life

Fig. 3-120 **Clown Fish and Anemone**

Occasionally the balance of nature is disrupted by nature herself. Where ideal growing conditions exist, the population of one or more species may increase to huge proportions, far beyond what is normal. When this happens, nature is able to rebalance herself. As the population increases, so does the demand on its food source. As the food source begins to diminish, so does the population, until everything regains its proper balance.

Left undisturbed, nature establishes a system in which the strongest survive. The weak are killed and eaten and the survivors produce successive generations which become more adept at survival. This system constantly improves the species.

All through the oceans you can see large and small creatures helping one another. A good example is the small clown fish which lives inside the poisonous sea anemone. The clown fish attracts other fish which are killed by the anemone. The remains of the victim serve as a food source for the clown fish, so each helps the other. The small cleaner wrasse operates stations throughout the oceans where the larger fish come to have parasites cleaned off their bodies. The large fish even allow the small wrasse to enter their mouths and remove food from between their teeth. They are serving each other, in what is known as symbiosis.

Man, in his effort to provide a better way of life for himself, is constantly upsetting the balance of nature. The dumping of excess waste, the process of construction in and around the water, and the search for natural resources, all disturb the natural chain of life in some way.

Nature has an amazing capacity for adapting to change both on land and in the water. However, if there are enough continuing changes, or changes that are severe enough, nature is often unable to adapt. When a permanent change occurs, it affects more than just a single species; it will interact and all creatures will tend to reduce each other.

COASTAL PROBLEMS

SEWAGE

The dumping of unrefined sewage into rivers or immediately offshore into the oceans is killing much of the marine life. The survivors are becoming mutations and disease is increasing among the fish. The affected creatures aren't fit for human consumption, but, worse, they aren't safe as food for each other. Healthy fish which eat the sick ones are also affected.

Fig. 3-121   Diseased Fish

The sewage pollution is affecting not only the fish living *in* the water, but also the people *around* the water. It causes rivers and beaches to be closed, decreasing recreational areas for swimming and, in some cases, for boating as well.

Fig. 3-122   Pollution

Many popular resort areas in foreign countries dump raw sewage into the rivers which eventually flows to the sea at or near swimming beaches. The result—swimmers in the area contract dysentery or even worse diseases.

CONSTRUCTION

Dumping and landfill along the shoreline to create new real estate disturbs homes of the shallow water animals and also destroys the natural food cycle.

Fig. 3-123   Landfills

Dredging along the coasts also disrupts the food cycle. In coral reef areas, the silt created by dredging drifts, settles along the reefs, and kills the coral. To kill the coral reefs and the shallow water creatures is to upset the chain of life. It affects not only animals in the immediate vicinity, but eventually creatures at greater ocean depths.

INDUSTRY

CHEMICAL DUMPING

Chemical dumping by industry produces much the same results as sewage. It kills marine life and causes deformation and disease. Fortunately, the United States Environmental Protection Agency has strict laws and is enforcing them with heavy fines for offenders. A constant watch, however, must be maintained to avoid chemical dumping not only in the form of direct dumping, but also from accidental runoff of pesticides into our rivers and coastal areas.

CRUDE OIL DAMAGE

Crude oil has caused a great deal of damage to the coastal areas' beauty, recreation, and marine life. Land animals that depend on the sea for their life suffer too.

There have been natural crude oil seepages for millions of years and the oceans have handled them gracefully. However, with the depletion of our natural oil reserves on land, man has reached into the oceans to tap its riches, and regardless of the care taken to safeguard against oil spills, they do happen.

Fig. 3-124   Crude Oil Spills

Until recently, it was believed that most of the oil problems stemmed from exploration and its resulting spills. It is now apparent, however, that another source of crude oil is much more severe and holds a greater potential danger than all the drilling put together.

Oil tankers transport about 2 billion tons of oil each year. They carry crude oil one way across the ocean and then use seawater for ballast on the return voyage. At the end of the voyage, they dump the seawater along with its oily residue back into the oceans. The oil industry estimates that 5 million tons of oil are disposed of in this manner each year and scientists estimate that ballast pumping accounts for five times as much oil pollution as the accidental spills which we hear about. This dumping is not only a matter of course, but is quite legal. Unless something is done, it will have long-range and drastic effects on the natural ecosystem of the oceans.

COMMERCIAL FISHING

Damage caused by pollution, accidental or intentional, is a major problem. Overharvesting of the seas presents an equally great threat to our existence. In recent years, sophisticated electronic equipment has improved the techniques

Fig. 3-125 Commercial Fishing

of long-line fishing boats, trawlers, and purse seiners. New, larger boats are able to process the fish as they are caught. These boats have catching and storage capabilities far beyond what fishermen of just a few years ago ever dreamed possible.

Even with today's improved fishing techniques, in 1972, fishing boats in some areas were able to take only about 10 percent of the amount harvested in 1965. Clearly, the oceans are being depleted of their available resources.

The seas currently provide only a small percentage of the animal protein used by the world. If the demand increases, conservation methods will have to be strictly enforced for fishermen throughout the world. It must be remembered that only about one-tenth of the ocean is really fertile—the rest is virtually barren.

Some forms of sea farming are practical, but not every species can be controlled. Consequently, fishermen must be careful not to deplete the stock of fish beyond chances for natural recovery.

SPORT DIVING

The threat to the oceans by sport divers is minimal. The amount of game the sport diver can take from the oceans by spearfishing or other means is inconsequential in comparison to what a single fishing boat can take. Still, the sport diver has a responsibility to respect sea life and not take just for the sake of taking. Spearfishing is fine for food, but to take fish just for sport is wrong. The same is true of crustaceans and shellfish. To take what you need to eat is a way of life, to take for sport is unique to man and is wrong. Along the coastal waters of the United States, fish and game departments have established limits and seasons. If the seasons are observed, the stocks won't be depleted and can be maintained for all.

Fig. 3-126 Don't Pollute

Sport divers must respect the new environment and avoid unnecessary damage. Don't remove anything natural unless there is a very good reason. Don't break off coral or disturb underwater growths. Remember that it took millions of years to grow the beautiful underwater life and it takes only moments to destroy it. If everyone was careless, before long we would have nothing but an underwater desert.

INLAND PROBLEMS

Problems in fresh water are much the same as in the oceans, including sewage and industrial dumping plus the additional problems created by the widespread use of insecticides.

Chemical fertilizers and runoff from cattle-feeding operations eventually settle in ponds and lakes. The runoffs are creating a problem known as eutrophication. Eutrophication is a process whereby too many nutrients enter a body of water, causing increased plant growth which dies and produces a lethal gas, which in turn kills the animal life.

If the intentional or accidental dumping of nutrients is not curtailed, it is only a matter of time until eutrophication begins to take its toll on larger bodies of water with long-range and disastrous effects on freshwater animal life as we know it today.

SOLUTIONS

It would be a wonderful thing if it were possible to list the causes of pollution, and then, just as easily, list the solutions to the problems. Unfortunately, such is not the case.

Fig. 3-127   Conserve and Enjoy

The solution to pollution problems are at least as complex as the problems themselves. Ecologists are painfully aware that dramatic action to eliminate the obvious may, in fact, create new problems that are equally bad, if not worse.

One point shines clearly amid the confused quest for answers. Pollution is everyone's problem, and each individual must do his or her part to keep pollution levels down to a point where nature can handle it. Until such time as answers are found, a program of active prevention must be maintained.

PART IV

the dive

introduction

By now you should have a good basic understanding of the equipment required to dive safely. You should also have a clear understanding of how water affects the diver and how the diver can function safely within the new environment.

This part will offer an insight into diving activities. It will discuss how to provide yourself with food from both the sea and from the fresh waters. It will provide further information on collecting techniques for aquariums and preserving specimens, as well as ways to capture your undersea experiences on film. For the more adventuresome diver who seeks the thrill of something more than just the normal open water environment, there is a presentation on cave diving, ice diving, wreck diving, treasure hunting, and other advanced diving techniques.

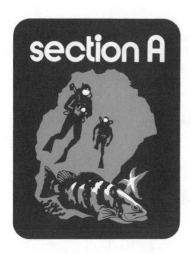

section A

food from sea and lake

- SPEARFISHING
- SHELLFISHING
- CRUSTACEANS
- COMMERCIAL FOOD FARMING

SPEARFISHING, ANIMAL TYPES, AND COMMERCIAL DEVELOPMENT

The seas and lakes provide an ever increasing amount of our daily food requirements. Even more food will be available as commercial fishing and undersea farming techniques improve but care must be taken in everything we do concerning the seas.

Environmentalists have recently made it clear that the seas are showing the adverse effects of too much commercial fishing. There can be little question that the problems they are creating must be solved, but the desire to protect our waters from abuse by large commercial fishing firms should not affect all forms of fishing. This includes a minority of sport divers who fish from the sea.

The sport diver, using selective techniques and careful conservation, does not threaten the ecosystem but can, in fact, help it. He can also help his personal economic situation by supplementing his food supply with what he is able to gather from the water. More important than economics is the thrill and satisfaction of using your own skills to provide your own food.

SPEARFISHING

Man has always looked to the sea for food, and one of the oldest methods of securing food was with a spear. Originally, this weapon was used at the surface while standing near or on the shore, as shown in figure 4-1. Man now may go beneath the surface of the water with spearguns. In the beginning, man spearfished *only* for food. Only in the past few decades has he regarded spearfishing as a sport.

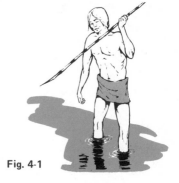

Fig. 4-1

Spearfishing offers many challenges, because man must function within an environment that belongs solely to the fish. However, it has recently become painfully apparent that the sea is unable to reproduce at a rate which corresponds with the pressures of commercial fishermen. While spearfishing as a sport has little or no effect in relation to the sophisticated commercial trawlers, each diver must do his share to avoid depleting the precious resources of our oceans. Therefore, it is suggested that spearfishing be used only to take food and not for sport, and that careful conservation methods be employed to protect the fish and allow them to reproduce in their own manner.

SALTWATER TECHNIQUES AND EQUIPMENT

The speargun is the most important piece of equipment and a large selection is available for the spearfisherman. The first spear was a large thin shaft with a point on the end. After a point that would hold the fish was designed, there came the desire for power. The development of rubber reached a stage where it could be used to power the shaft, and the Hawaiian sling was born.

The Hawaiian sling, featured in figure 4-2, resembles a slingshot with the shaft going through the handle and into a notch attached to the rubber. The shaft is pulled back in the manner of a slingshot and then released. It is a free spear (not attached by a line) and is legal only in salt water where the water is sufficiently clear to keep track of any game that may be speared.

While the Hawaiian sling is efficient, its use is difficult to master. In many areas of the world, spearfishing is limited to the use of the Hawaiian sling, and then only while skin diving. No tanks are allowed. (See figure 4-3.)

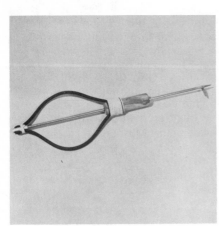

Fig. 4-2　Hawaiian Sling

Fig. 4-3　Using Hawaiian Sling

Rubber Guns

Because the Hawaiian sling must be pulled back and released each time, its power is limited by the strength of its user. To give the user more power, the rubber gun was invented. It is nothing more than a method of holding the shaft secure so that several rubber slings can be attached and released simultaneously at the proper moment. Rubber guns require strength and a good deal of time to load. The number of slings which propel the shaft limit the rubber gun's power. For these reasons, CO_2 guns were invented.

CO_2 Guns

CO_2 guns do have great power, but they also have several drawbacks. They must be recharged each time they are fired, and the gas released into the water creates a disturbance that obstructs the vision of the spearfisherman. Because of these and other problems, including the extreme power and effectiveness of the CO_2 guns, they have been outlawed in most parts of the world.

Spring-Powered Spearguns

The spring-powered gun was designed as a compromise between the CO_2 and rubber gun. A shaft forced against a spring inside the barrel compresses the spring; a trigger mechanism then holds the shaft. When released, the spring throws the shaft. Because the reserve energy of compressed steel is not great, and because salt water had a corrosive effect on the trigger mechanism and spring, the spring gun passed out of favor while the rubber gun remained.

The Pneumatic Speargun

The pneumatic speargun is a compromise between the rubber, CO_2, and spring gun. It offers the advantages of the spring gun because it loads faster than the rubber gun. It is much safer than the CO_2 gun because the gun retains expended air inside. The problem with this seemingly perfect gun is its power is also limited by the user's strength because it is loaded by forcing the shaft down the barrel against pressure.

FREE-SWIMMING AND ROCK FISH

In areas where the diver is free to choose the type of gun, he should consider the kind of fish to be taken. Fish generally can be placed into two categories: free-swimming fish which move around and hunt for food and bottom or rock fish which frequent reefs and rock outcroppings along coastal areas.

Free-swimming fish usually are found in waters along points and dropoffs. They search for food along protected areas such as coral reefs in warm waters, and rock outcroppings and kelp beds in colder waters. When hunting for fish while skin diving, remember—you can't possibly outswim the fish, they must come to you. Dive to a point slightly below the depth at which the fish normally swim, then just hang motionless in the water. It's important that you move as little as possible. Free swimmers are very spooky and will veer off at the slightest indication of danger. The idea is to shoot up toward the fish rather than down. Remember that free swimmers move quite fast, so you must take a careful lead.

A scuba diver does not always have an opportunity to shoot at free-swimming fish. They don't normally frequent the bottom areas scuba divers like to roam, and the fish may be frightened by exhalation noises.

When shooting large free-swimming fish, special spear points are required, as shown in figure 4-4. These fish possess great power, so the point must be detachable from the shaft. A point secured directly to the shaft would be snapped off almost instantly. There must be a flexible connection, such as a line between the point and the spear shaft. The line should be either strong nylon or cable approximately 18 inches long. Quite often a reel like the one shown in figure 4-5, is attached to the gun and will hold 150 to 250 feet of line. In this way the fish can be played in much the same manner as a fisherman with a rod and reel.

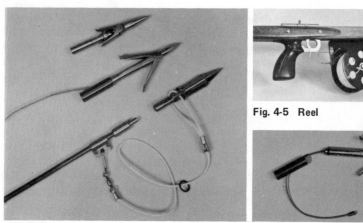

Fig. 4-5   Reel

Fig. 4-4   Spear Points

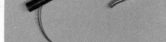

Fig. 4-6   Cable

Rock fish, or reef fish, present the spearfisherman with a different challenge. Where the diver remains still and allows free swimmers to come to him, he must hunt rock fish. Rock fish are territorial and are seldom found far from a hiding place. When stalking these fish, the diver must move carefully, be very quiet, and peek over every rock and ridge until the fish is located. The diver must move slowly with no sudden motion until he is within the fish's range.

When taking rock fish, you are seldom more than a few feet away, so the ranges are short in comparison to free swimmers. The equipment required is essentially the same except that the shaft should be shorter and heavier. The points used on the spear shaft should still be detachable, but the connecting cord should be made of cable rather than nylon to avoid being cut on rocks or coral, as illustrated in figure 4-6. Reels are not required when shooting rock fish because they don't normally go any great distance, but rather head directly for their hiding places.

FRESHWATER SPEARFISHING TECHNIQUES AND EQUIPMENT

Spearfishing in fresh water is really no different than in salt water. The fish are smaller and not quite as strong.

Many parts of the United States do not allow spearfishing. Of those that do, only a few allow the taking of game fish, even though it has been proven that line fishermen take more fish than spearfishermen. It has also been shown that spearfishermen are much more selective and can actually aid ecology rather than damage it, but until the laws are changed, the diver must adhere to them.

Locating Fish

Fresh water differs from the ocean because the thermoclines change radically according to the time of year and the fish vary in location according to temperature ranges. In the summer you may find fish in rather deep waters, while in the spring and fall they swim in much shallower water.

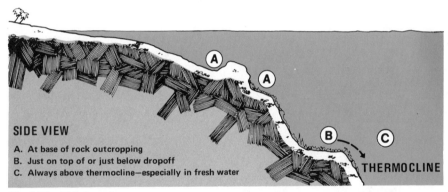

SIDE VIEW
A. At base of rock outcropping
B. Just on top of or just below dropoff
C. Always above thermocline—especially in fresh water
THERMOCLINE

Fig. 4-7A   Fish Locations

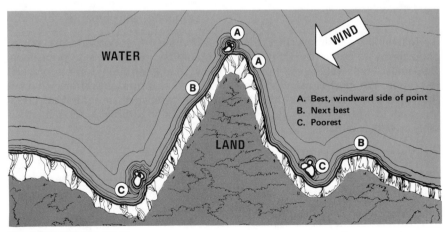

WATER

WIND

A. Best, windward side of point
B. Next best
C. Poorest

LAND

Fig. 4-7B   Fish Locations

Locating the particular fish you desire will vary depending on whether they are territorial fish and remain in a particular area, or if they are hunters which swim around searching for food. The chart in figure 4-7 A and B gives some indication of the areas various fish frequent. By seeking out these areas and using good spearfishing techniques, the diver increases his chance for success.

It is important to remember that fish can outswim the diver and it is fruitless to move along looking for the fish. The diver should remain in the most likely place and wait for the fish to come to him.

Equipment Required

The guns required for freshwater use are considerably smaller than those used in the ocean. The pneumatic spearguns are particularly suited to fresh water because they are fast-loading, extremely accurate, and powerful enough to take any freshwater fish. The points do not have to be detachable. While certain fish (such as catfish) do have enough power to damage your equipment, they are not found in sufficient numbers to warrant the special equipment.

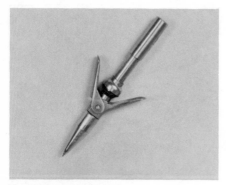

Fig. 4-8   Double-barb Point

The type of spear point used by the freshwater diver is important. It should be a point rugged enough to withstand contact with rocks and employ a double barb to keep the fish on the shaft, as shown in figure 4-8. There must be some method of holding the barbs down so the fish can be removed from the shaft. The freshwater spearfisherman can carry the fish with him, while the saltwater diver must remove fish from the water to avoid attracting any type of predator.

By following these simple rules, the spearfisherman in fresh or salt water has an opportunity to obtain food. Spearfishing should be used for this purpose alone. Remember—the waters are not an endless source of supply for sport and recreation. We must conserve our resources so that future generations will have the opportunity to observe these beautiful creatures in their natural surroundings and to insure that there is a sufficient supply to provide food for their table as well as ours.

SALTWATER SHELLFISH

ABALONE

Many edible shellfish inhabit salt waters. Among the most popular are abalone. They are excellent food and are found from Alaska to Mexico. Because of their excellent taste, they are in great demand and, as a result, supplies have been depleted drastically. Strict controls have been placed on abalone in U.S. waters.

Fig. 4-9 Abalone

California, for example, has rules controlling the depths at which abalone may be caught, and the size and number taken. Methods of taking them are also limited in California.

Abalone may be found hiding quite cleverly in cracks along rocks and under ledges, as shown in figure 4-9. Abalone which are removed from their hiding places must be replaced. If you drop them on the bottom, they will be eaten by predators. They are incapable of replacing themselves and are helpless and defenseless on the open ocean bottom.

CONCH

The conch, pictured in figure 4-10, is another excellent source of food. It is found crawling along the bottom, primarily in warmer waters. It varies in size from very small to several pounds. While there are a number of species of conch, you cannot eat all of them. It is a good idea to check with the local people to determine which are safe to eat.

Fig. 4-10 Conch

OYSTERS, SCALLOPS, AND CLAMS

The common oyster, scallop, and clam are three more ocean delicacies. Oysters and scallops dwell on rocks, while clams are normally found on the bottom, particularly along the shore areas in the mud, or in sand along the beach. Locating oysters, scallops, or clams varies according to the area. Again, checking with local divers is the best idea.

FRESHWATER SHELLFISH

The only shellfish found in fresh water in sufficient quantities or large enough to be of interest to divers are freshwater clams. They live in many lakes throughout the United States and vary in size from two to eight inches in length. Although they are a little tough, they are very tasty. Clams are found on the bottom areas in the bays of lakes and stillwater ponds. To determine if the clam is edible, see if it can be opened easily. Clams which cannot be opened easily are usually healthy, and those which can be opened with your fingers may be sick and should be avoided.

SALTWATER CRUSTACEANS

There are a number of edible crustaceans found in the oceans. Among these are lobster, crab, and shrimp.

LOBSTERS

There are two common types of lobsters. The spiny lobster lives along the west coast of the United States, down through Mexico, into the Caribbean, and up as far north as Virginia. The spiny lobster lacks the claws of the so-called Maine lobster, as illustrated in figure 4-11.

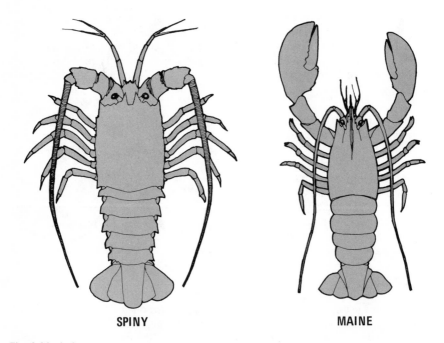

SPINY   MAINE

Fig. 4-11 Lobsters

Lobsters are primarily nocturnal. To locate them during the day you need a good light to search their favorite hiding places—little nooks and crannies along reefs and rock outcroppings. (See figure 4-12.) Lobsters, like abalone, are desirable because of their delicious flavor and have become quite scarce. Divers must pay strict attention to the laws protecting lobsters and take no more than they can eat.

CRABS

Another delicious crustacean is the crab. Crabs can be found virtually all over the world in one form or another. Not all crabs are edible and it is strongly suggested that you check with local people regarding the types available. Crabs and lobsters prefer similar environments. A crab in its natural habitat is shown in figure 4-13. However, they occasionally can be found outside their hideaway during the day. A careful eye must be kept to locate these deceptive creatures.

Fig. 4-12 Spiny Lobster   Fig. 4-13 Crab

SHRIMP

Shrimp are almost totally nocturnal and are rarely seen during the day. They range in size from almost microscopic to the size of a small lobster. Shrimp, similar to the one shown in figure 4-14, can be found all over the world. They are highly sought after for food. Their numbers, too, appear to be waning.

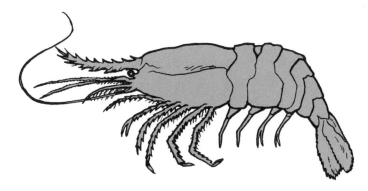

Fig. 4-14 Shrimp

There are a great many edible sea creatures besides those already mentioned. Many are considered delicacies, such as the sea urchin, turtle, squid, octopus, and a number of others which are not readily available to the commercial market. Each type of animal requires special handling and knowledge. Once again, it is suggested that information from local people be obtained prior to taking any creature unfamiliar to you.

COMMERCIAL DEVELOPMENT
OF THE SEAS FOR FOOD

There are numerous attempts being made to cultivate the seas for commercial use. Among the most successful sea farming ventures are turtle farming and the cultivation of shrimp and oyster beds. Seaweed is being used as a human food supplement and as a source of minerals and vitamins. New uses are sought daily. Attempts to cultivate lobsters have failed so far. Not enough is known about the lobster's growing and breeding habits to allow man to cultivate it commercially.

The world is just now awakening to the fact that the seas resources must not be indiscriminately wasted. Eventually, through research, man will discover techniques required to cultivate the sea sensibly. It is a new and virtually untapped area that offers a bright future for any young people today who may be interested in doing their part to help solve the world's problems.

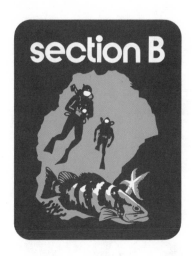

section B

collecting

● AQUARIUMS
● PRESERVING SPECIMENS

SALTWATER AQUARIUMS, FRESHWATER AQUARIUMS, AND PRESERVING SPECIMENS

For the avid diver, time away from water interrupts two of the things he loves most—diving and the opportunity to observe nature firsthand. But time away from water need not be wasted. It can, in fact, involve a hobby which brings the water to you.

Aquariums offer both entertainment and education. They provide the owner with an interesting hobby, an opportunity to witness nature on a continuing basis, and to learn how it functions.

SALTWATER AQUARIUMS

Before you run down to the local pet shop and lay out money for a new saltwater aquarium, there are some things you really should know. Select a dealer who has been in business long enough to gain practical experience. Be sure he really knows what he is talking about, and whoever you choose, stick with him for at least three months. Remember—if you do only *one* thing different than the dealer tells you, your aquarium could fail. His methods are tested and they work, but you cannot expect anything more from a dealer than what he is able to show you in his own display tanks.

EQUIPMENT

The basic equipment required for setting up a saltwater aquarium is shown in figure 4-15. The tank must be all glass and be able to hold at least 30 gallons. Inside the tank you need a platform type under-gravel filter which should cover the entire bottom of the aquarium. A filter media, or gravel, should cover the filter at the ratio of 20 pounds per square foot of bottom area. The mixture itself should be 40 percent onyx, 40 percent silica, and 20 percent oyster shell, although others will work. The onyx and silica should be of medium

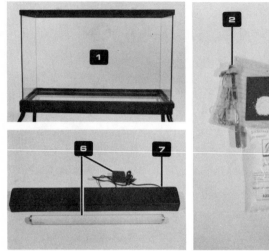
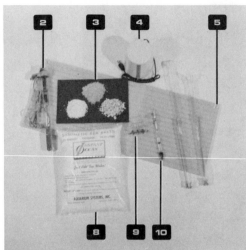

1	TANK	6	LIGHT FIXTURE AND BULB
2	HEATER	7	TANK COVER
3	GRAVEL	8	SALT
4	AIR PUMP	9	AIR VALVES
5	FILTER (PLATFORM TYPE)	10	HYDROMETER

Fig. 4-15 Saltwater Aquarium and Equipment

density—one-eighth inch granules, no smaller, no larger. The next requirement is an air pump and valves. Be sure to get the best your money can buy. To save a few dollars on your equipment only to lose one fish, would destroy any savings that you might enjoy initially.

A heater, light bulb, tank cover with fluorescent light, and a good hydrometer and salt for preparing the water come next. The salt should be a top quality, nationally known brand containing a separate trace element solution. Finally, of course, you need animals and food.

Setup Procedure

The setup should be done by your local dealer, but the procedure is as follows: First place the aquarium on something quite solid, capable of handling the weight, as illustrated by figure 4-16. Place the under-gravel filter in the aquarium and wash the gravel thoroughly. Pour in the gravel and fill the tank two-thirds full of water. Add the salt and let it dissolve. Then add the trace element solution, remove about one-half of the water, and place it in a plastic trashcan.

Add fresh water, checking the specific gravity or density ratio, with the hydrometer shown in figure 4-17, until it reaches 1.020. Continue to add salt water and fresh water until the tank is full and shows a specific gravity of 1.020. Let it run for 24 hours and make sure the temperature is at 72° to 76°F (22° to 24.5°C) with the specific gravity still at 1.020.

After the first 24 hours, introduce the seed: a handful of gravel from the bottom of an already established aquarium.

The biggest problem many aquarists initially confront is the result of ammonia nitrogen nitrite and nitrogen nitrite products. You must set up the nitrogen cycle before introducing the first fish. This requires establishing a synthetic waste product (ammonia) which matches fish waste, but lacks organic contaminants.

Once the aquarium is running at the desired temperature, and the proper specific gravity and dirty gravel have been introduced, feed a solution of ammonium chloride (six percent in water) into your aquarium. Add this at the rate of four drops per gallon of water each day for seven days. On the eighth day begin measuring the nitrogen nitrite with a nitrite test kit, as shown in figure 4-17. Wait for the nitrite to come up, peak out, and go all the way back to zero parts per 10 million. This process, known as curing a tank, requires

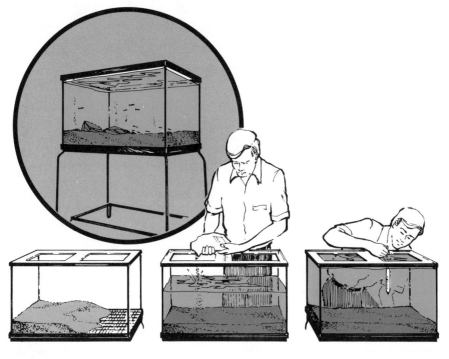

Fig. 4-16 Setup Procedure

approximately three weeks. It can be done more rapidly, but three weeks insures a good saltwater aquarium that will last indefinitely. Once the aquarium has cured, you may introduce your animals.

INTRODUCING MARINE LIFE

The techniques of introducing animals to the water are not too stringent. The main thing is to get them into the water as quickly as possible, and to be sure the water they come from is the same temperature and same specific gravity as the water they will inhabit.

Adjusting the temperature is simple. You merely float the bag containing new fish in the aquarium, as illustrated in figure 4-18. When the temperature has equalled, they may be dumped into the aquarium.

Fig. 4-17 Hydrometer
and Nitrite Test Kit

Fig. 4-18 Water Temperature Equalization

While the method of introducing the fish is important, it isn't nearly as important as the animals you choose. Don't buy an animal until the dealer has had it for at least 30 days. If there is a question in your mind about the animal, don't buy it. There are three time periods during which the fish may die. One is in the initial shipment time. These fish usually die within the first two days.

Within one week there will be another percentage of fish lost as a result of being massively overdrugged during capture. By the third week more fish will be lost. These deaths occur from a lesser degree of overdrugging. Those that survive the fourth week are generally in good health. It may cost a little more for a healthy fish, but it *is* going to live. It is possible to find some fantastic buys when the dealer first receives the fish, but chances are they may die.

Introduce the invertebrates first. The best invertebrates are shrimp, anemones, and featherduster worms, as shown in figure 4-19. Anemone crabs and spider crabs as shown in figure 4-19 are fine, but avoid crabs with claws, especially hermit crabs. They are too mean. For best results, stay away from crabs as much as possible. Also, live corals should be avoided because they are too difficult to feed.

The second week is the time to introduce fish. Clown fish like those pictured in figure 4-20 are good and will go with the anemones. Do not mix a tomato clown and a maroon clown, they do not get along. But any other clowns can be mixed. Yellow tangs and blue tangs portrayed in figure 4-20 are good, but it is recommended that the more exotic tangs be avoided.

Fig. 4-19 Typical Aquarium Invertebrates

Fig. 4-20 Typical Aquarium Fish

Fig. 4-21   Fish Not Recommended

Fig. 4-22   Harmful Marine Life

Fig. 4-23   Sea Horse

There are a number of fish which should not be part of your aquarium because they are either too mean, or their fatality rate is too high. Butterfly, damsel, and trigger fish are poor choices and eels are not recommended because they will eat everything they can get into their mouths. Anglers, trunkfish, and boxfish should also be avoided. (Note figure 4-21.)

There are other creatures which are quite dangerous and represent a serious hazard. Three of those are: the lionfish, stonefish, and the hapalochlaena or blue ring, a species of octopus. These fish are portrayed in figure 4-22. The lionfish, though not fatal, is dangerous, and can cause great pain. The stonefish can be fatal and the blue ring octopus is instantly fatal. Stay away from it. The sting is painless and death occurs within 90 minutes.

Stick with fish that are not vicious, that are not predators, and your tank will be more successful. You also will not have to buy goldfish for food. The life expectancy of fish should be from nine months to a year, on the average, with many lasting from three to four years in a properly controlled tank.

Feeding

With the exception of sea horses, marine fish don't require exotic foods. The top quality flake foods and frozen smelt or scallops found in grocery stores are sufficient. Sea horses, such as those in figure 4-23, require live brine shrimp. Live brine shrimp may introduce diseases and parasites which can kill your fish, so it is best to avoid this food and keep the sea horses in a separate tank.

In the wild, fish eat constantly, so the number of times a fish may be fed is not really important. A minimum of two times a day is required, but more often is acceptable. Most important is that they eat all the food given them. They should not be overfed. There should not be any waste, because waste can create poisonous gas in the water that can kill all life in the tank.

TANK MAINTENANCE

The secret to a good aquarium is maintenance. It has to be done on schedule. Remember, you do not *bring* a tank back to shape; it must be *kept* in shape. Most problems start from a dirty aquarium. This doesn't mean removing every little bit of debris in the aquarium. It means changing 25 percent of the water every four weeks. Fish consume the trace elements in the aquarium to grow and live. They assimilate a good deal of the solution, as do bacteria. You must replenish those trace elements—it cannot be done by simply adding a trace element solution. It is done by removing 25 percent of the water and replacing it with freshly mixed water.

Another reason for the change is the buildup of waste products that are not broken down. They must be diluted so the concentration does not stunt the fish's growth and cause stress. If the fish are under stress, they will become sick. The urge then is to medicate; but if you medicate, you kill bacteria. When the bacteria are killed, you are right back where you started.

To keep your aquarium healthy, never medicate. You don't have sick fish; you have a sick aquarium. Change the water to put the aquarium in proper condition.

It requires time and experience to become a good saltwater aquarist, and the fastest and safest way is to put your trust in a good dealer. He has the knowledge and experience to help you avoid the many pitfalls involved in setting up a new aquarium. Once the aquarium is in operation, it will afford you many hours of entertainment and endless opportunities of observing nature in action.

FRESHWATER AQUARIUMS

While freshwater fish may lack the color of saltwater fish, they are no less interesting or demanding than their saltwater counterpart. The variety of available freshwater fish is extraordinary and many are as strange and interesting as anything found in the sea.

EQUIPMENT

The equipment required for a freshwater aquarium is essentially the same as used for salt water. The all glass aquarium is best, but it may be smaller—10 gallons is sufficient in the beginning. Because there is no salt, the hydrometer and nitrite test kit is not required.

The mixture of onyx, silica, and oyster shell used in saltwater aquariums should not be used in fresh water. The gravel should be inert. An epoxy-coated gravel is best, because freshwater aquariums do not require the bacteria buildup saltwater aquariums do.

FEEDING

Freshwater fish eat much the same food as saltwater fish. The flake foods are excellent but freshwater fish can eat live brine shrimp which are strictly prohibited for saltwater fish.

MAINTENANCE

Outside of the fact that no special water mixture is required, the primary difference in maintenance between the saltwater and freshwater aquarium is that 25 percent of the water must be changed every week. A saltwater aquarium is changed once a month. The gravel should be cleaned at the same time. Like saltwater aquariums, most freshwater aquariums become sick due to uncleanliness.

Freshwater aquarium plants, as depicted in figure 4-24, are desirable for their oxygen production. They add a nice decorative touch to the aquarium but they are not essential.

As with the saltwater aquarium, the freshwater aquarist should begin with help from a good dealer. The dealer should do the initial setup.

Fig. 4-24   Freshwater Aquarium Plants

There are a great many things to learn about your new aquarium, but with patience and care it can provide endless hours of enjoyment and education. Aquariums are definitely one of the most fascinating hobbies available to divers.

PRESERVING SPECIMENS

Before entering into any discussion about the care and handling of specimens, it should be re-established that animal life is much more beautiful alive and in its natural environment, than dried or preserved sitting on a shelf.

It is virtually impossible to preserve the colors and original beauty of animals after they are removed from the water. Unless there is a valid reason for removing them, it would be much better to leave the creatures for others to see and enjoy.

Specimens may be preserved in a 70 percent solution of alcohol or a four percent solution of Formalin. Because the shells of mollusks and the bristles of worms tend to be corroded by Formalin, alcohol is more commonly used. Formalin preserves the specimen color more effectively than alcohol, but neither does a satisfactory job. To insure that specimens last, remove them from the solution after a time, rinse them, and refill the container with fresh preservative.

When drying a specimen, first soak it in a solution of alcohol, glycerine, Formalin, and water, then let it dry. By doing so, the specimens retain some of their original softness and color.

Many specimens will soften as they die. After a period of time they will reharden. In the case of sea urchins, sagging spines can be prevented by packing them in dry sand as you remove them from the water. (See figure 4-25.) The sand will help dry them and will keep the spines in their original position.

The animals must be removed from seashells. One way is to place the shell in water and heat it to the boiling point. The animal can be removed with the aid of a sharp instrument if you take care not to damage the shell. A weak solution of liquid bleach will serve to neutralize the smell of minute animal life on the outside of the shell.

Let it be stated again that animals are best left in their natural environment. The most desirable alternative is the aquarium. Specimens should be preserved as a last resort and only for educational reasons.

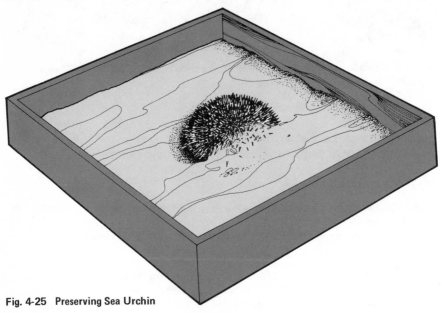

Fig. 4-25 Preserving Sea Urchin

section C

photography

- BASIC EQUIPMENT
- NATURAL LIGHT TECHNIQUE
- ARTIFICIAL LIGHT TECHNIQUE
- MOVEMENT OF CAMERA AND SUBJECT

EQUIPMENT, NATURAL AND ARTIFICIAL LIGHT PHOTOGRAPHY, AND MOVEMENT

Photography adds a new dimension to diving quite unlike any other diving activity. A diver is blessed with the opportunity of seeing more wildlife during his short watery visit than is seen on land over a long period of time. There is an endless parade of subjects passing. (Note figure 4-26.)

Photography offers the thrill of the hunt because it requires careful stalking and observation to capture your subject on film. It offers a chance to relive each adventure and to share the excitement of your discovery with others.

Capable underwater photographers are constantly in demand and there is good commercial potential. (See figure 4-27.) It is difficult to stage photographs below the surface, so the amateur has just as much opportunity to capture the sudden appearance of the award-winning photograph as the most advanced professional.

Fig. 4-26   Endless Parade of
Underwater Life

Fig. 4-27   Underwater Photographer
in Action

This section is designed to give some basic direction and to stir interest in this fascinating hobby. While photography is not difficult, it is involved and requires a good deal of study and information to handle the more sophisticated equipment. This section will answer questions about how to become involved and what equipment is the most practical for the money you are prepared to spend. Hints on how to get the most out of your equipment also will be discussed.

LAND CAMERAS IN HOUSINGS

CARTRIDGE TYPES

The popular cartridge type camera, as shown in figure 4-28, is an excellent choice for the beginning underwater photographer. It is relatively inexpensive and simple to operate. Since many people already own them, they are an excellent first choice for an underwater camera. Cartridge type cameras are available in pocket models along with the more advanced design features, including automatic exposure and automatic advance capabilities in more expensive models.

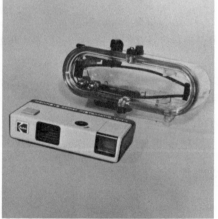

Fig. 4-28 Cartridge Type Camera   Fig. 4-29 Cartridge Type Camera Housing

Housings for cartridge type cameras are shown in figure 4-29 and are the least expensive housings available. They are compact, simple, and dependable. They give the owner an opportunity to experiment in underwater photography at a low cost.

Cartridge cameras offer the versatility of black and white, color prints, or slides, but the film is more expensive, and the cartridge offers a limited number of exposures. Because the shutter speed is rather slow, most cartridge type cameras must be held very still in order to assure sharp, clear pictures. They produce the best results in water less than 15 feet deep.

Fig. 4-30 Auto 35mm Cameras

AUTO 35MM RANGEFINDER TYPE

The auto 35mm rangefinder camera offers a more advanced method of taking pictures. A variety of shutter speeds is available and the exposure can be controlled. It also comes equipped with a flash synchronization and strobe lights can be used. It offers the more versatile 35mm format which provides up to 36 exposures and the cost of film is less because it is in roll rather than cartridge form. Most of the small auto 35mm cameras have automatic exposure control for natural light photography; many have automatic advance capabilities which are excellent for underwater photography.

The auto 35's, like those shown in figure 4-30, are medium price range cameras, varying from $80 to $150, which places them between the cartridge type and the single lens reflex camera in cost. The housings are inexpensive—about the same or slightly more than the cartridge type housings. They are dependable, small, and easy to handle. For the beginning photographer at the experimental stage who demands a little more quality in his pictures, the auto 35mm offers many advantages and excellent results.

SINGLE LENS REFLEX

The single lens reflex camera, or SLR, is the most versatile, available in 35, 120, and 70mm format. The SLR offers interchangeable lenses and through-the-lens viewing, as illustrated in figure 4-31, so you can see the exact image you will photograph and adjust the focus at the same time. Some models offer large capacity film magazines which let the photographer take up to 250 exposures without changing film. They also provide rapid advance motor drives which give the capability of automatic advancement; a very desirable feature for underwater photography.

A wide assortment of housings is available for SLR cameras. These range from the plexiglass housing, which is reasonably priced and completely reliable, to the very rugged metal housings, indicated in figure 4-32. Metal housings are more durable and longer lasting than plexiglass, but they are also much more expensive. Which one should be purchased depends entirely upon the amount and kind of use intended.

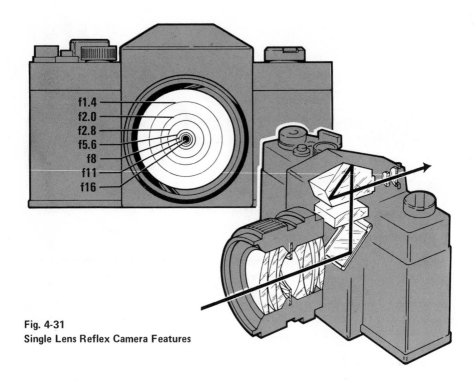

Fig. 4-31
Single Lens Reflex Camera Features

Compared to the cartridge and small auto 35's, the SLR camera is by far the most versatile and offers the best quality of photography. It is also the most expensive so you should think carefully about whether the use justifies the cost.

Fig. 4-32 Housings for the SLR Camera   **Fig. 4-33 Self-Contained Underwater Camera**

SELF-CONTAINED UNDERWATER CAMERAS

The advent of the self-contained underwater camera, portrayed in figure 4-33, has been a great boon to underwater photography. Many people desire the single lens reflex camera's photographic quality, but are not willing to take their expensive cameras under water. The self-contained camera seems to provide excellent quality at reasonable cost.

The self-contained camera is easy to handle. It is small and the controls are quite simple. It is rugged, dependable, and extremely versatile; it offers inter-changeable lenses, close-up attachments, flash synchronization, and complete adjustment of lens openings and shutter speeds.

While the self-contained camera does not offer through-the-lens viewing, it does produce extremely high quality and excellent pictures.

No matter what camera system you choose, one thing should be kept in mind at all times—underwater photography is an expensive hobby. While it is possible to take underwater pictures at low cost, those who become involved in underwater photography find the equipment required for quality pictures costs a great deal. Prior to purchasing equipment, the new photographer should prepare himself for a sizable investment.

All too many would-be photographers buy low cost, low quality equipment with the initial thought of saving money, because all they really want is a snapshot. Once they get involved, they wind up spending a great deal of additional money to replace low quality, inadequate equipment. It is much less expensive to buy good quality equipment which is adequate for the job.

NATURAL LIGHT PHOTOGRAPHY

PROBLEMS FOR BEGINNERS

Light

Taking pictures under water is much more difficult than on land. Water bends and absorbs the light rays as you can see in figure 4-34. The ripples on the surface tend to reflect the light and affect the amount of light that enters the water (see Part II, Section A). Because the eyes are able to compensate for the

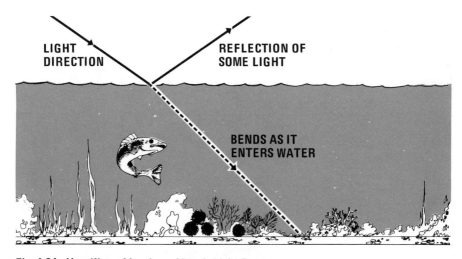

LIGHT
DIRECTION

REFLECTION OF
SOME LIGHT

BENDS AS IT
ENTERS WATER

Fig. 4-34 How Water Absorbs and Bends Light Rays

changes in light, the mind does not notice the changes; whereas the film has a fixed light absorption capability and the coming and going of light can greatly affect the exposure and the quality of the picture.

Most beginners assume the camera is able to capture what the eye sees and are disappointed with their first photographic attempts. Usually, they are too far away or too deep without enough light to expose the film properly. A rough guideline for exposure levels on various cameras indicates that the lower cost cartridge type cameras are effective above the 15 foot level in clear water, and the medium cost cameras, which offer lens opening and shutter speed adjustment, are effective down to 30 feet or more, depending on the clarity of the water.

Color

Another source of disappointment for the beginning photographer is that there is often very little color in their pictures. This is because color is lost very rapidly in water, as depicted in figure 4-35. The colors lost go right through the spectrum. Reds disappear for the photographer within the first 10 feet, then oranges, yellows, greens; near the 60 foot level nothing is left but blues and grays.

Color is affected to a large degree by particles in the water. Depending on what they are, suspended particles determine the color of the water itself. Certain animal life may actually turn the water green or red and that dominance of color affects the ultimate colors in your photograph.

To get maximum color into a photograph, the photographer must get as close to a subject as possible; the amount of color absorbed by the film is a function of not only the depth, but also the distance from the subject. So, to insure that you get maximum color and enjoyment from your pictures, remember to stay in shallow water and get close to your subject.

Fig. 4-35 Underwater Color

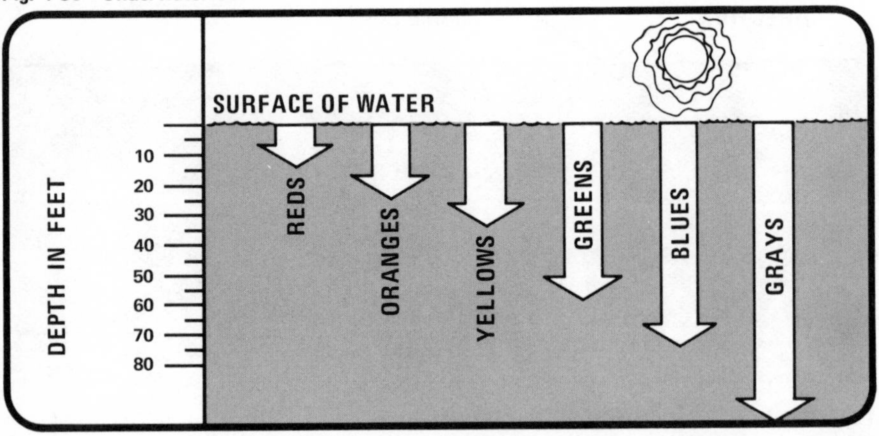

ARTIFICIAL LIGHT PHOTOGRAPHY

The primary reason for artificial light is an obvious one. As light is lost, it must be replaced. It also replaces color. At greater depths, both light and color are lost to the naked eye as well as to the camera. A good artificial light source, balanced to the sun's color temperature, can replace color and produce photographs of startling quality. The colors that exist in the ocean are almost beyond belief in their purity and brilliance.

TYPES OF LIGHT AVAILABLE

Flashbulbs

This applies to the expendable bulbs used to produce light for photography. They come in a variety of sizes, from small cubes to large press type bulbs. The problem with flashbulbs is that the light develops quite slowly, as indicated in figure 4-36. The light duration of the flashbulb is longer than the electronic flash and allows for subject movement. In addition, bulbs are more expensive on a per picture basis.

When using bulbs under water, you must be careful while handling them at depths and when removing used bulbs from the flash attachment. There is a vacuum inside the bulb and they are subject to implosion from the extreme pressure of depth. This is particularly true once they have been fired. A bulb imploding in a diver's hand could cause serious injury. Beyond the potential danger, there is a problem of litter. Bulbs tend to float and a diver must be careful to put spent bulbs in some type of holding sack.

In recent years the electronic flash has become quite popular for a number of reasons. While it does have a higher initial cost, it offers a much lower per picture cost factor than the bulb. The light reaches full intensity instantly and does not require a pre-burn. The short light duration helps stop subject motion, as indicated in figure 4-36.

Fig. 4-36 Light Duration with Electronic Flash and Bulb

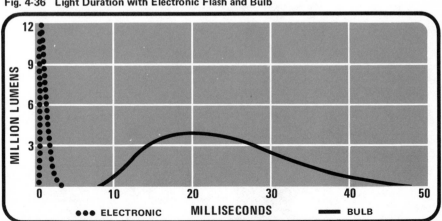

The color balance in an electronic flash unit is more natural than the bulb, and units are balanced exactly to the sun's color temperature, providing the purest of reds and other colors that may be present. In addition to its other advantages, many strobes can be adjusted for the amount of light and the way in which the light is dispersed. Electronic strobes quickly reactivate themselves and are ready for another picture. This is often quite important for action photography. Many outstanding pictures have been lost in the time it takes to replace a bulb.

MOVEMENT

The last and most common of the beginner's problems involves movement of either the camera or subject. It is very disappointing to remember all other aspects of good picture-taking only to wind up with a blurred picture because either you or the subject moved.

Camera movement is very common in natural light photography, and is normally caused by one of several things: slow shutter speed, weak grip on the camera, or the motion of water. Subject motion is normally the result of shutter speed being too slow or the light duration of the flash.

To avoid blurred pictures, weight yourself heavy so you can remain secure on the bottom; weight the camera to neutral buoyancy. If it is too buoyant, it tends to float upwards; if it is too negative, it tends to sink. It is important to maintain a secure hold on both the bottom and camera.

Photography is one of the most enjoyable hobbies available to the diver. It may in fact be *the* reason for diving. It offers a challenge to the diver unlike any other diving activity, and the results are vivid memories about lifetime adventures.

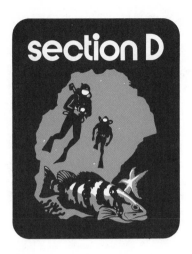

section D

specialty diving

● CAVES
● ICE
● WRECKS
● TREASURE HUNTING
● SEARCH AND RESCUE
● ADVANCED TRAINING

CAVE, ICE, WRECK DIVING, AND SEARCH AND RESCUE

Part of the fascination toward diving stems from the fact that it provides such a wide activity range. We have already explored the various hobbies which may be incorporated into the diving picture. Let us now look at some special diving activities which require a good deal more training and expertise than normal diving in open water.

Cave diving, ice diving, wreck diving, treasure hunting, and, of course, search and rescue, all require their own special brand of excellence. Each represents special diving conditions which introduce additional hazards the open water diver generally does not have to face.

This section offers ideas on how to become involved in something more than just open water diving. It is not intended to provide the technical means to participate in these activities. If you wish to participate in any activities listed, it cannot be emphasized too strongly that you obtain special training from experts.

CAVE DIVING

Caves have always been an irresistible magnet to people. Stemming possibly from the time when people lived in caves, there has always been the desire to explore what's there. With the advent of scuba diving, it became possible to explore underwater caves.

Underwater caves can be found all over the world. In the United States, the greatest concentration seems to be in the southeast. Florida is probably the best known for cave diving and more has been done there to promote cave diving and cave diving training.

TYPES OF CAVES

Caves fall into several categories. There are man-made caves, such as abandoned mines and quarries; there are natural springs and sinkholes. The difference, as shown in figure 4-37, is that mines were originally dry and as they were abandoned, they filled with water. Springs stem from underground rivers bubbling to the surface. A sinkhole is created by an underground river; the ground caves in and creates a hole down to the water's surface.

Cave Characteristics

Springs always have a flow where the water comes out of the ground, and a run where the water flows, creating a stream or river. Sinkholes never have a run, but they may have a flow and a siphon. The flow is the point where the water moves into the sinkhole and the siphon is where it moves out. Because of the siphon possibility, divers must be especially careful in sinkholes.

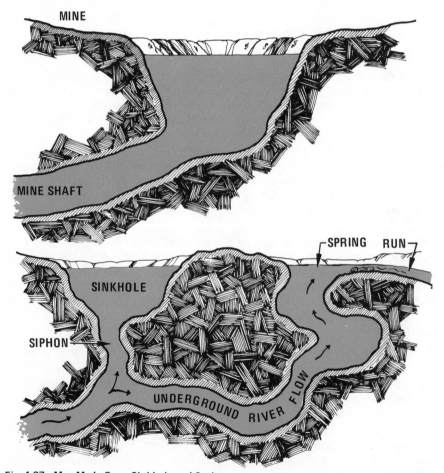

Fig. 4-37 Man-Made Cave, Sinkhole and Spring

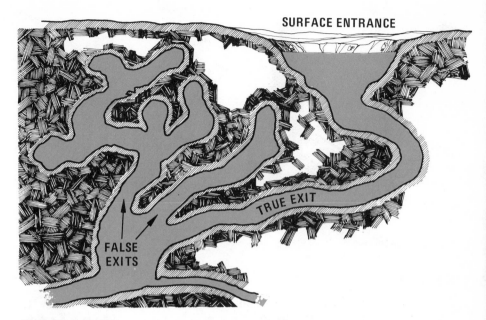

Fig. 4-38   False Exits

In both caves and springs, the entrance is only one of many attempts by the water to reach the surface. (Note figure 4-38.) The diver attempting to exit from the cave is liable to encounter any number of chambers that appear to be exits, but which actually are dead ends.

The floors of most caves are covered with a sediment, a very fine silt which, when stirred, can completely hide the outlet. Safety lines are the only way to insure your safe return to the surface. Another reason for safety lines is that you, as the diver, work in constant darkness even though you use powerful lights to offset the darkness.

ATTITUDE AND TRAINING

A strong mental attitude is required, because the possibility of the lights going out is quite real. If that happens to a cave diver who has a wrong mental attitude, it could spell disaster.

Because of the darkness and sheer uncertainty of what lies ahead in caves, much special training and equipment is required. Whatever prompts you to try cave diving, be certain to properly prepare yourself by seeking professional, specialized training.

Cave diving can be a great joy and thrill, despite its requirements. Caves may contain all sorts of things—from fossils to antiques. The thrill of exploration and the search for contents of caves is endless.

Fig. 4-39 Ice Divers

ICE DIVING

Diving under the ice is very much like cave diving, except it is colder. It requires similar equipment. The diver has only one exit and must use safety lines, as figure 4-39 shows. Because snow often covers the ice, it is very dark and lights are normally required.

Ice diving has a special appeal to the adventuresome diver. It can be done wherever ice forms. In areas where ice diving is done, water is iced over more often that it is open. There is a fascination to see what goes on beneath the ice; however, there is little reason beyond adventure to go ice diving. While the water is sometimes clearer, there is little to see. In cold weather, most fish hibernate.

REQUIREMENTS

In many ways ice diving is even more dangerous than cave diving. The cold does strange things to your mind, to your body, and to your equipment. The cold slows down the bodily functions, so the mind isn't able to react as quickly to any problem that might arise. When the mind does react, there is a physical slowdown that keeps the body from performing needed tasks. In addition, the equipment is subject to freezing and requires special maintenance and care to keep it in top condition.

The watery environment below the ice is totally hostile and the diver must prepare himself to survive in it. He should begin by diving in particularly cold water, training himself to function both mentally and physically under those conditions. He also must have special equipment instruction. Care must be taken to see that the regulator is dry and lubricated and that the tank is filled quite slowly so that no moisture can possibly form. The air must be totally dry to prevent condensation from freezing. The wet suit must be in perfect repair.

Extra layers are required to prevent the cold from creeping through. When adding the extra layers, the diver should have additional practice time in the open water to adapt to the extra equipment.

SAFETY PRECAUTIONS

A great many safety precautions must be taken prior to ice diving. Ice diving is done in teams, as illustrated in figure 4-40. Two divers in the water use the buddy system, and two more divers wait on the surface. You must use safety lines for both divers in the water and safety divers. All divers involved should have a complete knowledge of and be thoroughly drilled in procedure and signals. The reaction time between the line tender and the divers must be immediate. There is no time for trying to determine what was meant by that last tug on the rope. A wrong interpretation or slow reaction could spell disaster.

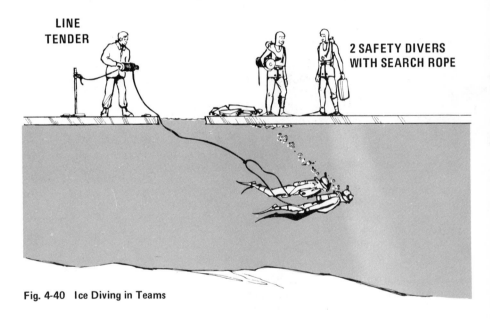

LINE TENDER

2 SAFETY DIVERS WITH SEARCH ROPE

Fig. 4-40 Ice Diving in Teams

If you are interested in ice diving, it is suggested that you seek an established ice diving unit. In most areas of the United States where ice diving has been going on for some time, there are people who have established good solid safety techniques. This reduces existing danger to a minimum. They can provide the special training and information required to ice dive in safety.

WRECK DIVING

Wreck diving has a great deal of fascination for almost all open water divers. The mystery and solitude of a wreck must be experienced to be appreciated. Wreck diving may be conducted in salt water or fresh water, on small boats or large ships, and may include recently sunken vessels or old wrecks with great historical value.

Special training is required because wreck diving is very much like cave diving. Conditions are normally quite poor. The water could be dirty and, in the ocean particularly, it is almost always moving and the water is often quite deep.

When entering a wreck, a diver must be especially careful of internal decay. Even steel ships have a great deal of wood inside them which rots after a period of time. Sometimes the rotting wood requires nothing more than a diver brushing against it to cause its collapse.

Fig. 4-41 Wreck Diving

Wrecks have long been a favorite of divers. They combine adventure with the search for history, and there is always the lure of treasure. Some divers are only interested in the more commercial possibility of salvage.

Whatever your reason for wreck diving, prior to making a dive, learn about the wreck itself. Learn about techniques required, and particularly any special techniques that may be involved for that wreck.

To avoid any possible danger and to insure that the dive will be a success, be sure your equipment is up to par and have sufficient safety equipment. Prior to removing anything from the water, information should be acquired to determine your legal rights to the items you have found. Depending on the area, there are strict laws in effect which govern the diver's right to the items he has located. In fresh water, the prior owner retains ownership at all times. Finding something does not automatically make it yours. Avoid any legal problems that might come up and establish your rights with the proper authorities.

Fig. 4-42 Underwater Treasure Hunting

TREASURE HUNTING

The search for sudden riches has been one of man's failings from the beginning of time, but it has also been one of his great joys. Underwater treasure hunting is no different, and great riches have been taken from the seas.

Treasure does not always come in the form of precious metals, although that is how we normally think of it. It may, in fact, come in the form of artifacts. It may mean prospecting, as shown in figure 4-43. Many divers are involved in dredging for gold in the streams and rivers in parts of the United States where gold is known to exist.

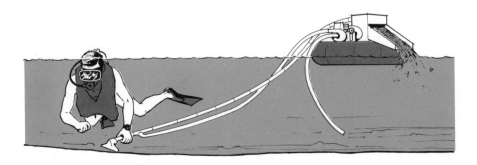

Fig. 4-43 Gold Dredge

While wreck diving for treasure involves a great deal of expense and research time, prospecting can be done on a very small budget. The rewards are more predictable if not as dramatic.

SEARCH AND RESCUE

More and more cities, counties, and states are establishing search and rescue units. These groups have been organized to take care of the least pleasant job in diving, but it is a job that must be done, and it must be done safely.

Water accidents invariably occur during the worst conditions. The water is often dirty, deep, cold, or moving. The bottom may contain plant life. Another problem arises when rescue must be made in icy waters. It could be done at night, but, regardless, rescue always seems to happen under the worst conditions.

When diving problems occur, emotional problems often follow, such as, handling the survivors, organizing the searchers, and maintaining order once the recovery has taken place.

The team efforts may not always involve recovery—they may involve rescue. First aid training is a necessary part of the diver's education as well as a general knowledge of emergency techniques.

Search and rescue diving doesn't appeal to everyone; those who do feel the responsibility and wish to become involved can contact their local law enforcement agencies who can put them in touch with the proper authority in charge of search and recovery teams in your area.

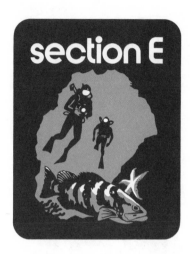

section E

careers

- SPORT DIVING
- LIGHT COMMERCIAL DIVING
- HEAVY COMMERCIAL DIVING
- OCEANOGRAPHY
- LIMNOLOGY

SPORT DIVING, COMMERCIAL WORK, SCIENCES

Diving is at once the most fascinating and exciting of sports, unique in its flexibility and diversity. It requires careful thought, complete training, and keen intelligence to be performed safely. It provides an ample source of recreation, allowing the diver to combine many of the land sports and hobbies that he might normally engage in with his water activity.

For many, diving represents a way to earn a living at something they really love. The employment opportunities in diving fall into four general categories: sport diving, which includes instruction and such things as writing and photography; light commercial work, which is work that can be accomplished under water with scuba gear; heavy commercial work, which requires mixed gas and/or hard hat gear; and the scientific area, which may include any of the sciences as applied to either oceans or fresh waters.

Whatever underwater employment you choose, you are in continual contact with nature, on the threshold of earth's last frontier. You are a real pioneer and part of the world's future.

SPORT DIVING

INSTRUCTION

There are several ways to earn a living in sport diving. Among these are teaching, writing, and photography. The first step in becoming a diving instructor is, of course, sport diver certification. After gaining further diving experience and perhaps serving as an assistant instructor to a fully certified diving instructor, you would attend an instructor certification course. These courses are offered by a number of local, national, and international schools and organizations listed on page 4-41.

Instructor certification courses last from several days to several weeks. They involve intensive learning experiences in the classroom and in open water and have extremely high standards and rigorous testing procedures.

Some instructor organizations offer student instructors a complete course, not only in diving instruction, but also in retail salesmanship, equipment repair, and

Fig. 4-44 The Instructor at Work

all aspects of effective dive store operation. They also act as dealer associations for the combined diving store and diving school. They aid in communication between dealers, help improve and police business practices, and help maintain high-quality diving education programs. Complete business and education programs like these are offered by the National Association of Skin Diving Schools (NASDS), Professional Association of Diving Instructors (PADI), Professional Diving Instructor College (PDIC), and Scuba Schools International (SSI).

Other instructor organizations focus on diver education for the individual, independent instructor who may or may not be affiliated with a dive store. Since these schools place all their emphasis on diver education instead of retail business operations, they are generally shorter, lasting days instead of weeks. As a result, instructor candidates must be mentally and physically prepared before beginning the short and intense training program, for course standards are as rigorous for these as for the more lengthy courses. Diver education courses for the independent instructor are offered by the Association of Canadian Underwater Councils (ACUC), Los Angeles County Underwater Unit (LACO), National Association of Underwater Instructors (NAUI), and Young Men's Christian Association (YMCA).

For specific details, admission, and course information regarding instructor certification schools, write to the following addresses:

Association of Canadian Underwater Councils (ACUC)
National Sport & Recreation Center
333 River Road
Vanier City, Ontario, Canada K1L 8B9

Professional Association of Diving Instructors (PADI)
P.O. Box 177
Costa Mesa, CA   92697

Los Angeles County Underwater Unit (LACO)
155 West Washington Boulevard
Los Angeles, CA   90015

Professional Diving Instructor College (PDIC)
320 Hoffman
Monterey, CA   93940

National Association of Skin Diving Schools (NASDS)
1757 Long Beach Boulevard
Long Beach, CA   90802

Scuba Schools International (SSI)
1634 South College
Fort Collins, CO   80521

National Association of Underwater Instructors (NAUI)
22809 Barton Road
Colton, CA   92324

Young Men's Christian Association (YMCA)
YMCA National Scuba Program
1611 Candler Building
Atlanta, GA   30303

JOURNALISM

As diving grows, so does the demand for information. Journalism and photography offer a field where the diver can convert his findings, adventures, and knowledge into money and, at the same time, enjoy the sport.

Journalistic areas open to the potential writer are education, adventure, and travel.

Education

Instructors everywhere are hungry for technical information. They are constantly in need of information regarding new teaching techniques and how other instructors are handling problems that arise in training safe divers. In addition, they need equipment information regarding modification and

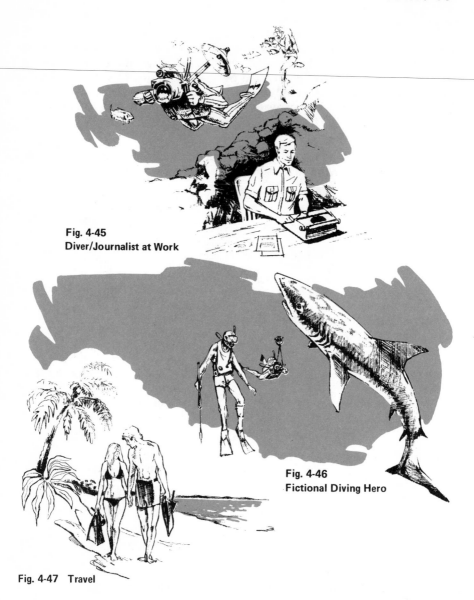

Fig. 4-45
Diver/Journalist at Work

Fig. 4-46
Fictional Diving Hero

Fig. 4-47   Travel

evaluation. Very few instructors are capable of personally purchasing and evaluating each new piece of equipment. Written information regarding personal findings and evaluations is very important.

Adventure

Every sport has its fictional heroes and diving is no exception, see figure 4-46. Many stories, both fact and fiction, are in demand. Every dive is an adventure and special adventures make excellent reading.

Travel

Travel information about different diving areas is important to everyone. Something new appears even in old diving areas. Divers need to know where to go and what to look for, including any special problems that might be involved and how to handle them.

PHOTOGRAPHY

Photography is the only suitable way to present the underwater world visually to the nondiver. Photographs are important because they highlight every article and story. Figure 4-48 is a good example.

Fig. 4-48 Photography

Fig. 4-49 Types of Light Commercial Work

Underwater photographic training begins with basic photography on land. A number of schools in the United States specialize in photography. Once the technique of handling the camera is mastered, most diving equipment stores offer training in underwater camera use. After the diver is familiar with the basic techniques involved, specialized training can be obtained from any of several schools. However, there is no substitute for experience and for the capable photographer, experience is the best teacher.

Almost every publication and television station is a potential buyer for underwater pictures. A career in journalism and photography begins with the basic training received at your local dive school.

LIGHT COMMERCIAL WORK

Light commercial work is normally defined as underwater work accomplished in a short amount of time or in shallow enough water so that decompression is unnecessary. It generally involves inspection of dams, pipelines, cables, and even sewage outfalls, as shown in figure 4-49. It may also consist of such things as salvaging small boats, underwater repair, and even some forms of underwater construction.

To the diver with an imagination, there is an almost endless array of jobs that can be completed with the use of scuba. However, every other certified diver is a potential competitor and, unless there is a big demand in your area, it is not a dependable source of income.

A competent light commercial diver needs advanced training and a keen mechanical ability. A light commercial worker must be a jack-of-all trades, skilled at construction techniques with a good sound knowledge of physics and photography.

Advanced scuba training for light commercial work is available at your local professional school and, of course, on the job. Again, there is no substitute for experience.

HEAVY COMMERCIAL WORK

Heavy commercial work is the highest paid and most hazardous of all commercial diving. Most work is done under adverse conditions where visibility is zero and water temperature may be low. The work involves salvage, repair, maintenance, construction, and may include saturation diving. Salvage work is normally done on ships or anything else worth recovering. Repair, maintenance, and construction work may involve oil rigs, piers, bridges, or any number of underwater objects.

The equipment has become quite sophisticated—beginning with scuba and the Kirby Morgan units and going to hard hat rigs which utilize both compressed air and mixed gas. (See figure 4-50.)

Fig. 4-50
Equipment for Heavy Commercial Work

Fig. 4-51 Scientists Research Earth's Last Frontier

Before applying to one of the many commercial schools, a diver should be thoroughly trained in scuba. You should have a good knowledge of what to expect in heavy commerical work with all its inherent conditions. Instruction includes welding, the use of hard hat and mixed gas units as well as heavy construction techniques.

There are several commercial training facilities in the United States, including these listed below:

California Institute for Men
(For prison inmates only)
14901 Central Avenue
P.O. Box 128
Chino, CA 91710

Commercial Diving Center
272 South Fries Avenue
Wilmington, CA 90744

Divers Institute of Technology, Inc.
Department S–P.O. Box 70312
Seattle, WA 98107

Divers Training Academy
Box 193–C, Link Port
Fort Pierce, FL 33450

Highline Community College
Redondo Pier
Midway, WA 98031

Ocean Corporation
2120 Peckham Street
Houston, TX 77019

Santa Barbara City College
Marine Technology Program
312 North Nopal Street
Santa Barbara, CA 93103

The Coastal School of Deep Sea Diving
320 29th Avenue
Oakland, CA 94601

SCIENCES

It has already been stated that the waters of the world are our last frontier on earth. Diving is one of the tools used by scientists to personally examine the happenings in the underwater world. More sciences now recognize the potential of the oceans and fresh waters. It is quite apparent that additional research must be done to allow us to tap that great potential.

OCEANOGRAPHY

When science is applied to the marine environment, it is known as oceanography; the scientists are oceanographers. The science involved includes such specializations as biology, botany, zoology, geology, geography, and archaeology, to name a few. Many nations have research vessels, similar to that portrayed in figure 4-52, operating on the oceans. They employ sophisticated equipment and highly trained scientists. The oceanographers of the world are attempting to unlock the mysteries of the deep, but they are confined to a very small segment of the ocean floor—primarily the area of the continental shelf.

LIMNOLOGY

Limnology is the application of the sciences to fresh water as opposed to the marine environment, and, just as there is a growing need for oceanographers, there is a great need for limnologists. The fresh waters, like the oceans, hold a key to our future. The challenges are great and exciting.

The most pressing research concerns pollution and feeding the world. Giant steps are being taken toward locating and stopping the causes of pollution in many areas of the world.

If you are interested in a career in the sciences, you must begin with a good solid background in the science of your choice, starting at the junior high level with all of the sciences that are available to you. For specific information, contact your local high school or university. They can supply you with the specific information required to begin a career in oceanography or limnology.

Fig. 4-52   Research Vessel

appendix

WATER TEMPERATURE PROTECTION CHART

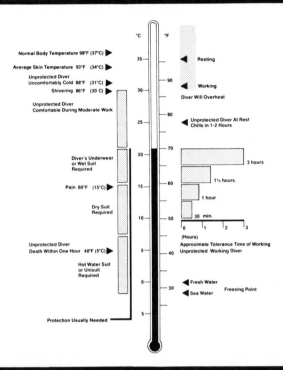

AIR PURITY STANDARDS

STANDARDS FOR AIR 5.2.1.2 Air used in SCUBA operations must meet these standards of purity for the U.S. Navy. This is true no matter what the source of the air or the method used for charging the cylinders. These standards are—

Oxygen concentration	20 - 22% by volume
Carbon dioxide	0.05% (500 ppm)
Carbon monoxide	0.002% (20 ppm)
Oil—mist or vapor	5 mg per cu meter max.
Solid and liquid particles	Not detectable except as noted above under oil—mist or vapor
Odor	Not objectionable

ARCHIMEDES PRINCIPLE, GAS LAWS, AND AIR CONSUMPTION FORMULA/TABLE

Archimedes Principle: Any object wholly or partially immersed in a liquid is buoyed up by a force equal to the weight of the liquid displaced. (a) A negatively buoyant body sinks in a fluid because the weight of the fluid it displaces is less than the weight of the body. (b) A neutrally buoyant submerged body remains in equilibrium, neither rising nor sinking, because the weight of the fluid it displaces is exactly equal to its own weight. (c) A positively buoyant submerged body weighs less than the volume of liquid it displaces. It will rise and float with part of its volume above the surface. A floating body displaces its own weight of a liquid.

Boyle's Law: If the temperature is kept constant, the volume of a gas will vary inversely as the ABSOLUTE pressure while the density will vary directly as the pressure. Since the pressure and volume of a gas are inversely related—the higher the pressure, the smaller the volume, and vice-versa. The formula for Boyle's Law is:

PV=C
Where P= absolute pressure
V= volume
C= a constant

Charles' Law: If the pressure is kept constant, the volume of a gas will vary directly as the ABSOLUTE temperature. The amount of change in either volume or pressure is directly related to the change in absolute pressure. For example, if absolute temperature is doubled, then either the volume or the pressure is also doubled. The formula for Charles' Law is:

PV=RT or $\frac{PV=R}{T}$

Where P= absolute pressure
V= volume
T= absolute temperature
R= a universal constant for all gases

General Gas Law: Boyle's Law illustrates pressure/volume relationships, and Charles' Law basically describes the effect of temperature changes on pressure and/or volume. The General Gas Law is a combination of these two laws. It is used to predict the behavior of a given quantity of gas when changes may be expected in any or all of the variables. The formula for the General Gas Law is:

$$\frac{P_1V_1}{T_1} = \frac{P_2V_2}{T_2}$$

Where P_1 = initial pressure (absolute)
V_1 = initial volume
T_1 = initial temperature (absolute)
P_2 = final pressure (absolute)
V_2 = final volume
T_2 = final temperature (absolute)

Dalton's Law: The total pressure exerted by a mixture of gases is equal to the sum of the pressures of each of the different gases making up the mixture—each gas acting as if it alone was present and occupied the total volume. The whole is equal to the sum of its parts and each part is not affected by any of the other parts. The pressure of any gas in the mixture is proportional to the number of molecules of that gas in the total volume. The pressure of each gas is called its partial pressure (pp), meaning its part of the whole. Dalton's Law is sometimes referred to as "the law of partial pressures." The formula for Dalton's Law is:

$$P_{Total} = PP_A + PP_B + PP_C .....$$

and

$$PP_A = P_{Total} \times \frac{\%Vol._A}{100\%}$$

Where P_{Total} = Total absolute pressure of gas mixture
PP_A = Partial pressure of gas A
PP_B = Partial pressure of gas B
PP_C = Partial pressure of gas C

Henry's Law: The amount of a gas that will dissolve in a liquid at a given temperature is almost directly proportional to the partial pressure of that gas. If one unit of gas dissolves in a liquid at one atmosphere, then two units will dissolve at two atmospheres, three units at three atmospheres, etc.

AIR CONSUMPTION FORMULA

Knowing your air consumption rate is very important. By determining your consumption rate at the surface, it becomes a simple matter to calculate what it will be at any given depth. Since pressure gauges are calibrated in pounds per square inch (PSI), your consumption rate must be in PSI too. The formula is as follows:

$$\frac{PSI \div TIME}{33/33 + DEPTH/33}$$

PSI = PSI consumed in timed swim at a constant depth.

TIME = Duration of timed swim.

DEPTH = Depth of timed swim.

EXAMPLE:
A diver swims at a depth of 10 feet for 10 minutes and consumes 300 PSI of air. You want to determine his surface consumption expressed in PSI.

$$\frac{300 \text{ (PSI used)} \div 10 \text{ (Time)} = 30}{33/33 + 10 \text{ (Depth)}/33 = 43/33} = \frac{30 \times 33}{43} = \frac{990}{43} = 23.02$$

23.02 PSI = PSI CONSUMED PER MINUTE AT SURFACE

NOTE: Consumption rate must be recalculated if tank size is changed.

AIR CONSUMPTION TABLE AT DEPTH

DEPTH IN FEET

Surface	10	15	20	25	30	40	50	60 ·	70	80	90	100	120	140	160
15	19.5	21.8	24.0	27.0	28.5	33.0	37.5	42.0	46.5	51	55.5	60	69	78	87
16	20.8	23.2	25.6	28.8	30.4	35.2	40.0	44.8	49.6	54.4	59.2	64	73.6	83.2	92.8
17	22.1	24.7	27.2	30.6	32.3	37.4	42.5	47.6	52.7	57.8	62.9	68	78.2	88.4	98.6
18	23.4	26.1	28.8	32.4	34.2	39.6	45.0	50.4	55.8	61.2	66.6	72	82.8	93.6	104.4
19	24.7	27.6	30.4	34.2	36.1	41.8	47.5	53.2	58.9	64.6	70.3	76	87.4	98.8	110.2
20	26.	29.0	32.0	36.0	38.0	44.0	50.0	56.0	62.0	68.0	74.0	80	92	104	116
21	27.3	30.5	33.6	37.8	39.9	46.2	52.5	58.8	65.1	71.4	77.7	84	96.6	109.2	121.8
22	28.6	31.9	35.2	39.6	41.8	48.4	55.0	61.6	68.2	74.8	81.4	88	101.2	114.4	127.6
23	29.9	33.4	36.8	41.4	43.7	50.6	57.5	64.4	71.3	78.2	85.1	92	105.8	119.6	133.4
24	31.2	34.8	38.4	43.2	45.6	52.8	60.	67.2	74.4	81.6	88.8	96	110.4	124.8	139.2
25	32.5	36.3	40.0	45.0	47.5	55.0	62.5	70.0	77.5	85.0	92.5	100	115	130	145
26	33.8	37.7	41.6	46.8	49.4	57.2	65.0	72.8	80.6	88.4	96.2	104	119.6	135.2	150.8
27	35.1	39.2	43.2	48.6	51.3	59.4	67.5	75.6	83.7	91.8	99.9	108	124.2	140.4	156.6
28	36.4	40.6	44.8	50.4	53.2	61.6	70.	78.4	86.8	95.2	103.6	112	128.8	145.6	162.4
29	37.7	42.1	46.4	52.2	55.1	63.8	72.5	81.2	89.9	98.6	107.3	116	133.4	150.8	168.2
30	39.	43.5	48.0	54.	57.0	66.0	75.0	84.0	93.0	102.0	111.0	120	138	156	174
31	40.3	45.0	49.6	55.8	58.9	68.2	77.5	86.8	96.1	105.4	114.7	124	142.6	161.2	179.8
32	41.6	46.4	51.2	57.6	60.8	70.4	80.0	89.6	99.2	108.8	118.4	128	147.2	166.4	185.6
33	42.9	47.9	52.8	59.4	62.7	72.6	82.5	92.4	102.3	112.2	122.1	132	151.8	171.6	191.4
34	44.2	49.3	54.4	61.2	64.6	74.8	85.0	95.2	105.4	115.6	125.8	136	156.4	176.8	197.2
35	45.5	50.8	56.0	63.0	66.5	77.0	87.5	98.0	108.5	119.0	129.5	140	161	182	203
36	46.8	52.2	57.6	64.8	68.4	79.2	90.0	100.8	111.6	122.4	133.2	144	165.6	187.2	208.8
37	48.1	53.7	59.2	66.6	70.3	81.4	92.5	103.6	114.7	125.8	136.9	148	170.2	192.4	214.6
38	49.4	55.1	60.8	68.4	72.2	83.6	95.0	106.4	117.8	129.2	140.6	152	174.8	197.6	220.4
39	50.7	56.6	62.4	70.2	74.1	85.8	97.5	109.2	120.9	132.6	144.3	156	179.4	202.8	226.2
40	52	58.	64.0	72.0	76.0	88.0	100.	112.0	124.0	136.	148.0	160	184	208	232

CONSUMPTION RATE AT SURFACE (PSI PER MINUTE)

U.S. NAVY AIR DECOMPRESSION TABLES

No-Decompression Limits and Repetitive Group Designation Table for No-Decompression Air Dives 7.5.2 The No-Decompression Table serves two purposes. First, it summarizes all the depth and bottom time combinations for which no decompression is required. Secondly, it provides the repetitive group designation for each no-decompression dive. Even though decompression is not required, an amount of nitrogen remains in the diver's tissues after every dive. If he dives again within a 12 hour period, the diver must consider this residual nitrogen when calculating his decompression.

Each depth listed in the No-Decompression Table has a corresponding no-decompression limit given in minutes. This limit is the maximum bottom time that a diver may spend at that depth without requiring decompression. The columns to the right of the no-decompression limits column are used to determine the repetitive group designation which must be assigned to a diver subsequent to every dive. To find the repetitive group designation enter the table at the depth equal to or next greater than the actual depth of the dive. Follow that row to the right to the bottom time equal to or next greater than the actual bottom time of the dive. Follow that column upward to the repetitive group designation.

Depths above 35 feet do not have a specific no-decompression limit. They are, however, restricted in that they only provide repetitive group designations for bottom times up to between 5 and 6 hours. These bottom times are considered the limitations of the No-Decompression Table and no field requirement for diving should extend beyond them.

Any dive below 35 feet which has a bottom time greater than the no-decompression limit given in this table is a decompression dive and should be conducted in accordance with the Standard Air Table.

Example—
Problem— In planning a dive, the Master Diver wants to conduct a brief inspection of the work site, located 160 feet below the surface. What is the maximum bottom time which he may use without requiring decompression? What is his repetitive group designation after the dive?

Solution— The no-decompression limit corresponding to the 160 foot depth in the No-Decompression Table is 5 minutes. Therefore, the Master Diver must descend to 160 feet, make his inspection and begin his ascent within 5 minutes without having to undergo decompression.

Following the 160 foot depth row to the 5 minute column, the repetitive group designation at the top of this column is D.

NO-DECOMPRESSION LIMITS AND REPETITIVE GROUP DESIGNATION TABLE FOR NO-DECOMPRESSION AIR DIVES

Depth (feet)	No-decompression limits (min)	A	B	C	D	E	F	G	H	I	J	K	L	M	N	O
10		60	120	210	300											
15		35	70	110	160	225	350									
20		25	50	75	100	135	180	240	325							
25		20	35	55	75	100	125	160	195	245	315					
30		15	30	45	60	75	95	120	145	170	205	250	310			
35	310	5	15	25	40	50	60	80	100	120	140	160	190	220	270	310
40	200	5	15	25	30	40	50	70	80	100	110	130	150	170	200	
50	100		10	15	25	30	40	50	60	70	80	90	100			
60	60		10	15	20	25	30	40	50	55	60					
70	50			5	10	15	20	30	35	40	45	50				
80	40			5	10	15	20	25	30	35	40					
90	30			5	10	12	15	20	25	30						
100	25			5	7	10	15	20	22	25						
110	20				5	10	13	15	20							
120	15				5	10	12	15								
130	10					5	8	10								
140	10					5	7	10								
150	5					5										
160	5				5											
170	5				5											
180	5				5											
190	5				5											

> **TO CONVERT FEET TO METERS, MULTIPLY FEET BY 0.3048**

Residual Nitrogen Timetable for Repetitive Air Dives 7.3.5 The quantity of residual nitrogen in a diver's body immediately after a dive is expressed by the repetitive group designation assigned to him by either the Standard Air Table or the No-Decompression Table. The upper portion of the Residual Nitrogen Table is composed of various intervals between 10 minutes and 12 hours, expressed in minutes: hours (2:21 = 2 hours 21 minutes). Each interval has two limits; a minimum time (top limit) and a maximum time (bottom limit).

Residual nitrogen times, corresponding to the depth of the repetitive dive, are given in the body of the lower portion of the table. To determine the residual nitrogen time for a repetitive dive, locate the diver's repetitive group designation from his previous dive along the diagonal line above the table. Read horizontally to the interval in which the diver's surface interval lies. The time spent on the surface must be between or equal to the limits of the selected interval.

Next, read vertically downwards to the new repetitive group designation. This designation corresponds to the present quantity of residual nitrogen in the diver's body. Continue downward in this same column to the row which represents the depth of the repetitive dive. The time given at the intersection is the residual nitrogen time, in minutes, to be applied to the repetitive dive.

If the surface interval is less than 10 minutes, the residual nitrogen time is the bottom time of the previous dive. All of the residual nitrogen will be passed out of the diver's body after 12 hours, so a dive conducted after a 12 hour surface interval is not a repetitive dive.

There is one exception to this table. In some instances, when the repetitive dive is to the same or greater depth than the previous dive, the residual nitrogen time may be longer than the actual bottom time of the previous dive. In this event, add the actual bottom time of the previous dive to the actual bottom time of the repetitive dive to obtain the equivalent single dive time.

Example—
Problem— A repetitive dive is to be made to 98 fsw for an estimated bottom time of 15 minutes. The previous dive was to a depth of 102 fsw and had a 48 minute bottom time. The diver's surface interval is 6 hours 28 minutes (6:38). What decompression schedule should be used for the repetitive dive?

Solution— Using the repetitive dive worksheet—

REPETITIVE DIVE WORKSHEET

I. PREVIOUS DIVE:
_48_ minutes ☑ Standard Air Table
_102_ feet ☐ No-Decompression Table
_M_ repetitive group designation

II. SURFACE INTERVAL:
_6_ hours _28_ minutes on surface.
Repetitive group from I _M_
New repetitive group from surface
Residual Nitrogen Timetable _B_

III. RESIDUAL NITROGEN TIME:
_98_ feet (depth of repetitive dive)
New repetitive group from II. _B_
Residual nitrogen time from
Residual Nitrogen Timetable _7_

IV. EQUIVALENT SINGLE DIVE TIME:
_7_ minutes, residual nitrogen time from III.
+ _15_ minutes, actual bottom time of repetitive dive.
= _22_ minutes, equivalent single dive time.

V. DECOMPRESSION FOR REPETITIVE DIVE:
_22_ minutes, equivalent single dive time from IV.
_98_ feet, depth of repetitive dive

Decompression from (check one):
☐ Standard Air Table
☐ No-Decompression Table
☐ Surface Table Using Oxygen
☐ Surface Table Using Air
☑ No decompression required

Decompression Stops:
_____ feet _____ minutes
_____ feet _____ minutes
_____ feet _____ minutes
_____ feet _____ minutes
_____ feet _____ minutes

Schedule used _____
Repetitive group _____

RESIDUAL NITROGEN TIMETABLE FOR REPETITIVE AIR DIVES

*Dives following surface intervals of more than 12 hours are not repetitive dives. Use actual bottom times in the Standard Air Decompression Tables to compute decompression for such dives.

Repetitive group at the beginning of the surface interval

Group	Surface interval ranges
A	0:10–12:00*
B	0:10–2:10 2:11–12:00*
C	0:10–1:39 1:40–2:49 2:50–12:00*
D	0:10–1:09 1:10–2:38 2:39–5:48 5:49–12:00*
E	0:10–0:54 0:55–1:57 1:58–3:22 3:23–6:32 6:33–12:00*
F	0:10–0:45 0:46–1:29 1:30–2:28 2:29–3:57 3:58–7:05 7:06–12:00*
G	0:10–0:40 0:41–1:15 1:16–1:59 2:00–2:58 2:59–4:25 4:26–7:35 7:36–12:00*
H	0:10–0:36 0:37–1:06 1:07–1:41 1:42–2:23 2:24–3:20 3:21–4:49 4:50–7:59 8:00–12:00*
I	0:10–0:33 0:34–0:59 1:00–1:29 1:30–2:02 2:03–2:44 2:45–3:43 3:44–5:12 5:13–8:21 8:22–12:00*
J	0:10–0:31 0:32–0:54 0:55–1:19 1:20–1:47 1:48–2:20 2:21–3:04 3:05–4:02 4:03–5:40 5:41–8:40 8:41–12:00*
K	0:10–0:28 0:29–0:49 0:50–1:11 1:12–1:35 1:36–2:03 2:04–2:38 2:39–3:21 3:22–4:19 4:20–5:48 5:49–8:58 8:59–12:00*
L	0:10–0:26 0:27–0:45 0:46–1:04 1:05–1:25 1:26–1:49 1:50–2:19 2:20–2:53 2:54–3:36 3:37–4:35 4:36–6:02 6:03–9:12 9:13–12:00*
M	0:10–0:25 0:26–0:42 0:43–0:59 1:00–1:18 1:19–1:39 1:40–2:05 2:06–2:34 2:35–3:08 3:09–3:52 3:53–4:49 4:50–6:18 6:19–9:28 9:29–12:00*
N	0:10–0:24 0:25–0:39 0:40–0:54 0:55–1:11 1:12–1:30 1:31–1:53 1:54–2:18 2:19–2:47 2:48–3:22 3:23–4:04 4:05–5:03 5:04–6:32 6:33–9:43 9:44–12:00*
O	0:10–0:23 0:24–0:36 0:37–0:51 0:52–1:07 1:08–1:24 1:25–1:43 1:44–2:04 2:05–2:29 2:30–2:59 3:00–3:33 3:34–4:17 4:18–5:16 5:17–6:44 6:45–9:54 9:55–12:00*
Z	0:10–0:22 0:23–0:34 0:35–0:48 0:49–1:02 1:03–1:18 1:19–1:36 1:37–1:55 1:56–2:17 2:18–2:42 2:43–3:10 3:11–3:45 3:46–4:29 4:30–5:27 5:28–6:56 6:57–10:05 10:06–12:00*

NEW ➔ GROUP DESIGNATION

| Z | O | N | M | L | K | J | I | H | G | F | E | D | C | B | A |

REPETITIVE DIVE DEPTH

Depth	Z	O	N	M	L	K	J	I	H	G	F	E	D	C	B	A
40	257	241	213	187	161	138	116	101	87	73	61	49	37	25	17	7
50	169	160	142	124	111	99	87	76	66	56	47	38	29	21	13	6
60	122	117	107	97	88	79	70	61	52	44	36	30	24	17	11	5
70	100	96	87	80	72	64	57	50	43	37	31	26	20	15	9	4
80	84	80	73	68	61	54	48	43	38	32	28	23	18	13	8	4
90	73	70	64	58	53	47	43	38	33	29	24	20	16	11	7	3
100	64	62	57	52	48	43	38	34	30	26	22	18	14	10	7	3
110	57	55	51	47	42	38	34	31	27	24	20	16	13	10	6	3
120	52	50	46	43	39	35	32	28	25	21	18	15	12	9	6	3
130	46	44	40	38	35	31	28	25	22	19	16	13	11	8	6	3
140	42	40	38	35	32	29	26	23	20	18	15	12	10	7	5	2
150	40	38	35	32	30	27	24	22	19	17	14	12	9	7	5	2
160	37	36	33	31	28	26	23	20	18	16	13	11	9	6	4	2
170	35	34	31	29	26	24	22	19	17	15	13	10	8	6	4	2
180	32	31	29	27	25	22	20	18	16	14	12	10	8	6	4	2
190	31	30	28	26	24	21	19	17	15	13	11	10	8	6	4	2

RESIDUAL NITROGEN TIMES (MINUTES)

110 TABLE

U.S. NAVY STANDARD AIR DECOMPRESSION TABLE

Depth (feet)	Bottom time (min)	Time first stop (min:sec)	Decompression stops (feet) 50	40	30	20	10	Total ascent (min:sec)	Repetitive group
40	200						0	0:40	*
	210	0:30					2	2:40	N
	230	0:30					7	7:40	N
	250	0:30					11	11:40	O
	270	0:30					15	15:40	O
	300	0:30					19	19:40	Z
50	100						0	0:50	*
	110	0:40					3	3:50	L
	120	0:40					5	5:50	M
	140	0:40					10	10:50	M
	160	0:40					21	21:50	N
	180	0:40					29	29:50	O
	200	0:40					35	35:50	O
	220	0:40					40	40:50	Z
	240	0:40					47	47:50	Z
60	60						0	1:00	*
	70	0:50					2	3:00	K
	80	0:50					7	8:00	L
	100	0:50					14	15:00	M
	120	0:50					26	27:00	N
	140	0:50					39	40:00	O
	160	0:50					48	49:00	Z
	180	0:50					56	57:00	Z
	200	0:40				1	69	71:00	Z
70	50						0	1:10	*
	60	1:00					8	9:10	K
	70	1:00					14	15:10	L
	80	1:00					18	19:10	M
	90	1:00					23	24:10	N
	100	1:00					33	34:10	N
	110	0:50				2	41	44:10	O
	120	0:50				4	47	52:10	O
	130	0:50				6	52	59:10	O
	140	0:50				8	56	65:10	Z
	150	0:50				9	61	71:10	Z
	160	0:50				13	72	86:10	Z
	170	0:50				19	79	99:10	Z
80	40						0	1:20	*
	50	1:10					10	11:20	K
	60	1:10					17	18:20	L
	70	1:10					23	24:20	M
	80	1:00				2	31	34:20	N
	90	1:00				7	39	47:20	N
	100	1:00				11	46	58:20	O
	110	1:00				13	53	67:20	O
	120	1:00				17	56	74:20	Z
	130	1:00				19	63	83:20	Z
	140	1:00				26	69	96:20	Z
	150	1:00				32	77	110:20	Z
90	30						0	1:30	*
	40	1:20					7	8:30	J
	50	1:20					18	19:30	L
	60	1:20					25	26:30	M
	70	1:10				7	30	38:30	N
	80	1:10				13	40	54:30	N
	90	1:10				18	48	67:30	O
	100	1:10				21	54	76:30	Z
	110	1:10				24	61	86:30	Z
	120	1:10				32	68	101:30	Z
	130	1:00				5	36	74	116:30	Z

* See No Decompression Table for repetitive groups

U.S. NAVY STANDARD AIR DECOMPRESSION TABLE

Depth (feet)	Bottom time (min)	Time to first stop (min:sec)	Decompression stops (feet)							Total ascent (min:sec)	Repetitive group
			70	60	50	40	30	20	10		
100	25								0	1:40	*
	30	1:30							3	4:40	I
	40	1:30							15	16:40	K
	50	1:20						2	24	27:40	L
	60	1:20						9	28	38:40	N
	70	1:20						17	39	57:40	O
	80	1:20						23	48	72:40	O
	90	1:10					3	23	57	84:40	Z
	100	1:10					7	23	66	97:40	Z
	110	1:10					10	34	72	117:40	Z
	120	1:10					12	41	78	132:40	Z
110	20								0	1:50	*
	25	1:40							3	4:50	H
	30	1:40							7	8:50	J
	40	1:30						2	21	24:50	L
	50	1:30						8	26	35:50	M
	60	1:30						18	36	55:50	N
	70	1:20					1	23	48	73:50	O
	80	1:20					7	23	57	88:50	Z
	90	1:20					12	30	64	107:50	Z
	100	1:20					15	37	72	125:50	Z
120	15								0	2:00	*
	20	1:50							2	4:00	H
	25	1:50							6	8:00	I
	30	1:50							14	16:00	J
	40	1:40						5	25	32:00	L
	50	1:40						15	31	48:00	N
	60	1:30					2	22	45	71:00	O
	70	1:30					9	23	55	89:00	O
	80	1:30					15	27	63	107:00	Z
	90	1:30					19	37	74	132:00	Z
	100	1:30					23	45	80	150:00	Z
130	10								0	2:10	*
	15	2:00							1	3:10	F
	20	2:00							4	6:10	H
	25	2:00							10	12:10	J
	30	1:50						3	18	23:10	M
	40	1:50						10	25	37:10	N
	50	1:40					3	21	37	63:10	O
	60	1:40					9	23	52	86:10	Z
	70	1:40					16	24	61	103:10	Z
	80	1:30				3	19	35	72	131:10	Z
	90	1:30				8	19	45	80	154:10	Z
140	10								0	2:20	*
	15	2:10							2	4:20	G
	20	2:10							6	8:20	I
	25	2:00						2	14	18:20	J
	30	2:00						5	21	28:20	K
	40	1:50					2	16	26	46:20	N
	50	1:50					6	24	44	76:20	O
	60	1:50					16	23	56	97:20	Z
	70	1:40				4	19	32	68	125:20	Z
	80	1:40				10	23	41	79	155:20	Z

* See No Decompression Table for repetitive groups

U.S. NAVY STANDARD AIR DECOMPRESSION TABLE

Depth (feet)	Bottom time (min)	Time to first stop (min:sec)	60	50	40	30	20	10	Total ascent (min:sec)	Repetitive group
150	5							0	2:30	C
	10	2:20						1	3:30	E
	15	2:20						3	5:30	G
	20	2:10					2	7	11:30	H
	25	2:10					4	17	23:30	K
	30	2:10					8	24	34:30	L
	40	2:00				5	19	33	59:30	N
	50	2:00				12	23	51	88:30	O
	60	1:50			3	19	26	62	112:30	Z
	70	1:50			11	19	39	75	146:30	Z
	80	1:40		1	17	19	50	84	173:30	Z
160	5							0	2:40	D
	10	2:30						1	3:40	F
	15	2:20					1	4	7:40	H
	20	2:20					3	11	16:40	J
	25	2:20					7	20	29:40	K
	30	2:10				2	11	25	40:40	M
	40	2:10				7	23	39	71:40	N
	50	2:00			2	16	23	55	98:40	Z
	60	2:00			9	19	33	69	132:40	Z
	70	1:50		1	17	22	44	80	166:40	Z
170	5							0	2:50	D
	10	2:40						2	4:50	F
	15	2:30					2	5	9:50	H
	20	2:30					4	15	21:50	J
	25	2:20				2	7	23	34:50	L
	30	2:20				4	13	26	45:50	M
	40	2:10			1	10	23	45	81:50	O
	50	2:10			5	18	23	61	109:50	Z
	60	2:00		2	15	22	37	74	152:50	Z
	70	2:00		8	17	19	51	86	183:50	Z
180	5							0	3:00	D
	10	2:50						3	6:00	F
	15	2:40					3	6	12:00	I
	20	2:30				1	5	17	26:00	K
	25	2:30				3	10	24	40:00	L
	30	2:30				6	17	27	53:00	N
	40	2:20			3	14	23	50	93:00	O
	50	2:10		2	9	19	30	65	128:00	Z
	60	2:10		5	16	19	44	81	168:00	Z
190	5							0	3:10	D
	10	2:50					1	3	7:10	G
	15	2:50					4	7	14:10	I
	20	2:40				2	6	20	31:10	K
	25	2:40				5	11	25	44:10	M*
	30	2:30			1	8	19	43	63:10	N
	40	2:30			8	14	23	55	103:10	O
	50	2:20		4	13	22	33	72	147:10	Z
	60	2:20		10	17	19	50	84	183:10	Z

*See No Decompression Table for repetitive groups

LOCATING YOUR NEAREST RECOMPRESSION CHAMBER

The following numbers may be called 24 hours a day, seven days a week. Physicians are on call and consultation can be provided on air embolism or decompression sickness cases. Each maintains a world-wide listing of recompression chambers.

Brooks Air Force Base
LEO-FAST-Command Post
AC512-536-3278

U.S. Navy Experimental Diving Unit
EDU Duty Phone
AC904-234-4353

SAFE DIVING PRACTICES

Every dive can be a safe and interesting event if every effort is made to recognize and control the variables, and the greatest variable is you.

Know yourself completely. Learn exactly what you are capable of. Be absolutely honest in your appraisal of your condition. Be aware of the precise effects of drugs, or alcohol, and avoid them completely before diving. Smoking and diet also impose certain limits. Smoking, for instance, interferes with the body's ability to transfer oxygen. If you smoke, admit your reduced efficiency. Certain foods are definitely gas-producing; some people are affected more than others. Remember their effect and avoid those foods before diving or limit yourself accordingly.

Know your personal limitations and abide by them. If you have certain phobias, fatigue easily, or are overly susceptible to cold, admit it and plan accordingly and never overextend yourself. Don't try to match performance with people who have set no personal restrictions. Try to swim with a buddy who falls into your physical and skill categories.

Also, know your swimming fitness and knowledge limitations. Again, refrain from overextending yourself. Constantly strive to upgrade and improve all your skills. Practice emergency procedures with your buddy on every dive—don't wait for emergencies to happen. Stay current on the latest emergency procedures. Take courses in lifesaving, cardio-pulmonary resuscitation, and first aid.

Never dive without a buddy, and try to dive with a buddy you have practiced with many times; someone whom you know well enough to know their strong points, weaknesses, and probable reactions. Practice buddy breathing for at least a couple of minutes on every dive. Don't wait until an emergency occurs to find that you and your buddy have different conceptions of the proper way to handle these emergencies.

Preplan every dive no matter how short or insignificant it may appear to be. An essential of predive planning is a thorough equipment check. Don't dive with marginal equipment. There are enough unsuspected things that can happen without further complicating a situation with equipment malfunction.

Approach every dive with a positive and bright attitude. If you don't feel good about it, don't dive! A positive attitude promotes quick reactions; a negative attitude can slow the reactions considerably. Under stress, reactions can be warped enough without any other contributing factors being present.

Understand yourself, your equipment, and your environment to insure yourself of the maximum enjoyment of diving.

The following step-by-step summary of safe diving practices will help you quickly review these important points. Use the summary periodically to recall any forgotten details.

1. **BE WELL TRAINED.** Be trained in scuba diving by a certified instructor of scuba diving and certified by a nationally recognized certifying organization.

2. **NEVER DIVE ALONE.** Always dive with a buddy who is completely familiar with you and your diving practices.

3. **NEVER HOLD YOUR BREATH WHILE USING SCUBA.** Breathe regularly. Exhale during emergency ascents. Do not hyperventilate excessively before breath-hold dives.

4. **DON'T DIVE BEYOND YOUR LIMITS.** Maintain good mental and physical condition for diving. Only dive when feeling well. Do not use any intoxicating liquor or dangerous drug before diving. Have a regular medical examination for diving. Be sure to exercise regularly, keep well rested, and maintain a well-balanced diet.

5. **AVOID DEPTHS DEEPER THAN 100 FEET.** This is the recommended sport diving limit.

6. **USE PROPER EQUIPMENT.** Use correct, complete, and proper diving equipment which is checked before each dive and well-maintained. Do not loan your scuba equipment to a non-certified diver. Have your scuba equipment regularly serviced by a qualified person. When scuba diving in open water, use flotation equipment (vest or buoyancy compensator) and a submersible pressure gauge and/or reserve warning mechanism.

7. **PLAN YOUR DIVE.** Know the area. Establish emergency procedures. Know the limitations of yourself, your buddy, and your equipment. Use the best possible judgement and common sense in planning and setting the limitations of each dive, allowing a margin of safety in order to be prepared for emergencies. Set reasonable limits for depth and time in the water. Always buddy dive—know each other's equipment, know hand signals, and stay in contact.

8. **ALWAYS WEAR A BUOYANCY COMPENSATOR.** Control your buoyancy to make diving as easy as possible. Be prepared to ditch your weight belt, make an emergency ascent, buddy breathe, clear your mask and mouthpiece, or take other emergency action if needed. In an emergency: stop and think; get control; take action.

9. **PUT YOUR WEIGHT BELT ON LAST.** Ditch your weight belt when a potential emergency arises. Be sure to unclasp it completely and throw it well away from your body.

10. **USE A DIVER'S FLAG AND FLOAT.** Make sure that your diving area is well-identified to avoid potential hazards from boats in the area.

11. **HAVE YOUR TANKS VISUALLY INSPECTED AT LEAST ONCE A YEAR AND HYDROSTATICALLY TESTED EVERY FIVE YEARS.** The hydrostat test every five years is required by law, but a visual inspection every year can head off trouble before it happens.

12. **USE ONLY CLEAN, DRY, FILTERED AIR IN SCUBA TANKS.** Be sure any source of compressed air always meets established standards for diving air.

13. **NEVER USE EARPLUGS OR GOGGLES.** Air pressure squeezes can cause damage in any area that cannot be vented.

14. **DON'T CARRY KILLED GAME.** Killed game can attract creatures that can become aggressive when they sense food.

15. **CANCEL DIVES WHEN WATER AND WEATHER CONDITIONS ARE QUESTIONABLE.** Too many unknowns can happen without aggravating the situation. It is far better to have everything in your favor which will make emergencies less serious.

16. **BE FAMILIAR WITH THE AREA.** Know your diving location. Avoid dangerous places and poor conditions. Take whatever special precautions are required.

17. **ASCEND PROPERLY.** When surfacing, look up and around, move slowly and listen, hold your hand up if any possible hazards exist. Do not hold your breath with scuba. Be sure to equalize pressure early and often both during ascent and descent.

18. **KNOW DECOMPRESSION PROCEDURES.** Be familiar with decompression tables and emergency procedures. Make all possible dives "no-decompression" dives. Avoid stage decompression particularly on repetitive dives, at altitude, or when flying after the dive.

19. **DON'T OVEREXTEND YOURSELF.** If you are cold, tired, injured, out of air, or not feeling well, get out of the water. Diving is no longer fun or safe. If any abnormality persists, get medical attention.

20. **AVOID TOUCHING UNKNOWN CREATURES UNDER WATER.** Be especially careful of anything very beautiful or very ugly.

21. **KNOW YOUR BOAT AND REGULATIONS.** Be sure any boat used for diving is legally and adequately equipped for diving.

22. **BE A GOOD CITIZEN DIVER AND SPORTSMAN.** Comply with laws and regulations concerning diving. Be friendly and respect personal property. When diving have your certification card, diving log, and identification nearby.

23. **BE AN ACTIVE DIVER.** Keep actively diving and logging your dives with your buddy's signature by each logged dive. Try to dive no less than 12 times per year.

24. **CONTINUE YOUR TRAINING.** Continue your scuba diving training by taking advanced, open water, or specialty courses.

EQUIPMENT CHECKLIST

DIVING EQUIPMENT

____ SWIM SUIT
____ MASK & ANTI-FOG SOLUTION
____ SNORKEL & KEEPER
____ FINS
____ WET SUIT
  ____ JACKET
  ____ BOOTS
  ____ GLOVES
  ____ PANTS
  ____ VEST
  ____ HOOD
____ WEIGHT BELT & WEIGHTS
____ BUOYANCY COMPENSATOR
____ FULL SCUBA TANK & BACKPACK
____ REGULATOR
____ SUBMERSIBLE PRESSURE GAUGE
____ WATCH
____ DEPTH GAUGE
____ COMPASS
____ DECOMPRESSION TABLES
____ DIVER'S FLAG/FLOAT &
       ANCHOR/LINE
____ WHISTLE
____ KNIFE
____ LOGBOOK & PENCIL
____ GEAR BAG

OTHER ITEMS

____ DRY CLOTHES
____ TOWELS
____ FOOD & DRINKING WATER
____ SUNGLASSES
____ SUNTAN LOTION
____ LOGBOOK
____ CERTIFICATION CARD
____ SPORT DIVING MANUAL

SPECIALTY EQUIPMENT

____ DECOMPRESSION COMPUTER
____ THERMOMETER
____ EMERGENCY FLARE
____ LIGHT & BATTERIES
____ SLATE & PENCIL
____ SAFETY LINE (200 FT.)
____ BUDDY LINE (6 FT.)

____ LIFT BAG
____ PHOTOGRAPHY EQUIPMENT
  ____ FLASH
  ____ CAMERA
  ____ FILM
  ____ FLASHBULBS
  ____ BATTERIES
____ SPEARFISHING GEAR
  ____ SPEAR
  ____ FISHING LICENSE
  ____ GAME BAG

SPARE PARTS & REPAIR KIT

____ MASK STRAP & BUCKLE
____ FIN STRAP & BUCKLE
____ "O" RINGS
____ CO_2 CARTRIDGES
____ REGULATOR HIGH PRESSURE PLUG
____ SILICONE SPRAY OR GREASE
____ WET SUIT CEMENT
____ NEEDLE & THREAD
____ EXTRA MASK LENS
____ WATERPROOF PLASTIC TAPE
____ PLIERS
____ WRENCH
____ SCREWDRIVER
____ SMALL KNIFE
____ BUOYANCY VEST PATCHES

FIRST AID KIT

____ ADHESIVE TAPE
____ ALCOHOL SOLUTION (70%)
____ AMMONIA SOLUTION
____ ANTISEPTIC SPRAY
____ ADHESIVE STRIPS
____ BUTTERFLY CLOSURES
____ COMPRESSES
____ COTTON SWABS
____ RAZOR BLADE
____ SCISSORS
____ SNAKEBITE KIT
____ SPLINTS
____ SOAP
____ SEASICK PILLS
____ DIMES & EMERGENCY PHONE NUMBERS
____ BAKING SODA
____ NASAL DECONGESTANT

METRIC SYSTEM

UNIT	ABBREVIATION	NUMBER OF	APPROXIMATE U.S. EQUIVALENT

LENGTH

UNIT	ABBREVIATION	NUMBER OF	APPROXIMATE U.S. EQUIVALENT
myriameter	mym	10,000 meters	6.2 miles
kilometer	km	1,000 meters	0.62 mile
hectometer	hm	100 meters	109.36 yards
dekameter	dam	10 meters	32.81 feet
meter	m	1 meters	39.37 inches
decimeter	dm	0.1 meters	3.94 inches
centimeter	cm	0.01 meters	0.39 inch
millimeter	mm	0.001 meters	0.04 inch

AREA

UNIT	ABBREVIATION	NUMBER OF	APPROXIMATE U.S. EQUIVALENT
square kilometer	sq km or km^2	1,000,000 sq. meters	0.3861 square mile
hectare	ha	10,000 sq. meters	2.47 acres
arc	a	100 sq. meters	119.60 square yards
centare	ca	1 sq. meters	10.76 square feet
square centimeter	sq cm or cm^2	0.0001 sq. meters	0.155 square inch

VOLUME

UNIT	ABBREVIATION	NUMBER OF	APPROXIMATE U.S. EQUIVALENT
dekastere	das	10 cubic meters	13.10 cubic yards
stere	s	1 cubic meters	1.31 cubic yards
decistere	ds	0.10 cubic meters	3.53 cubic feet
cubic centimeter	cu cm or cm' also cc	0.000001 cubic meters	0.061 cubic inch

CAPACITY

UNIT	ABBREVIATION	NUMBER OF	CUBIC	DRY	LIQUID
kiloliter	kl	1,000 liters	1.31 cubic yards		
hectoliter	hl	100 liters	3.53 cubic feet	2.84 bushels	
dekaliter	dal	10 liters	0.35 cubic foot	1.14 pecks	2.64 gallons
liter	l	1 liters	61.02 cubic inches	0.908 quart	1.057 quarts
deciliter	dl	0.10 liters	6.1 cubic inches	0.18 pint	0.21 pint
centiliter	cl	0.01 liters	0.6 cubic inch		0.338 fluidounce
milliliter	ml	0.001 liters	0.06 cubic inch		0.27 fluidram

U.S. WEIGHTS AND MEASURES

UNIT	ABBREVIATION OR SYMBOL	U.S. EQUIVALENT	APPROXIMATE METRIC EQUIVALENT
LENGTH			
mile	mi	5280 feet, 320 rods, 1760 yards	1,609 kilometers
rod	rd	5.50 yards, 16.5 feet	5.029 meters
yard	yd	3 feet, 36 inches	0.914 meters
foot	ft or '	12 inches, 0.333 yards	30.480 centimeters
inch	in or "	0.083 feet, 0.027 yards	2.540 centimeters
AREA			
square mile	sq mi or mi^2	640 acres, 102,400 square rods	2.590 square kilometers
acre		4840 square yards, 43,560 square feet	0.405 hectares, 4047 square meters
square rod	sq rd or rd^2	30.25 square yards, 0.006 acres	25.293 square meters
square yard	sq yd or yd^2	1296 square inches, 9 square feet	0.836 square meters
square foot	sq ft or ft^2	144 square inches, 0.111 square yards	0.093 square meters
square inch	sq in or in^2	0.007 square feet, 0.00077 square yards	6.451 square centimeters
VOLUME			
cubic yard	cu yd or yd^3	27 cubic feet, 46,656 cubic inches	0.765 cubic meters
cubic foot	cu ft or ft^3	1728 cubic inches, 0.0370 cubic yards	0.028 cubic meters
cubic inch	cu in or in^3	0.00058 cubic feet, 0.000021 cubic yards	16.387 cubic centimeters
CAPACITY			
		U.S. liquid measure	
gallon	gal	4 quarts (231 cubic inches)	3.785 liters
quart	qt	2 pints (57.75 cubic inches)	0.946 liters
pint	pt	4 gills (28.875 cubic inches)	0.473 liters
gill	gi	4 fluidounces (7.218 cubic inches)	118.291 milliliters
fluidounce	fl oz	8 fluidrams (1.804 cubic inches)	29.573 milliliters
fluidram	fl dr	60 minims (0.225 cubic inches)	3.696 milliliters
minim	min	1/00 fluidram (0.003759 cubic inches)	0.061610 milliliters
WEIGHT			
		Avoirdupois	
ton			
short ton		20 short hundredweight, 2000 pounds	0.907 metric tons
long ton		20 long hundredweight, 2240 pounds	1.016 metric tons
hundredweight	cwt		
short hundredweight		100 pounds, 0.05 short tons	45.159 kilograms
long hundredweight		112 pounds, 0.05 long tons	50.802 kilograms
pound	lb	16 ounces, 7000 grains	0.453 kilograms
ounce	ox	16 drams, 437.5 grains	28.349 grams
dram	dr	27.343 grains, 0.0625 ounces	1.771 grams
grain	gr	0.036 drams, 0.002285 ounces	0.0648 grams
		Troy	
pound	lb t	12 ounces, 240 pennyweight, 5760 grains	0.373 kilograms
ounce	oz t	20 pennyweight, 480 grains	31.103 grams
pennyweight	dwt also pwt	24 grains, 0.05 ounces	1.555 grams
grain	gr	0.042 pennyweight, 0.002083 ounces	0.0648 grams

index

A

B